MR DARCY I.

&

OTHER JANE AUSTEN STUDIES

By the same author

Shakespeare's God, a study of the four great tragedies

Jane Austen & the Interplay of Character

Hamlet, King of Denmark, a new tragicomical ending

Mr Darcy in Love
&
Other Jane Austen Studies

Critical Inquiries into the Novels' World

IVOR MORRIS

The Jane Austen Society of North America has kindly given permission for publication in this book of four studies which first appeared in its journal *Persuasions On-Line*: vols. 23 (2002), 25 (2004), 26 (2005), and 'Occasional Papers iv' (2001).

British Library Cataloguing-in-Publication Data
A CIP catalogue record for this book is available
from the British Library

ISBN 978-0-9575220-9-1

Printed and published by Sarsen Press
22 Hyde Street, Winchester SO23 7DR

To

C. V. H.

Contents

Along with her comedy sense she possessed a subtle insight into the moral nature of man. The union of the two is the distinguishing characteristic of her achievement; and it makes these lively unpretentious comedies of social and domestic life the vehicle of profound and illuminating comments on the human drama.

Lord David Cecil, A *Portrait of Jane Austen*, 1978.

Preface

It is with personality, as it projects and manifests itself through the written word, that this book is essentially concerned. To a present-day understanding, it is a unique possession, a 'given' of a man or woman's identity. But for Jane Austen it was not a matter of fixed distinctiveness. She and the readership she addressed tended to regard persons as conditioned and moulded by the society they were part of: its conventions, norms and pressures. As they journeyed through life, therefore, theirs was not so much a state of being as of becoming: one of consistently attaining to character rather than simply possessing it. To such a perception, man in fact was less an entity in himself than a social phenomenon, partly at least drawing selfhood from his dealings with those around him.

That this idea of individuality belonged to an age which has vanished does not mean it was mistaken. Could it, on the contrary, be closer to the truth than the view most of us hold today? And might it be to a real extent responsible for the freshness, modernity, and enduring appeal of the world and the people Jane Austen sets before us?

The main business of the younger element is, for the reader, their pursuit of love and marriage. It is a process which, in Shakespeare's words, should not admit of impediment: but the chief interest, indeed the fascination, of a novel lies in the overcoming of obstacles, personal and social, that lie in the way of the man and woman concerned. The principal one, without doubt, is uncertainty regarding each other's true feelings. For much of the time, all are in a state of acute unknowing as to the disposition of the beloved; and for some, it takes the sequence of events to bring them to the point of discovering the nature of their own affections.

Of none is this more true than the best known couple, Mr. Darcy and Elizabeth Bennet. Darcy is the most unlikely of lovers in scornfully rejecting his soul-mate as being not handsome enough to dance with, and making his subsequent advances – if that is what they are – beneath an attitude of indifference and hauteur. Yet his suddenly asking the astonished Elizabeth for her hand is no idle declaration, but proof of a deep and true falling in love. The signs of it have been present in him, for all his aloofness, and despite the author's preoccupation with the sentiments of her heroine: and identifying them could be found rewarding in giving fuller understanding of his character, and for the insight it provides into Jane Austen's consummate artistry.

At the close of his Memoir in the 1818 posthumous edition of Northanger Abbey and Persuasion, Jane Austen's brother Henry wrote that Winchester Cathedral, where his sister lies entombed, "does not contain the ashes of a brighter genius or a sincerer Christian". Are these striking and poignant claims justified? There can be no question as to the first: the novels speak for themselves. But no corresponding evidence for the other appears in them. If indeed any is presumed to exist, it is to be gleaned only by inference from the pages of an author whose religious promptings, even more than her personal thoughts, seem excluded from her literary vision.

Nor need this be surprising. The creator of comedy is under almost the same necessity as the tragedian of keeping to the secular, and resolving issues of life and living that arise in the novel in terms of its own imaginary world. The suggestion of an order beyond the present would dissipate its power.

Jane Austen elsewhere committed herself to statements formally though succinctly reflecting the faith she held; and the endeavour is made here to afford them full expression. Her testimony is eloquent of deep conviction; but if it can scarcely fail to place the novels in surer perspective, it does not – with what might be thought a minor exception – have the explicit bearing upon incident or sentiment that would make for fresh appraisal. The hope is however that its setting forth will reveal something of the inner light of the mind which produced the novels, and that readers will through this means be enabled to share the present writer's feeling of having come closer at once to the woman who was Jane Austen and the origin of her outlook upon life and people.

The bracketed numbers accompanying quotations relate to the pages of R.W. Chapman's standard Oxford edition (1932 –) of the novels, and will enable the text to be readily consulted upon issues under review.

It is a pleasure to record my indebtedness to friend and assistant Ceri Thomson, herself a Jane Austen devotee of wide literary interests, for her accomplished presentation of the manuscript and encouragement in this undertaking.

Ivor Morris.

i

Jane Austen and Her Men

"Faults are in flesh", laments the bard, "as motes be in the sun". Jane Austen's distinction lies in her showing that this need not be a cry of despair. She presents us with the auspicious paradox of a sharp-eyed realist relentlessly critical of humankind, yet benignly compassionate towards it – and able, what is more, to call forth unwonted fellow-feeling in ourselves. All who have experience of that summons must wonder at it; and even where it might not be present, a book of hers will rarely be set aside without the thought, "That strain I heard was of a higher mood"[1]. Consciousness that she is dealing with, and reconciling us to, a flawed humanity is at once part of the secret of her dedication and a source of the enduring interest and appeal of her portrayal of men and women. And if her Mr. Knightley can find his domestic bliss in an Emma who is "faultless in spite of all her faults", we may be in no doubt that Mrs. Knightley will in due time have cause enough to come to a corresponding appreciation of the man who is now her life's companion.

The subject of Jane Austen's men recalls to mind a shrewd elderly widow of my early acquaintance, who on occasion would give me the benefit of her wisdom. Once, the topic of matrimony having arisen, she confided, "It's dead easy for a woman to keep a man". "Is that so?" I inquired politely. "Simple", was the rejoinder. "Just flatter them. Make them think they're wonderful". I was mildly affronted at an estimate of my sex that made them out to be helpless victims of the vanity and pride Mary Bennet had so platitudinously pronounced human nature to be prone to. But I must confess to having pondered the matter since then.

Jane Austen does, to be sure, give us examples of vanity rampant in men. One need only consider Sir William Lucas, who, having upon being knighted developed a distaste for residence in a small country town, removed from Meryton to Lucas Lodge, "where he could think with pleasure of his own importance"; or a person more grandly addicted, of whose character we are told, "Vanity was the beginning and the end". The handsomeness and the baronetcy which he enjoyed were for him the highest of blessings: "and the Sir Walter Elliot, who united these gifts, was the constant object of his warmest respect and devotion". The same may be concluded of Mr. Collins, who not only cannot conceive that any woman should reject him as suitor, but regards the office of parson "as equal in point of dignity with the highest rank in the kingdom".

These lesser characters embodying an extreme of vanity put one in mind of Shakespeare's Dogberry who, on being named an ass by his betters, protests with felicitous fury,

> I am a wise fellow, and, which is more, an officer, and, which is more, a householder, and, which is more, as pretty a piece of flesh as any is in Messina, and one that knows the law, go to; and a rich fellow enough, go to; and a fellow that hath had losses, and one that hath two gowns and everything handsome about him[2].

When it comes to the vanity or pride of possession, he speaks for many greater than himself who are to be found in Jane Austen's novels. General Tilney, certainly, derives no small satisfaction from the vast Abbey he is master of, and the magnificence of its dining room, "of which... the General could not forego the pleasure of pacing out the length, for the more certain information" of the unconcerned Catherine Morland. But can we for a moment doubt that, in quieter ways, pride of ownership also suffuses Mr. Darcy, Sir Thomas Bertram and Mr. Rushworth, the possessors of Pemberley, Mansfield Park and Sotherton Court? And the prospective possessors, too – like Miss Eliza Bennet, who upon her first setting eyes on it, "felt, that to be mistress of Pemberley might be something!" or Emma Woodhouse, whom "the respectable size and style" of Mr. Knightley's Donwell Abbey, her destined home, moves to an "honest pride and complacency", no less; or Maria Bertram, whose "Rushworth-feelings" become so obviously pronounced in the vicinity of Sotherton, and whose spirits, as the barouche drives up to its principal entrance, are " in as happy a flutter as vanity and pride could furnish"?

From pride and vanity in this and other forms few can be free; and the comedian's task is to set the snares of ridicule for it in the social context, and laugh us back to sense. But it is a long step from a Dogberry to a Malvolio or a Shylock – to personalities in whom self-regard has become obsessive, and a controlling force. Neither the entreaties of good-nature nor the techniques of the happy ending can assuage the hurt they suffer: comedy fades, and drama takes on tragic tones as they leave the stage unappeased, vowing or dreaming of revenge. They draw us with them away from the fragile fabric of man's society to the sheer cliff face of things: for tragedy's role is to display the essence of our human nature to us. Its protagonist heroes we can identify with, for, though built on a bigger scale, they are entirely like ourselves. And their motivation can be summed up in a single word: pride.

Othello goes forward with an absolute belief in himself – in what he consciously terms, "My parts, my title, and my perfect soul"[3]. Lear's self-concept is an innate royalty of disposition: in his madness he professes himself, significantly, "Ay, every inch a king: / When I do stare, see how the subject quakes"[4]. Disaster for him comes through a refusal to be treated as anything less than his own estimate of himself. Macbeth murders his way to the "golden round" because it will, as he assumes, confer a deserved greatness upon him. Hamlet alone abandons the path of pride. Though he can find it in himself, like the others, to "do such bitter business as the day / Would quake to look on"[5] in propitiation of his own image, he turns from the tragic self-assertion to become, in Dr. Johnson's words, "an instrument rather than an agent"[6] – acted upon, rather than himself acting.

It is a woman, in the person of Lady Macbeth, who makes plain what lies at the heart of the heroic pretence. Her husband hesitates at his appalling task: it is for her to steel him to resolution. She does so by appealing to the basic quality of manhood within him – and succeeds by taunting him with the lack of it:

> Art thou afeard
> To be the same in thine own act and valour
> As thou art in desire?[7]

Are you afraid to assert what you have it in you to do, and to be? In that scornful challenge is revealed that it is pride in himself which makes her man, and any man, what he is: that self-esteem is the dominant constituent of the male ego: that, in truth, men most characteristically need to have the feeling that they are wonderful!

Why, in discussing Jane Austen's men, do I argue from Shakespeare? Because he was her tutor. As she says in Henry Crawford, speaking for herself, "Shakespeare one gets acquainted with without knowing how. It is a part of an Englishman's constitution..... one is intimate with him by instinct". And, as a fellow dramatist, though writing in novel form – Macaulay is not alone in rating her second only to him[8] – she likewise will fathom the soul of man, as of woman. Do, then, her heroes also exhibit the heroic pride? For an answer, I would point to what is less than half a hero – to the young Lucas who happens to overhear Elizabeth and Mrs. Bennet in agreement upon the detestable pride of the rich Mr. Darcy, and Mary's ensuing observations upon that failing. "If I were as rich as Mr. Darcy", he pipes up, "I should not care how proud I was. I would keep a pack of foxhounds, and drink a bottle of wine every day". And when Mrs. Bennet interposes that he would be drinking a good deal more than he ought, and that if she were to see him at it she would take away his bottle directly, " The boy protested that she should not; she continued to declare that she would, and the argument ended only with the visit". This young gentleman will patently not be afeard to be the same in his own act and valour as he is in desire. The child here is father of the man, is he not? More than that: he is the very archetype.

4

Is he, though? Surely this exalted notion of the self is not evident in Jane Austen's men. She is appraising, not man in the abstract, but in the drawing room and dining room: not the bedrock condition, but that fashioned by education, culture, social modes and pressures: personages of the leisure reading of a polite age. Tragic heroes may indeed pursue their own shadow, take a lofty self-regard to its logical conclusion, and go down to splendid or gory destruction; but they are not her concern, her heroes do not imitate them. Indeed, the men of her novels would consciously reject any such grandiose pretension and vaingloriousness as absurd, scorn it as being in the worst possible taste.

Consciously, they would; but what about their more inward promptings? Might it not be that their literary creator is better aware than they of what lurks beneath the urbane surface of their demeanour? Would she not have known, as all do, that her men, like all men, are grown-up schoolboys – and found the demon of their spirits, in almost every case, to be that proud and aspiring Lucas imp? Certain it is that she entertained no sanguine expectation of the youthful male. When the school term ended, and "a countless number of Postchaises full of Boys" from Winchester passed by the cottage at Chawton, she saw them "full of future Heroes, Legislators, Fools, & Vilains"[9]. Can it be that she saw her fictional heroes as exemplars of the vice of pride? Of whom else should we inquire, for a beginning, than the mature Fitzwilliam Darcy?

*   *   *

There is not the least bit of vanity in Mr. Darcy. Why should there be, when he has no need of it – when his rank and his income render him indifferent to what others may think of him? But pride – well-regulated pride – he will admit to: proudly. Not so as to claim to be altogether free of faults: "Perhaps", he concedes accommodatingly to Elizabeth, "that is not possible for any one". But, he assures her, he has made it the study of his life to avoid the more contemptible kinds of weakness.

How far short is Darcy here of asserting, with Othello, "My parts, my title, and my perfect soul"? Not much. Especially when you bear in mind the associated characteristic of an unyielding temper which he so readily confesses: "My good opinion once lost", he affirms, "is lost for ever". For what is Othello's reaction when he loses his good opinion of his friend and comrade, Cassio? It is,

> Cassio, I love thee;
> But never more be officer of mine.[10]

In the earlier Darcy, at least, the heroic pride is strongly evident. There is not only an implicit self-admiration in his attitudes, but a striving after éclat in his speech which Elizabeth has noticed, and had good cause to: a use of scathing unreserve against foe and friend which can impartially charge Bingley with the indirect boast in relation to his handwriting, accuse young ladies of walking about for the purpose of showing off their figures – and remark, concerning his future bride, "*She* a beauty! – I should as soon call her mother a wit". His behaviour at the Netherfield ball proclaims the man. "He walked here, and he walked there, fancying himself so very great!" declares Mrs. Bennet in reporting it. She speaks, as Margaret Kennedy comments, with unusual accuracy[11]. Here struts the pride which goes before a fall.

It is in a woman of course that he meets his Waterloo. Not Caroline Bingley – though with commendable feminine discernment she has offered what would have been the right treatment for a more ordinary mortal, in those flattering compliments upon the speed, the evenness, the delightfulness of his writing, as she watches the progress of his letter to his sister; and upon his possessing, furthermore, qualities of mind and disposition so beyond any reproof as to enable him, were he so disposed, to "hug himself". The difficulty for Caroline is that Darcy is convinced of his being admirable to the point of needing no telling, and has met so many girls who try this tactic as to be heartily weary of it. When, though, he encounters one who will attempt no such thing, but will rather tell him in words as explicit as his own precisely what she thinks of him – who dispels the enrapturing notion of his own consequence – he's lost: goes down like a ninepin.

From a Darcy to a Knightley is a far cry. Here is no pretentious spirit, but "a sensible man about seven or eight and thirty", as plain-dealing and principled as they come. But the question does arise in the novel – in relation to his status, moreover – and it is his own Emma who sees through him. Knightley is a countryman, given to walking round his estate – and to social functions, in disregard of the dignity requisite in that era for persons of any consideration in the world. To the Coles' dinner party, however, he does drive up in a carriage. Emma Woodhouse, following in her own, is pleased; and as he hands her out, observes, "This is coming as you should do, ... like a gentleman". Knightley senses and meets the challenge instantly. A carriage, he insists, is irrelevant to the issue: "if we had met first in the drawing room", he tells her, "I doubt whether you would have discerned me to be more of a gentleman than usual". "Yes, I should", she replies – seizing upon an effect Jane Austen herself had often noted in such circumstances. "There is always a look of consciousness or bustle when people come in a way which they know to be beneath them. You think you carry it off very well, I dare say, but with you it is a sort of bravado, an air of affected unconcern..... *Now* you have nothing to try for. You are not afraid of being supposed ashamed. You are not striving to look taller than any body else. *Now* I shall really be very happy to walk into the same room with you".

She has caught him out, in a minor yet pompous affectation. What reply can he make? He doesn't hate her; and he has grace enough to be amused at his own discomfiture. So he just says, "Nonsensical girl!" as must any man when a woman has had the better of the argument. He had presupposed that arriving in a plebeian way could not affect him personally – rather in the manner of Julius Caesar, who, alluding to any menace that might lie in Cassius's disapproval of him, avers to Mark Anthony,

> I rather tell thee what is to be fear'd
> Than what I fear; for always I am Caesar.[12]

So Knightley – though not any kind of tragic hero – had been telling himself, "Whatever style I choose to arrive in, I fear no loss of dignity in my own or others' eyes: for always I am Knightley". He may be replete with estimable qualities, but amongst them pride has some habitation.

But can it inhabit a person in whom we consistently find (to use the author's own words) "the gentleness of an excellent nature"? The fact that Edmund Bertram is a man of the cloth is no indication one way or the other: Jane Austen had been in the company of far too many clergymen to be under illusion that the cleric is from that cause "a thing ensky'd and sainted"[13]. More to the point for her is that Edmund is inescapably his father's son. There is an evident likeness: a mutual trust and understanding exists between them, and both are reflective, moralizing natures. Nothing in fact could have exceeded Sir Thomas's concern that instruction in moral and religious principles should form part of his children's education; but the novel demonstrates how warped his judgment and personal morality can be by the dictates of social consequence. Seeing full well that Maria has neither love nor respect for James Rushworth, he is nevertheless happy to consent to a marriage "which would bring him such an addition of respectability and influence, and very happy to think any thing of his daughter's disposition that was most favourable for the proposal". The same consideration determines his attitude to Fanny Price before she is even in the house. At all costs her being nurtured amongst them must not bring social degradation: Sir Thomas's main object is "to preserve in the minds of my *daughters* the consciousness of what they are". – How acute is Margaret Kennedy's remark that, though he believes he is bringing up his daughters to serve God, "he is really more bent upon fitting them to serve Mansfield Park".

His son she finds to be "in search of some better repository of the good"[14]. He is indeed. But Edmund's quest for it can be bedevilled, believe it or not, by this very consciousness, in his father's terms, of "what he is". Consider the problem that faces him when, through his declining to act in *Lover's Vows*, it is proposed that that most gentlemanly commoner Charles Maddox be invited to make good the deficiency. Edmund is alarmed at the prospect. He has pained awareness

> "of the mischief that *may*, of the unpleasantness that *must*, arise from a young man's being received in this manner – domesticated among us – authorized to come at all hours – and placed suddenly upon a footing which must do away all restraints".

Every rehearsal in such a situation would tend to create what he terms "licence". The magnanimity with which he admits to knowing no harm of Charles Maddox will not extend to toleration of this "excessive intimacy" and its dread outcome, "familiarity". "I cannot think of it with any patience", he cries – "and it does appear to me an evil of such magnitude as must, *if possible,* be prevented".

Edmund's concept of evil would not withstand theological scrutiny; but in the social context it has an inflexible logic. These are the accents of pride: here speaks the arrogance of rank. In the disdainful idiom of Shakespeare's Prince of Arragon, Edmund has reacted as he does

> Because I will not jump with common spirits
> And rank me with the barbarous multitude.[15]

This imperative obliges him to withdraw his objection over 'Lovers' Vows' and take the part of Anhalt against his judgment: a decision which materially affects the progress of events. Fanny sees, and grieves over, her beloved's lapse. And Jane Austen is sympathetically aware of the absurdity in itself of that ingrained presumption in Edmund which has helped to make him what he is. Her confidence and ours rests in the small likelihood of anything similar arising, in the sphere in which he and Fanny will afterwards move, to discompose the graciousness of that excellent nature.

Would Henry Tilney have found as much to unnerve and offend him in a commoner's proximity? In so humoursome, as well as charming a man, we might be inclined to expect a reaction of more amused sort.

For Tilney is genuinely witty. Now if wit can be supposed a fault, is it possible, in Hamlet's phrase, for a person to "take corruption" from it?[16] Tilney can be viewed as having succumbed, to the point of turning into a dedicated satirist. Who has so viewed him? Why, Catherine Morland. At the start of their acquaintance Catherine fears "that he indulged himself a little too much with the foibles of others", while she listens to the grave assent he confers upon Mrs. Allen's divulgings as to the properties of muslin and the amenities of Bath. In their first conversation he has been busily running intellectual rings round Catherine to his own complete satisfaction and gratification, if not hers: diverting her with Assembly Room chatter and posturings, teasing her with what she might privately think of him, and enthusing upon the perfection of women's letter-writing save for the three characteristics of its deficiency of subject, inattention to punctuation and ignorance of grammar.

With what delighted energy he pounces upon any infelicity in Catherine's speech. Her pleonastic concept of a "faithful promise" from Isabella Thorpe receives, perhaps, the short shrift it merits. But her undiscriminating use of "nice" is met with open ridicule; and her declaring that she has "just learnt to love a hyacinth" by the mockingly ironical, "And how might you learn? – By accident or argument?"

The spirited humour of Henry's upbraidings seems to free them from offence. Who could really be solemn about his protestation, on being charged to state his acknowledgement of women's intelligence, that "no one can think more highly of the understanding of women than I do. In my opinion, nature has given them so much, that they never find it necessary to use more than half". And we dismiss it as brotherly banter when he sports with Eleanor's alarmed incomprehension of Catherine's prophecy that "something very shocking indeed" – by which she means an horrific novel – "will soon come out in London". "Forgive her stupidity", he urges Catherine. "The fears of the sister have added to the weakness of the woman; but she is by no means a simpleton in general".

This trenchancy may, however, be somewhat less agreeable – bring in asperity of tone, and manner bordering on the inquisitorial, as for example in Henry's relentless questioning upon finding Catherine in an unexpected part of the Abbey. But the cleverness which discomfits her then can, on occasion, be too much even for himself. When he is driving her to Northanger, he diverts her with an extempore Gothic tale so compelling that he has to break off through being able no longer to "command solemnity of subject or voice". His very triumph in the jest incapacitates him. To adapt a definition from a different context, he becomes inebriated with the exuberance of his own virtuosity.

What symptoms are these but of pride in high intelligence: of a self-congratulation on his own brilliancy in the style of Shakespeare's Benedick? But while Benedick meets his match in both senses in Beatrice, Tilney is properly vanquished by his very antithesis in Catherine Morland. As Jane Austen coolly remarks as to their encounter,

> Where people wish to attach, they should always be ignorant. To come with a well-informed mind, is to come with an inability of administering to the vanity of others, which a sensible person would always wish to avoid. A woman especially, if she have the misfortune of knowing any thing, should conceal it as well as she can.

Catherine has no cleverness to conceal from Henry, and no art to conceal it if she possessed it. Not for nothing is she made to reply, when he declares that he understands her perfectly, "Me? – yes; I cannot speak well enough to be unintelligible". Her entire response to him is an innocent flattery: in his company she is "listening with sparkling eyes to every thing he said; and, in finding him irresistible, becoming so herself". When, therefore, he comes to propose to her, he is soliciting a heart "which, perhaps, they pretty equally knew was already entirely his own". His is a deep and true affection; but as to its origin, we are told "that a persuasion of her partiality for him had been the only cause of giving her a serious thought". He loves Catherine for those fine attributes which flow from unpretentiousness in human nature – but also, to some degree at least, because she is, and happily cannot help being, a living confirmation of his high opinion of himself.

Henry Crawford is not the hero of the novel, but he might well have been. When that other Henry, Jane Austen's brother, got to book three of *Mansfield Park*, he thought that Crawford might win Fanny Price in the end; and we owe to Margaret Kennedy the insight that he would have made a better husband for someone of her qualities than Edmund Bertram[17]. And yet the author shows us that vanity, pure and simple, is largely determinative of his actions and hopes. The giving free rein to it accounts for his characteristic unwillingness to look beyond the present moment, and his consequent drifting course through the story. It explains also his fickle relations with Maria and Julia Bertram. The sisters "were an amusement to his sated mind": his pleasure in their company stems from the deeper joy he evinces in the adroit exercise of his engaging powers, in conferring attentions sufficient to attract both girls while never seeming directed at either. Jane Austen's term for behaviour of this type is "to trifle"; and what could better describe the blandishments Crawford bestows on Maria that day at Sotherton Court? It is vanity, again, or pique arising from its frustration, which provokes him to gain the satisfaction of "making a small hole in Fanny's heart": for despite his best efforts he had unaccountably got nowhere with her. Attempting it he finds himself, more unaccountably, in love for the first time. But he brings to the task of courtship a mind "sanguine and pre-assured", which can first imagine affection to exist beneath Fanny's manifest indifference, and then find "so much delight in the idea of obliging her to love him in a very short time, that her not loving him now was scarcely regretted". It cannot at any stage enter his thoughts that "Love such as his, in a man like himself", should ever fail of a return.

Crawford is the perpetrator of what perhaps is the most fulsome act of incivility in the novels. While Lady Bertram peacefully slumbers on the drawing room sofa at Mansfield, and Edmund, indulgently taking what is going on to be the lovers' tiff that it is not, hides himself in a newspaper, Crawford remorselessly cross-examines the helpless Fanny Price as to her impression of him. He persists in forcing a confidence in utter disregard of her embarrassment, anguished feelings, and appeals – and in defiance of manners, as of manliness. For rudeness is none other than the external indication of people's being wrapped up in and existing for themselves.

And it is vanity which brings Crawford to his ruin. He loves Fanny still; but the same compulsion which led him first to exert his charm upon her obliges him to try to re-animate Maria's former regard when they meet at Mrs. Fraser's party, and he is received by her with dismissive coldness. He is, we are told,

> mortified, he could not bear to be thrown off by the woman whose smiles had been so wholly at his command; he must assert himself to subdue so proud a display of resentment.

So he begins the attack in which he is overwhelmed by the strength of feelings in Maria Bertram beyond what he had supposed to exist. The self-concern which so aided him in his trifling had been all along deluding him as to the realities of relationship. A justice of inexorable consequence brings it about, therefore, that at the end, "He was entangled by his own vanity".

Anyone listing the instances through the novel of conduct in Crawford deriving from this feature of his personality would find they had something like the outline of an allegorical figure from a Morality play. But there is nothing abstract about Henry Crawford: with his manifold accomplishments he is solidly human – all too human. If, nonetheless, his portrayal should offer the least suggestion of the Morality, it will be neither as Vice nor Vanity, but, alas, much nearer an Everyman.

There is no point in looking for pride and vanity in Edward Ferrars. A sceptic might say it is not easy to find much else, or wonder in the common phrase what Elinor sees in him. But so culpable an innocence could be the legacy of two disadvantages he almost throughout labours under: that of being engaged to another according to the strict standards of the times, and that of being without fortune and thus dependent on a parent's whim. That the rigours and inhibitions of the latter state are not readily discerned today is hardly surprising, when they could escape the notice of contemporaries. Emma Woodhouse can admonish her friend with, "You are the worst judge in the world, Mr. Knightley, of the difficulties of dependence". Its disabling force is perhaps visible in Captain Tilney, upon his father's denouncing him for coming down late to breakfast. He listens in silence, attempts no defence; and, we learn, Catherine "scarcely heard his voice while his father remained in the room,…so much were his spirits affected". Making allowance for the restrictions life imposes on Edward Ferrars permits one to think there could be more to him than meets the eye. The contrasting effusiveness of his younger brother is explainable as simply the token of Robert's deeper kinship in stupidity with his all-powerful mother.

But there is not the slightest prospect of Edward Ferrars bearing comparison with Frederick Wentworth, the most heroic of Jane Austen's heroes: a man, according to Margaret Kennedy, "completely masculine in all he says and does"[18]. If this is so – and few would deny it – should there not be found in him a correspondingly greater impulsion, typical of his gender, to look well in his own eyes, or in the eyes of others, or both? Wentworth does, in fact, contrive to leave the inhabitants of the Great House at Uppercross in no doubt as to his abilities. He talks happily and unrestrainedly about his doings: about his "taking privateers enough to be very entertaining" when in command of the Asp, and of having "such a lovely cruise" off the Western Islands in the Laconia. "How fast I made money in her!" he assures the assembled party. – But you've to be careful with a man like this. When you consider that these expressions "entertaining", "lovely", and "making money" are euphemisms for fights at sea, and that he is giving very keen listeners an account of events, and making no bones about it, in the manner of any sailor telling a yarn, you find you are in the presence of something that merits respect. If there is a trace of vanity in Wentworth's disposition to talk freely of his exploits, it is the product, at least, of exceptional achievement. He wouldn't be human if he were not conscious of personal claim and merit: in Charlotte Lucas's words, "If I may so express it, he has a *right* to be proud". It would never come into his mind, though, to use this implied prerogative for the purpose of boasting. We know it would be quite beneath him; and we are left with the fact of Wentworth's natural impressiveness.

This fact, perhaps, is mainly responsible for the singular lapse on his part with respect to the Miss Musgroves – a fault for which Ann Elliot, predisposed as she is in his favour, knows not how to excuse him. "He was only wrong", she concludes, "in accepting the attentions – (for accepting must be the word) of two young women at once". But he had hardly been acting by design, and is shocked when the import becomes clear. The involvement is one which seems to have grown around him in the general warmth of regard at Uppercross, there being "so much of friendliness, and of flattery, and of every thing most bewitching in his reception there". Indeed, Jane Austen queries, "If he were a little spoilt by such universal, such eager admiration, who could wonder?" While Wentworth is blamable for his insensitivity, his willingness to bear the consequence frees him from discredit.

When, eight years after their broken engagement, he had come to stay with the Crofts at Kellynch Hall, Ann Elliot wondered what his wishes were with respect to meeting her again. She tries to work them out by adopting his standpoint and reasoning from it.

> Had he wished ever to see her again [she tells herself] he need not have waited till this time; he would have done what she could not but believe that in his place she should have done long ago, when events had been early giving him the independence which alone had been wanting.

Her conclusion is that therefore, "He must be either indifferent or unwilling". But in this she is wrong: the very opposite is true. She is in error on a vital matter, simply because it is a woman's mind that she has employed upon it. As a woman she knows of nothing that would have prevented her from renewing acquaintance if she had desired to; it takes a man to make her aware of what the impediment had been, – the man being Wentworth himself. During the card party at Camden Place, when they have drawn aside from the other guests, he asks her the very question she had posed to herself: would she have renewed the engagement if he had written after a couple of years? And her smiling response draws from him a passionate confession not only as to his wishes, but as to his nature.

> "It is not that I did not think of it, or desire it, as what could alone crown all my other success. But I was proud, too proud to ask again."

Self-esteem in Wentworth issued the command which had to be obeyed, in defiance of every other appeal of his being. The whole story of *Persuasion* turns upon the reality and consequence of masculine pride.

*   *   *

By this stage some will be saying, "Wait a moment. What's going on? An insidious attempt, it would seem, to typify Jane Austen's men – excellent fellows – as pitifully presuming and vainglorious sorts of creatures. Is this to be endured?" So, before I am drummed out of the regiment, let me hasten to say that the women in principle are just as bad. Think of Lady Catherine sallying forth to confront the fractious residents of Hunsford, and "settle their differences, silence their complaints, and scold them into harmony and plenty" by that awesome sincerity and frankness for which her character has ever been celebrated. With some slight adjustment of rank (overdue, without doubt, in her estimation), would she not make a fitting consort for a monarch, and be heard declaring herself, "Ay, every inch a queen", as with complacency she perceives the trembling of her subjects? Or consider Mrs. Elton, a parvenue in Longbourn, presuming to detach the social initiative from its rightful and incensed custodian, with her, "Miss Woodhouse, we must exert ourselves", and her detestable "You and I's". Isn't it the first article of her faith that she is wonderful? And this applies to the Miss Bertrams, who were popular wherever they went because "Their vanity was in such good order, that they seemed to be quite free from it, and gave themselves no airs", as it does to Mary Musgrove, whose tenacity about the deference due to her as a baronet's daughter is constantly causing annoyance even among those close to her.

Yes, Jane Austen's women are as vain and proud as the men in principle – but not quite so in fact. Not because they are better, but merely because it was, and is, harder for a woman to fulfil the requirements of self-magnification. They are not really compatible with the feminine role of bringing harmony, social and musical, into the life of the household; or that of bearing children; or of dealing with demanding husbands enjoying a freedom they were denied. And, to a woman's quicker and finer sensibilities, the very notion of glorifying the self will tend to appear a little suspect. Her duties and perceptions alike are of a humbling kind: and the more salutary for being so.

This, presumably, is why an American professorial friend once confided to me that he had no trouble choosing whom to vote for in an election. "If there's a woman candidate, I vote for her, regardless of party". His explanation was as follows: "Because it's impossible for a woman to be worse than the men; and there's a slight chance she might be better".

And this is also the reason why Jane Austen, who is not strictly a satirist, here and there allows herself the luxury of parodying her own male characters. You hear its ring in the protestations of the necessitous Sir Walter Elliot that, "It had not been possible for him to spend less; he had done nothing but what Sir Walter Elliot was imperiously called on to do; but blameless as he was", and so on. But it is at Mansfield Parsonage, in the course of one of Sir Thomas Bertram's "dignified musings", this time upon attentions Fanny Price appears to be receiving, that the mimicry is more pronounced.

> ...though infinitely above scheming or contriving for any the most advantageous matrimonial establishment that could be among the possibilities of any one most dear to him, and disdaining even as a littleness the being quick-sighted on such points, he could not avoid perceiving in a grand and careless way that Mr. Crawford was somewhat distinguishing his niece.

That she will parody wherever it is merited, regardless of sex, is delightfully demonstrated in the set-piece of Mrs. Elton's dulcet utterances amidst Donwell Abbey's strawberry-beds. But the men more aptly incur such ridicule because of her knowledge that they are more inclined than women to build a pretentious and brittle self-image, and that in this respect they are vulnerable, and women stronger.

For proof one has only to compare the quarrel between Anne and Elizabeth Elliot in *Persuasion* with that between Edmund and Tom Bertram in *Mansfield Park*. The circumstances are similar. In both, the younger tries to warn and advise the elder about a course of conduct which could be personally and socially harmful: in the one case, embarking on amateur theatricals in Sir Thomas's absence, and in the other, permitting the commoner Mrs. Clay to remain a member of the household. But for the sisters the issue is far more serious. Tom Bertram risks no more than arousing his father's and the neighbourhood's displeasure; but what threatens Elizabeth is not only the disgrace of complicity in Sir Walter's marrying beneath him, but loss of all her rights as mistress of Kellynch Hall, and even at Camden Place.

Yet where most is at stake, there is least offence given or taken. Elizabeth, vexed by the reflection on her judgment and what she must regard as an upstart endeavour in Anne, conveys her displeasure in answers of shortness and warmth. But, compared to what takes place between the brothers, the combat is ceremonious, the exchanges ritual. Anger seems to have been at once anticipated; it is allowed for, and promptly dismissed: the contenders part confirmed, naturally, in their own attitudes, but unshaken and unscathed.

With the men it is otherwise. Although annoyance is as much as possible dissimulated at the behest of good breeding, there is nothing ceremonious about their encounter. Tom, in surprise and irritation at the challenge, from the start makes a defiantly contradictory riposte: to the plea of Maria's delicate situation it is, "I have no fears, and no scruples"; to the argument that his father will disapprove, "And I am convinced to the contrary". When Edmund persists in urging Sir Thomas's strong sense of decorum, Tom is, in Jane Austen's understated term, "displeased". His answer is a scathing affirmation of his status as Mansfield's heir and acting head that shows him touched to the quick. "I'll take care that his daughters do nothing to distress him. Manage your own concerns, Edmund, and I'll take care of the rest of the family". Against his brother's charge that staging a play would be taking liberties with his father's house, Tom, "in a decided tone", attempts a studied sarcasm. "His house shall not be hurt. I have quite as great an interest in being careful of his house as you can have". But vehemence and ridicule bursts forth in his cries of "Absolute nonsense!" and of "prodigious!" at the likely expense; and the last, as he walks out of the room, is plain denunciation. "Don't imagine that nobody in this house can see or judge but yourself. Don't act yourself if you do not like it, but don't expect to govern every body else".

There's no mistaking it. Here are the throbbings, the whirls and eddies of humiliation and pain: both young men experience raw emotions which bring them near the limit of the tolerable. It is with an image of animal savagery that the author, appropriately, concludes this scene. "Family squabbling is the greatest evil of all", Edmund confides to Fanny Price, "and we had better do any thing than be altogether by the ears". One wonders how things would have gone if she had not been there; but even with her present, Jane Austen is revealing a man's world to us – and the depth of her understanding of the male ego. For it is wounded vanity and pride which makes this quarrel so much more damaging that the other. Not that women don't also have their pride: it is just that in their natures pride tends not to dominate.

Love, rather, preponderates with women, does it not? – a thing apart in the lives of men, but for women their whole existence, if Byron is to be believed. Surely, men are in this respect the hardier, the less susceptible? Only an affirmative, seemingly, can come from the novels, for the sentiments of woman are Jane Austen's main theme: she will not normally enter into male preserves, or much into the minds of her male characters. The tendernesses and apprehensions of love and falling in love are registered in all her heroines, and its pains movingly displayed in a Marianne Dashwood – or in an Anne Elliot, when she undergoes "All the overpowering, blinding, bewildering first effects of strong surprise" upon glimpsing Captain Wentworth in Milsom Street. But perturbation is also apparent in Wentworth as, seconds later, he recognizes her. It is described from without; yet the words, "He was more obviously struck and confused by the sight of her, than she had ever observed before" convey a great deal – as does Darcy's similar reaction to Elizabeth upon his encountering her at Pemberley.

Are Jane Austen's men to any extent freer from love's tyranny than her women? Is the passion less potent or compelling for them? It is a hard question, as Anne Elliot and Captain Harville find in their conversation at the White Hart. But a parallel may be drawn between the pathetic state of Marianne Dashwood and that of Edmund Bertram, who, under love's constraining, is through much of the novel a shadow of the man he was. He becomes a creature of desperate confessions and confidences, the agonized victim, even, of every new token of Mary Crawford's inclining towards him, or otherwise. Rarely can the horror of a perceived imperfection in the beloved have found such expression as it does in him. "She does not *think* evil", he tells Fanny, "but she speaks it – speaks it in playfulness – and though I know it to be playfulness, it grieves me to the soul". Nor can the predicament of the anxious lover have been often better exemplified. Despite all his self-knowledge, and knowledge of Mary's failings, he knows not how to come to terms with his promptings or settle on a purposive action, and is left clinging to fitful hope like a drowning man to a straw. – Or we might take note of Harville himself, speaking from his soul of a love which for him is in no sense a thing apart; whose one wish – words failing as they must, and his composure with them – is that he might convey "all that a man can bear and do, and glories to do for the sake of these treasures of his existence!"

It is, though, the ending of that discussion at the White Hart which would appear to be decisive. Love's like hold upon men is not to be doubted, at least – to use Anne Elliot's words – "while the woman you love lives, and lives for you". She claims for her sex what she calls an unenviable privilege, which Harville cannot bring himself to deny her: "that of loving longest, when existence or when hope is gone". But there is more than a hint of the privilege's not being woman's alone, in, of all people, Willoughby – the man who has knowingly sported with Marianne's affections, and discarded her as deliberately, to marry upon financial consideration a woman he does not care for. His precipitate journey to Somerset upon news of Marianne's dangerous illness may have a touch of bravado about it, as may his manner to Elinor during their strange interview at Cleveland that stormy night; but what quickly becomes clear is the bitter thoughts and torturing regret which animate him. Realization of his true state softens Elinor – more, moves her beyond pity to the near-affection which she has to struggle against. But it is Willoughby's final plea which is most instructive. He desires to know that Marianne has forgiven him. He is assured, with sympathy, that she has. But he wants something beyond this: to be able to fancy, as he puts it, that "a better knowledge of my heart, and of my present feelings, will draw from her a more spontaneous, more natural, more gentle, less dignified, forgiveness".

Only love itself could so wish, so crave, so rejoice in such a relenting, in one for ever separated – could find her regard still so infinitely meaningful when hope is at an end. Anne Elliot's assertion on behalf of her sex of loving longest well attests her own constancy, and gives Captain Wentworth, as he sits writing at the nearby table, the intimation vital for its finding a return. But the claim she makes is one which Jane Austen, from her own observation of love in men and women, knows to be untrue.

* * *

This awareness of equality between men and women where the profoundest instincts of the heart are evoked might seem hard to reconcile with a disparity in the presentation of the sexes in the novels. Jane Austen certainly appears to devote less attention to her men, and depicts them almost invariably from external vision. But that her achievement in characterization is more pronounced with women has more to do with the obligation she was under of conformity with her generation's idea of the novel, than with lesser ability in delineating men, by whatever method. In Mr. Bennet, if not elsewhere, we assuredly have a demonstration of the extent of her powers. Elizabeth Jenkins sets it down as "next door to impossible" for him to have been created by a woman. His having been drawn by a man would be more credible, she goes on, "except that it is difficult to think of a man who could have drawn him so well"[19]. We have all been entertained by the idiosyncrasy that expresses itself now in a distant and dismissive courtesy, now in elaborate irony and sarcasm, now in a judicial expansiveness, as occasion serves; and we are aware of the sudden impatience, and the capacity for fierce self-reproach and momentary gloom which belongs to a personality at once forceful and withdrawn. But nowhere else in the novels – and, one suspects, in anyone else's novels – do we come upon such chameleon-like change of attitude as occurs in Mr. Bennet when he is challenged to the depth of his being by his favourite daughter's seeming abandonment of her standards, in suddenly wanting to marry the man she has hitherto hated.

"What are you doing? Are you out of your senses, to be accepting this man?" he asks her, in shock and grief. But his mood, as Elizabeth rather confusedly assures him of her attachment, is instantly that of disdain. "Or in other words", he puts it to her, "you are determined to have him. He is rich, to be sure". Upon her steadfastly declaring her love for Darcy, Elizabeth hears accents of the tenderest fatherly concern. He has given Darcy his consent; he is prepared to give it to her; but, forewarning of the miseries of an unsuitable match, he pleads, "My child, let me not have the grief of seeing *you* unable to respect your partner in life. You know not what you are about". It is he, however, who is prevailed on to think again when Elizabeth, much moved, explains the change which has come about in herself, and urges Darcy's constancy and his good qualities. Bennet, still unconvinced, gives grudging approval: "I have no more to say. If this be the case, he deserves you". The tone is now that of resigned disappointment; but as Elizabeth recounts what Darcy has done for Lydia, it transmutes itself into elation. "And so Darcy did everything; made up the match, gave the money, paid the fellow's debts, and got him his commission!" There follows, in rapid succession, relief blended with humour: "So much the better. It will save me a world of trouble and economy"; an outburst of hilarity, as he laughs "some time" at Elizabeth over her earlier embarrassment at the warnings against Darcy in Mr. Collins's letter; and, finally, a comfortable relapse into the ironic courtesy of his customary manner: "If any young men come for Mary or Kitty, send them in, for I am quite at leisure".

The most fanciful and volatile of womankind in the novels could scarcely display such variation of mood. Yet these manifold states are truly Mr. Bennet: in them all, he is consistently himself, behaving exactly as we would expect him to behave – and entirely masculine. By no stretch of the imagination can his conduct (to use Elizabeth's previous words about her father) "be mistaken for the affectation and coquetry of an elegant female". And in none of her heroines does Jane Austen evince a greater triumph of comprehension.

She is as successful with men as with women in the concise rendering of character. The description of Mrs. Bennet as "a woman of mean understanding, little information, and uncertain temper" sets us smiling, and speaks eloquently. More might be held to devolve from the single point of taciturnity in Mrs. Ferrars: "She was not a woman of many words: for, unlike people in general, she proportioned them to the number of her ideas". This piece of summarizing does not, however, outdo her performance with respect to Sir William Lucas and Sir Walter Elliot – or in Admiral Croft's illuminating self-caricature through speeches like, "A new sort of way this, for a young fellow to be making love, by breaking his mistress's head! – is not it, Miss Elliot? – This is breaking a head and giving a plaister truly!" But her introduction of John Thorpe perhaps exceeds these in inspired inventiveness. This plain, rather stout individual "seemed fearful of being too handsome unless he wore the dress of a groom, and too much like a gentleman unless he were easy where he ought to be civil, and impudent where he might be allowed to be easy". The man's native worth, and the manner of his subsequent conduct, are alike deducible from this searing definition.

Not only her men's differentiation, but their similarity, can prove the measure of Jane Austen's skill. In a notable respect they are less outwardly distinguished from one another than their counterparts among the ladies. By air and accent, Charles Musgrove, Edmund Bertram, Edward Ferrars, Charles Bingley and Edward Gardiner are not easy to tell apart. They share the unassuming matter-of-factness and moderation which typified the country gentlemen of Jane Austen's personal acquaintance. Nevertheless, they are quite unlike as individuals: each seems to exist within a unique mental climate. The fact denotes an extraordinary sureness of touch.

So also does the variety of splendidly realized male types to be found in the novels. They are as abundant as those of the women; and comparison will show that for most female categories there is a male equivalent. For that of mindlessness and vacuity, we may have the agreeable occupation of choosing between Lady Bertram and Mrs. Allen on the one side, and Sir William Lucas and Mr. Rushworth on the other. When it comes to egotism and the will to dominate, Lady Catherine and General Tilney have much in common; some of his performances might conceivably be deemed to outclass hers. The principled and deliberative personality is at least as well exemplified in Sir Thomas Bertram as it is in Lady Russell. If the comportment of

Mrs. Weston may (as Emma maintains) be regarded as the model of "propriety, simplicity, and elegance" in a female, that of Mr. Gardiner for much the same reason is to be recommended to any man. In terms of what is avowedly ladylike and gentlemanly, Anne Elliot and Mr. Knightley would appear to be outstanding; and if Mrs. Grant merits praise for the preservation of cheerfulness despite being married to a perverse husband, Charles Musgrove, espoused to a fretful wife, is the man so distinguished.

Vulgarity, as Jane Austen was all too aware, is a plant which can never cease to flourish; and many, amidst its convoluted branches, share an occult relationship. Those fine cronies, Mrs. Jennings and Sir John Middleton, are not alone in displaying a consanguinity defiant of the widest divergence in the social scale: the gushing Anne Steele and vaunting Robert Ferrars are likewise linked in the species of vulgarity that feeds upon silliness and finds fulfilment in garrulity. That which is the mere offspring of underbreeding is demonstrated by the siblings Isabella and John Thorpe respectively in their consummate coquetry and rattledom; while the sort produced unawares by those engaged in the nefarious art of social posturing and pretence is personified in Mrs. Elton and her *caro sposo*.

But, human nature being what it is, gentility itself can carry the seeds of infelicities too numerous to recount; and many are the ramifications of those who, endowed with manners, yet sin against them. Some contrive to do so by excess, like Sir Walter and Elizabeth, in whom may be observed the self-congratulating haughtiness which can freeze a crowded room into silence, or the adulation of rank that makes Anne Elliot so oddly wish that her family had more pride. Far from being a garb of innocence, manners can mask the duplicity of the mercenary predator, a creature as well represented amongst the men by Wickham and Willoughby as it is by Mrs. Clay and – yes, it must be said, Charlotte Lucas amongst the women. Mannerliness may even beget a blatant self-assurance which spurns the very intimations that give it life: Marianne and Willoughby have both indulged in this refined abandon.

For representatives of that ease and cleverness in otherwise charming people which can be tempted into the reprehensible, one need look no further than to Emma Woodhouse and Frank Churchill. When the deceptions he secretly so much enjoyed are known and forgiven, she makes a statement for which he has no other answer than a bow of assent: "to tell you the truth, I think it might have been some amusement to myself in the same situation. I think there is a little likeness between us". They are so alike in this that it is well they go separate ways. And of the rather more questionable quipping and quibbling propensity, which twenty thousand pounds and the assurance it gives has created in Mary Crawford, we have as positive a masculine representation in the jovial irresponsibility and barbed outspokenness which comes so naturally to Tom Bertram as elder son. His observing that the "desperate dull life her's must be with the doctor" shows Mrs. Grant's dire need of a lover, and Mary's likening Maria's marriage and Edmund's ordination upon Sir Thomas's return from abroad to sacrificial offerings made to some heathen deity, are about equal in irreverence, if not quite so in ingenuity. That the paths of this pair diverge is also, one must think, probably a merciful provision.

But Miss Bates and Mr. Woodhouse are eternally neighbours and friends, twin and potent reminders as they are of how socially disastrous good nature can be if unaccompanied by both of two other needful complementary qualities. Miss Bates has perception in plenty, but not the least discretion; in Mr. Woodhouse is a teeming discretion that is without any perception to work upon. As characters they are not too ossified to be compatible: put together, they get on famously – though, curiously enough, not without a little straining of good nature on either side. For whereas she must grieve at his not letting her eat the delicacies which are put before her at Hartfield, he is driven to confessing with some irritation that she talks a little too quick.

For some of course there is not a corresponding person of the other sex. There is to be found no woman like Admiral Croft in his endearing and sometimes alarming breeziness – or man comparable to Lydia Bennet, "this robust, noisy, natural creature", as she has been called[20]. Mrs. Norris also is without a masculine counterpart in her presumption and petulance as indigent sister. Similarly, it is pointless looking for a true female version of Mr. Collins, for the reason that women are simply not capable of being so maladroit. And there is no gentleman remotely resembling Mrs. Bennet – but who on earth would expect one? The striking thing, however, about these novels concerned with the amours of women is the range of male characters drawn from many social conditions they set before us.

*   *   *

One category makes what might be thought an improbable appearance: that of the evil man. In *Lady Susan*, Jane Austen had drawn a wicked woman who pursues her designs with cold subtlety; General Tilney betrays a malevolence crude and unrestrained. But use of such terms in relation to him can readily appear an exaggeration. Is he not, after all, something of a joke, designedly and actually: a character whose purpose is to show Catherine being so naively under the influence of Mrs. Radcliffe's Gothic horrors as to suppose the General, "slowly pacing the drawing-room for an hour together in silent thoughtfulness, with downcast eyes and contracted brow", another villainous Montoni, when he is merely thinking over the latest batch of political papers and pamphlets – and turning out, in the end, to be no more than a petulant old buffer, anyway?

Henry Tilney is right when he accuses Catherine of having formed a surmise of such horror as makes him at a loss for words. The General is innocent of the despicable murder she had suspected him of; but we should be unwise to dismiss those suspicions as vain without giving some thought to what they are grounded on. At an early stage Catherine is aware of an effect seemingly without cause. General Tilney's children are oppressed in his company; and she herself finds it "a release to get away from him", despite his pointed courtesies. Indeed, it is through his absence, Jane Austen declares, that she derives "the first experimental conviction that a loss may be sometimes a gain".

Catherine finds nothing sinister in the incidents of their journey to Northanger – his wrath about the carriage, "his discontent at whatever the inn afforded, and his angry impatience at the waiters" – but accepts them as the given fact of a life-style she is unfamiliar with. Though this brand of assertiveness compares strangely with the civility which can rise to such height of compliment as beg her, while in Bath, to "quit this scene of public triumph" in order to be his guest, and bestow on her "one of the most graceful bows she had ever beheld", it does not detract from her pleasure in being so honoured, or cause her to fancy a hollowness in his attentions.

Might she not have sensed pride of possession, at least, beneath the mock-modesty which could concede the Abbey's palatial dining room to be "by no means an ill-sized room", and the apologetic of, "Why, as he *had* such rooms, he thought it would be simple not to make use of them"? And was she at all led to wonder at the persistence of the Generals's questioning about her friend Mr. Allen's rooms, his garden, and his succession houses, as he showed her round his own – or, on her assuring him of their inferiority, at his exclaiming of Mr. Allen, "'He is a happy man!' with a look of very happy contempt"?

The answers must be in the negative. It would have been beyond Catherine, in her innocence, to make anything of the evidence which even the accomplished reader is disinclined to take in: evidence of a fierce hunger for distinction, a huge gratification in its attainment, and a consonant apprehension of its loss which puts him instantly on the defensive at the slightest hint of criticism. But astonished she is when, after his urging Henry to go to no trouble in receiving him at Woodston, that "Whatever you may happen to have in the house will be enough", she sees the festive abundance there which he attacks with such obvious inconsistency and relish.

Little does Catherine know that General Tilney's condescension towards her has been of the same quality as these other manifestations: called forth, that is, by exultant anticipation of receiving an heiress into the family in her person. The full force of his disappointment in this prospect she is soon to feel in his suddenly turning her out of the house; but her own distress at this juncture is somewhat less than the General's. The being informed that she is a virtual pauper has, Jane Austen states, "terrified" him. Even this calculated use of the word cannot convey the enormity of such an assault upon such a mind. Here is a man whose manners are in every respect artifice, beneath whose outward politeness broods a barren nature swept by storms of passion: blind will to dominate, zest in self-assertion, greed to possess, rage at hindrance to a wish, – and, underlying all, the primordial fear, adjunct of unhallowed condition, which lends intensity to these malign satisfactions and strivings.

We may smile at Catherine's detecting a Montoni in Henry's father. He is, beyond denial, as his son rather aggrievedly points out, an English gentleman and a Christian. But were it to be removed from its particular environment and culture and placed under a less favoured dispensation, this personality would quickly decline upon its native barbarism. The best thing Catherine does in the novel is to fall in love with Henry Tilney: the next best is to develop the revulsion towards the General she feels almost throughout.

Another piece of remarkable veracity, though of quite different sort, may reside in the character of Mr. Darcy and his treatment of Elizabeth Bennet. His specifying and detailing to her the social inferiority of her family in the midst of proposing has been deemed unlikely conduct in a hero. Darcy appears to be sinning against the manners and decorum of the age, and against probability in a person of his type: what he might have thought, that is, it would never have occurred to him to speak. The seeming lapse has been explained by critics, the present one included, as due to Jane Austen's need to make Darcy at this moment the embodiment of the arrogance of rank and wealth she deplores, and her contriving to do so through an action uncharacteristic in someone like him. But is it uncharacteristic? Is there not such a thing as the pride which will not stoop to dissembling – and the constraint to be true to oneself in a searching encounter? Darcy's is an aloofness of spirit, as well as of attitude. And given, further, that uprightness and even severity of mind which can pronounce, at such a point, "disguise of every sort is my abhorrence!" and the ardour for truth and scorn of pretence in Elizabeth which Darcy has recognized and holds in esteem, might it not rather be that the "understanding" of a coming-together between such a pair can scarcely subsist without a real understanding of each other's position?

At least it may be said without contradiction that Darcy tells her not a thing about her family's deficiencies and shortcomings that she does not know and has not ruefully acknowledged to herself – though it is inevitable that she will react with anger to the open breach of decorum his candour is. Nor can it be denied that Darcy by this forthrightness succeeds in apprising Elizabeth of the reality of his love for her. Almost immediately she is experiencing a different form of agitation at the thought of having "inspired unconsciously so strong an affection".

Far from dealing here with an artificiality of characterization, we are being confronted with a phenomenal naturalness. There can be no swervings or zigzaggings of politeness with these two when it comes to matters so close to the heart, and to principle: such 'mannerliness' would itself have been an artificiality in terms of the people they are. The plainness Darcy uses, and desires, in proposing to Elizabeth at the end proclaims the man: "You are too generous", be tells her, "to trifle with me". That their married life will, indeed, never be a refuge from home truths is indicated soon thereafter by the style of this newly-betrothed young woman's complaisance towards her beloved, when, inquiring what had made him begin to be in love with her, she points out, with devastating frankness, "My beauty you had early withstood". Can it be that in Elizabeth Bennet we have another Lady Catherine de Bourgh in the making? Perish the thought! Hers is too intelligent and responsive a mind to incur such a destiny. But in this connection it would appear that Elizabeth has found in Darcy, not just her man, but her soul-mate.

Should some hesitate to accept this reading of Mr. Darcy, on the grounds that, whatever might be pleaded in extenuation, no true gentleman could have behaved so, they may be advised to dismiss their scruple as they can. And to rid themselves permanently of the notion all they need do is devote the odd hour to researching confrontations of Whig and Tory in the House of Commons.

*   *   *

Darcy, Knightley, Wentworth, Bertram, Tilney – even Ferrars: each is markedly individual: yet do they together represent an ideal of manliness for Jane Austen? What, to conclude, are the attributes in men she seems most to approve? Answers will be easily forthcoming, since they are embodied in the gentlemen themselves; but nothing can be better at the outset than to take note of Elizabeth's plea to Mr. Collins, that he regard her as "a rational creature speaking the truth from her heart". The heroes shun the established complimentary mode of address that sets women in a separate and subordinate class. In contrast to the strained gallantry of Mr. Elton, which made Emma want to run away and laugh, there is placed before us with obvious approval the manner towards Mary Crawford and women in general of Edmund Bertram: "he was not pleasant by any common rule, he talked no nonsense, he paid no compliments, his opinions were unbending, his attentions tranquil and simple".

Equally demanded, we may gather, is the capacity in a man to laugh at himself or tolerate being laughed at. The latter we are assured Mr. Darcy will gravitate towards; but both exist in Mr. Knightley, the former being overlaid by a magisterial outspokenness. Therefore we should not miss the chuckle when, in advising Emma to obtain from Harriet those "minute particulars" of her engagement to Robert Martin "which only woman's language can make interesting", he adds on behalf of men, "In our communications we deal only in the great". And Frederick Wentworth, wishing to impress upon Louisa Musgrove the desirability of firmness, and by way of illustration plucking a perfect nut from a bough, next moment is brought by sudden sense of incongruity to refer to it as being "still in possession of all the happiness that a hazel-nut can be supposed capable of ". In a woman, a sense of humour is an attraction; but for a man it is, according to Jane Austen's thinking, a prerequisite.

So is integrity in human dealings. It is the knowledge of its presence in Mr. Knightley which allows Emma at once to dismiss the thought of his being the giver of the unexplained present of a piano to Jane Fairfax. He would, she is sure, never have acted in so devious a way. And the revelation of Frank Churchill's past course of double-dealing consequent upon the secret engagement rouses Emma to condemnation in Mrs. Weston's very presence, so horrified is she at the thought of the absence in him of "that upright integrity, that strict adherence to truth and principle, that disdain of trick and littleness, which a man should display in every transaction of his life". She voices here the mind of her creator, all of whose heroes are typified by a principled directness. So are they by a readiness to accept responsibility for their mistakes or impulsive actions. Having allowed his attentions to Louisa Musgrove to appear too meaningful, Wentworth is resigned. "I was hers in honour if she wanted it", he says. "I had been unguarded". In the same way, Henry Tilney will take it upon himself to atone for his father's clear favouritism and subsequent gross misconduct towards Catherine: to her "He felt himself bound as much in honour as in affection", we are informed.

Such probity is part of the good manners always requisite in a man. They go beyond the politeness observable at surface level; and even there they are not admissible if they express elaborateness rather than the simplicity that is itself befitting, in its betokening the sincere. Manners do, of course, involve some pretence – a masking for social convenience, if not repressing, of genuine feeling, as when Wentworth responds to Mary Musgrove's depreciation of her relatives the Hayters with "an artificial, assenting smile, followed by a contemptuous glance, as he turned away". It is a requirement of good manners also not to defy public opinion "in any point of worldly decorum": and here, Marianne's flaunting "particularity" with Willoughby shows her utterly in the wrong. But, as her sister so earnestly tries to impress on her, such abiding by the conventions does not mean allowing them to prevail over personal belief or taste. It is on the contrary imperative, especially in a man, to be able while respecting society's norms and refinements to see beyond them, and where appropriate act accordingly – above all with regard to the human worth which might perhaps fall short of them, and to the human arrogance which might operate behind them. The respect which Knightley has for Robert Martin, and which he comes to entertain for Harriet, or Elizabeth's being unaffected by "the mere stateliness of money and rank" at Rosings, and stirred to contempt by the pretensions she encounters there, show them to be, in Jane Austen's eyes, mannered in the highest degree.

A formal mannerliness which however is unaccompanied by kindness takes on the appearance of monstrosity wherever it occurs: whether it be the unsisterly correctness of Elizabeth Elliot, or the polite indifference of her cousin to the distress of his former friend Mrs. Smith consequent upon her loss of husband and affluence. The behaviour of the heroes and heroines alike in this connection seems to confirm Geoffrey Chaucer's dictum that "pitee renneth sone in gentil herte"[21]. One would expect it to be less with men, and perhaps least in the manliest of them all; but Frederick Wentworth provides some of the most notable instances. He does so when Mrs. Musgrove's regrets over her lost son interpose in the conversation at the Great House, as, despite a flicker of amusement at recollecting the midshipman he had been at pains to get rid of, he seats himself by her and talks "with so much sympathy and natural grace, as shewed the kindest consideration for all that was real and unabsurd in the parent's feelings". His action later during the walking party's return from Winthrop, in prevailing on the Crofts to give Anne a seat in their gig upon perceiving her tiredness, is "a proof of his own warm and amiable heart". While still blaming Anne for the past, and indifferent to her in the present, he yet "could not see her suffer, without the desire of giving her relief". But more eloquent of that heart's amiability are the words which burst from him at Louisa's apparent lifelessness after her fall from the Cobb at Lyme. Staggering against the wall for support, he exclaims "in the bitterest agony, 'Oh God! Her father and mother!'" This incident, according to Margaret Kennedy, shows that in Jane Austen's view, kindness and even tenderness is not the prerogative of women[22]. The evidence from Wentworth's character, certainly, is that it is in no wise unbecoming in a man.

Nor, for Jane Austen, is that spontaneity and element of impulsiveness which, though it can make mistakes, confirms a correspondence between outward and inward in a man's comportment. The same Captain Wentworth had unawares inflicted deep pain upon Anne Elliot after the first meeting at Uppercross, when he described her to another as being "so altered he should not have known you again". Ignoring the possibility that his words might be conveyed to her, he "had spoken as he felt". But it is precisely this naturalness of his, his "enthusiasm" as she terms it, which has endeared him to her: she prizes "the frank, the open-hearted, the eager character beyond all others". The charm it holds for her alone makes it possible for Wentworth to hope. Had she not experienced unease at the absence of "any burst of feeling, any warmth of indignation or delight" in Mr. Elliot, she might, chillingly, have been led by the "eligibilities and proprieties of the match" to accept him.

All these qualities, and many more, a man may have; but, put together, they will be unavailing without one further excellence: that of steadfastness. Here we come back to Lady Macbeth, as she strives finally in vain to urge on her faltering lord, and expresses a world of scorn in her accusation, "Infirm of purpose!"[23] Such wavering in a man's nature – above all in relation to the woman he loves – renders him unacceptable and contemptible in Jane Austen's estimation. A resoluteness – and a readiness as it were to take their lives into their hands in its service at the critical moment – is what qualifies her men as heroes, and enables them, often enough, to win their fair ones. Wentworth, finding himself suddenly released from Louisa, within five minutes has said to himself, "I will be in Bath on Wednesday". At the White Hart, hearing Ann's emotion-charged tones upon constancy in love, he seizes a pen and writes, "I must speak to you by such means as are within my reach" – and asks there and then for her hand, concluding, "A word, a look will be enough". Darcy, determinedly, twice makes moments to propose to Elizabeth by calling on her when she is alone at the Parsonage. On both occasions the attitude he meets there frustrates his intention; but he wastes no time when, at Longbourn, she has found courage enough to thank him for what he has done for them. Mr. Knightley, coming to Hartfield to console Emma after what he assumes has been Frank Churchill's betrayal, and finding to his astonishment that she is fancy-free, on "the immediate effect of what he heard" speaks for himself: his proposal is "the work of the moment". Henry Tilney, ordered by his father to acquiesce in the treatment he has meted out to Catherine, instead declares his intention to propose to her. Arrived at Fullerton, he invites her to walk with him the quarter of a mile to the Allen's house. "Some explanation on his father's account he had to give" during the course of it, Jane Austen remarks wryly; "but his first purpose was to explain himself, and before they reached Mr. Allen's grounds he had done it so well, that Catherine did not think it could ever be repeated too often".

To such a happy conclusion Henry Crawford has come near enough – when, while devoted to Fanny Price, he allows himself to be swayed from his overriding desire by one purely ephemeral. So, too, Willoughby, knowing himself united to Marianne by every tie of affection and mind, makes himself the willing victim of circumstance, incurring the world's and his own contempt. And Frank Churchill is of their kindred. It is the irresoluteness she has detected in his character which is largely responsible for distancing Emma from his influence. Heedless of the obligations of secrecy as of love, he can let a mere jocular whim, while the company at Hartfield is playing at alphabets, cause Jane Fairfax embarrassment and alarm, and jeopardize their situation; and his resentment at her declining to arouse suspicions by walking with him from Donwell all but drives them apart. He would have ruined both their lives, had not the death of the formidable Mrs. Churchill made their way clear for them. Mr. Knightley, with justification, terms Frank Churchill "the favourite of fortune". Margaret Kennedy, with the same justification, declares him to be "very nearly a villain"[24].

It is as if, in her estimation of men, and men in love, Jane Austen had taken as crowning truth words of her master Shakespeare upon creatures so sadly erratic and self-appeasing:

> O heaven! were man
> But constant, he were perfect: that one error
> Fills him with faults.[25]

*   *   *

The charge may be made against this assessment of Jane Austen's men that it gives undue prominence to Mary Bennet's commonplaces upon pride and vanity. But even greater opprobrium may be impending. For it cannot be brought to an end without a bold assertion: that, despite the limitations which literary convention subjected her to, and all that contemporary tastes and attitudes imposed on her as a woman, and whatever disqualification her own being a woman implies, Jane Austen understood men as well as she understood women. The novels, I would claim, show this to be so. And I must venture even further, though upon grounds more commonplace. The number of women who can say of the man in their life, "I can read him like a book" is, by common knowledge, legion. But the tally of men able with conviction to return the compliment will make a relatively modest showing. For, as Oscar Wilde defined the matter, "men can be analysed, women… merely adored"[26]. I will therefore go so far as to declare that in all probability Jane Austen's understanding of men exceeded that of her women.

Is this an Aunt Sally by way of conclusion? Or treachery? Or heresy? Upon so grave an issue, I can only, as Mr. Bennet to his spouse, reply to the indignant questioner," I leave it to yourself to determine". But I am perfectly sure that, however much feelings may intensify and convictions clash, argument upon such a writer as Jane Austen will never degenerate into dispute: for, with this supreme creator of comedy, truth is at one with good-humour. So if there be matter here for contention, let that battle rage from which each combatant can only emerge victorious.

ii

Persuasion's Unwritten Story

> "Westgate Buildings!" said he; "and who is Miss Anne Elliot to be visiting in Westgate Buildings? – A Mrs. Smith. A widow Mrs. Smith, – and who was her husband? One of the five thousand Mr. Smiths whose names are to be met with every where… A poor widow, barely able to live, between thirty and forty – a mere Mrs. Smith, an every day Mrs. Smith, of all people and names in the world, to be the chosen friend of Miss Anne Elliot, and to be preferred by her, to her own family connexions among the nobility of England and Ireland! Mrs. Smith, such a name!" (157-8)

The expostulation of Sir Walter Elliot in response to his daughter's declining Lady Dalrymple's invitation in order to visit a former school friend in reduced circumstances. This demonstration of the full flow of his rhetorical and indeed intellectual powers does no more than confirm to the reader the first half of Admiral Croft's earlier observation, that "the baronet will never set the Thames on fire"; but the other half, that "there seems no harm in him", is disproved by the tirade's so wounding the feelings of the otherwise self-possessed Mrs. Clay as to make it impossible for her to stay in the room. In terms of the fortunes of its auditors, it is a far more potent pronouncement than immediately appears. Well considered, it might be found to constitute a turning point in the story.

Not that there is a great deal of substance in the remark; it would have been surprising if there were. True enough, when the author wishes to attribute the status of a nobody to one of her characters, Smith is the surname she seems to fall back upon – as with Emma Woodhouse's protégée Harriet, the mere parlour-boarder at Mrs. Goddard's school, and illegitimate daughter of a "respectable tradesman". But, the matter of status apart, the name itself demonstrably signifies little, if anything. In the course of the novel, Harriet displays such qualities of simplicity, good-nature and tenderness as can cause Emma on occasion to believe Harriet her superior, and capable of attaching men of wealth and social pretension. Roused by Mr. Knightley's attack on their friendship as an impropriety, she not only asserts that "such a girl as Harriet is exactly what every man delights in", but tells him, "Were you yourself ever to marry, she is the very woman for you" (64). Nor, as the world goes, does her opinion seem greatly to err. What reader of *Emma* would deny Harriet's natural and touching dignity towards the close, when she confides her hopes of Knightley's heart – or would at that point reject as a possibility what Emma, despite her every wish, cannot bring herself to do?

The conclusion must be – is it not part of the truth Jane Austen is presenting to us? – that, as it is with her Christian names, so with the surnames, they are in themselves no guide to the assessment of personality, or necessarily of social standing: that, in fact, the rose given another name, or placed within a different category, will smell as sweet. And of this there is corroboration in the other Smith in the novels: the very Mrs. Smith to whom Sir Walter Elliot without knowing her is moved to take such strong objection. Despite her being through poverty and misfortune resident in the unthinkable Westgate Buildings, she shows herself in manners, mind and disposition to be indisputably a lady, and even Anne's superior by right of seniority and knowledge of the world.

This, if a possible doubt – and a serious one – can first be laid to rest. It concerns the soundness or otherwise of her judgment in a prolonged declining to divulge her knowledge of Mr. Elliot's past selfish and cold-hearted demeanour to the friend she believes all but engaged to him in his new situation and persona. When the confidence is at last bestowed, there is amongst Anne's varied emotions so strong a puzzlement at its not having been forthcoming, and, more, at Mrs. Smith's having "seemed to recommend and praise" Mr. Elliot in the interim, that, well-mannered as she is, she cannot withhold an exclamation of surprise. Is she not justified? Can there be anything admirable in default upon so vital an issue, and whatever might lie behind it?

*   *   *

On the face of it, Mrs. Smith's behaviour is inconsistent. Instead of the needful communication, Anne has been offered a series of oblique queries and surmises all oddly indicating approval of the approaching marriage. She hopes and trusts her dear Miss Elliott "will be very happy". When might she speak of it as settled: "Next week?" Why should Miss Elliot be "cruel" enough to affect indifference to Mr. Elliot? Where would she "look for a more suitable match", or "expect a more gentlemanlike, agreeable man?" The change to incommunicativeness and silence that succeeds makes all the more shocking the vehemence of Mrs. Smith's denunciation when it bursts forth.

> "Mr. Elliot is a man without heart or conscience; a designing, wary, cold-blooded being, who thinks only of himself; who, for his own interest or ease, would be guilty of any cruelty, or any treachery, that could be perpetrated without risk of his general character...He is totally beyond the reach of any sentiment of justice or compassion. Oh! he is black at heart, hollow and black!" (199)

It should not escape us, however, that, no sooner are these accusations out of her mouth, than Mrs. Smith is begging her startled friend to "allow for an injured woman". In this recognition of her conduct having gone beyond decorous bounds, might we detect awareness that the position she is taking towards the person who has provoked it is likewise extreme? What, after all, are the offences she has taxed him with? We should do well to inquire, and consider whether they amount to what the poet might term "direct villainy".

There are a number of them. In his early years, Elliot had been guilty of a spendthrift style of living, and of an inclination also undeniable to escape from the trammelling constraints and expectations imposed by the accident of birth. His having found Sir Walter insufferable, insulting as this might seem to Anne Elliot, would elsewhere be deemed a sign of discernment and good taste. The desire to marry for money which subsequently motivated him, while naturally censurable, was one of those things which even Mrs. Smith admitted to be "too common" for outright condemnation, and which so discriminating a young woman as Elizabeth Bennet could view to be allowable in "A man in distressed circumstances", as Elliot was then by Mrs. Smith's account. The fact of his unkindness to his first wife, blemish though it may be, she is likewise from personal knowledge in a position to explain, and excuse. All these faults, while they show Mr. Elliot to be deserving of the title *homme moyen sensuel*, do not mark him down as a villain.

The monstrosity in his nature, if that is what it is, resides in his stern and unpitying refusal to come to the newly-widowed Mrs. Smith's aid, after the bankruptcy and death of the husband who had been his close friend. Estimable in any light such conduct cannot be; but in a certain light it could be seen as defensible. Now affluent, having, as Mrs. Smith puts it, "long had as much money as he could spend, nothing to wish for on the side of avarice or indulgence" (206), he has with the passing of years become intent upon the dignity destined for him in the future baronetcy. With entire propriety, therefore, he had proceeded to drop his former acquaintance upon her impoverishment and loss of social status: her becoming, so to speak, a mere Smith. In acting thus he had reverted to type and class: had "given her up", in the common phrase, with as little thought or compunction as Lady Bertram gave up the sister who had so "disobliged her family" as to bestow her affections upon a Lieutenant of Marines – or as Emma would have had to give up her dear Harriet if she had accepted Mr. Martin's letter of proposal.

Elliot's conduct had been deeply wounding and humiliating, deserving, perhaps, of a term like inhumanity; certainly in the estimation of Anne Elliot, face to face as she was now with grief and despair in her friend. But was she truly in any position to judge? Had she not, it might be asked, herself been guilty of inflicting real suffering, and upon much the same principle, in giving up her friend and lover, Frederick Wentworth, for the sake of "the independence which alone had been wanting"? And done so, in a daughter's more dependent situation, through conformity with the wisdom of that age, and of its spokesman in the figure of Lady Russell? The grief occasioned had not been his alone. Anne had borne a burden of sorrow long thereafter; but, at the time, she had "had to encounter all the additional pain of feelings, on his side, totally unconvinced and unbending, and of his feeling himself ill-used by so forced a relinquishment" (28). While still of course exercising fitting restraint, might he not in his exasperation have harboured the very supposition Mrs. Smith was to entertain of another, that Anne was "a woman without heart or conscience, a designing, wary, cold-blooded being who thinks only of herself"? What he did say, we are left to surmise; but to judge by what we know of his disposition, his parting comments will have been reasonably explicit; and, once having uttered them, he certainly showed no disposition to linger. When he reappears after a long interval, the affront still rankles in him.

So it is with Mrs. Smith, too; but she is sufficiently aware of her world, and has lived in it long enough, to know that, while Mr. Elliot's behaviour was reprehensible, he did not and could not exemplify the charge she has made against him. Her knowledge is Jane Austen's own. Readers and critics can be excused for sometimes forgetting, in the midst of being so well entertained, that in her novels she was not writing about novels, but about life: where, as her fanciful Catherine Morland was brought perforce to admit, it is not a question of persons either being "as spotless as an angel" or "having the disposition of a fiend", but of their partaking of "a general mixture of good and bad" (NA 200). In ordinary social intercourse, some may incur our dislike, a few perhaps justifiably our ire; but we should be unfortunate indeed to find ourselves confronted with a Montoni.

Through most of the fateful interview in her noisy parlour, however, Mr. Elliot was not Mrs. Smith's chief concern, though having been her first. The extremity of her need had made her resolve upon a renewed application, through Anne, to the man who had once spurned her appeal for help; but the presence of this very Miss Elliot was soon to impose upon her a problem far more critical and urgent: nothing less than that of making or marring the life's happiness of the friend she had rejoiced so unexpectedly to encounter. The engagement which she had gathered from all the indications to be about to take place, though apparently not yet a settled thing, was still very likely to happen; and she must now immediately decide whether, and by what right, she might take it upon herself to ensure that it never did.

In that ceremonious age, marriage was deemed not the product of romance, but a matter of family alliance. Within the bounds of her experience it would have been all but impossible for Mrs. Smith to have come upon a match of greater acceptability to the two immediately concerned, or to their family and acquaintances, who were from her certain information delighted at the prospect. All Anne's disavowals notwithstanding, the betrothal seemed near; in her features glowed the radiance of a young woman deeply in love. It betokened also the funds of future happiness which, despite the reservations Mrs. Smith entertained, might well be in store for the pair. For her merely to mention them would be a work of negation: of the destruction of possibility, with consequences unknown.

In its every detail, her subsequent conduct incurs no fault. First, dismissal of the subject of her previous friendship with Mr. Elliot: "It is a great time since we met", she tells Anne. Next comes the hesitation, and the inconsequential remarks often indicative of profound thought, to be followed by those inferences and refined delvings as to the state of Anne's emotions, legitimate in the circumstances, through which she hopes to arrive at a certainty. Then the composed responses to the rallying liveliness of Anne's inquiries, the less than polite short answers, and, finally, the muteness to which she is driven. But not before Anne, in her embarrassment at what was being asked of her, has made clear that her feelings relate to someone else, that "it is not Mr. Elliot that –"; and Mrs. Smith, in sensitive and mannered reaction, has instantly accepted her word, "and with all the semblance of seeing nothing beyond" (194-8).

Almost as soon, her decision has been made, and she is talking "in her natural tone of cordiality": asking pardon, confessing her previous uncertainty as to what to do, pleading the dislike any decent person feels "to be officious, to be giving bad impressions, making mischief" in the lives of others, and, at last, speaking without reserve her condemnation of the man by whom she has been wronged. The account is lengthy; by the time it is over her mood has changed to a considerate solemnity. The last we hear from her, drawn forth by Anne's wonderment at her first seeming commendation of Mr. Elliot, deserves not to be ignored.

> "My dear," was Mrs. Smith's reply, "there was nothing else to be done. I considered your marrying him as certain, though he might not yet have made the offer, and I could no more speak the truth of him, than if he had been your husband. My heart bled for you, as I talked of happiness. And yet, he is sensible, he is agreeable, and with such a woman as you, it was not absolutely hopeless. He was unkind to his first wife. They were wretched together. But she was too ignorant and giddy for respect, and he had never loved her. I was willing to hope that you must fare better." (211)

For Mrs. Smith to have come through so severe and agonising a test of friendship as this is nothing less than a triumph of good sense and good breeding. Where in the novels is there to be found a better example of sensitivity, discretion, principle, and kindness?

*　　　*　　　*

None would deny that the surname of Smith, which Sir Walter finds so offensively plebeian, is undistinguished: but there is another in *Persuasion* which, if anything, is even more so. Not that it is borne by so many persons; but, in respect of the associations of the word, what can be commoner than Clay? which name Jane Austen accords to the widowed daughter of Sir Walter's steward, frequent visitor at Kellynch Hall, and long-term resident in Camden Place. From these particulars a somewhat unfortunate juxtaposition might be deduced. But the lady is a rung or two up the social ladder in her father's being a lawyer – a minor profession, at least, despite its provoking the merriment of Caroline Bingley and Mrs. Hurst at Netherfield Hall, and the scorn of Emma Woodhouse for its representative in Highbury, the pert William Cox. In the novels' world, Mrs. Clay might be no more than on a par with Elizabeth Bennet's rather deplorable uncle Phillips: but she is also the equal of Elizabeth's first love and eventual brother-in-law, George Wickham, the possessor of manners more appealing than those of Mr. Darcy, and of social powers far more considerable.

In these latter respects, Mrs. Clay on her first appearance is as impressive. Quite at her ease in the rarefied atmosphere of Kellynch, she is as ready to promote her father's interests by extolling the virtues of a sailor tenant, as to contradict the baronet in mock remonstrance at his strictures upon the Navy, with her, "Nay, Sir Walter, this is being severe indeed. Have a little mercy on the poor men. We are not all born to be handsome". Clearly, a pronounced if not laudable ability is being displayed, in that this and her other rallyings are at the same time instinct with flattery. Having gone through the list of occupations, with their blighting effects upon the practitioners, she turns to the situation of "those who are not obliged to follow any, who can live in a regular way, in the country, choosing their own hours, following their own pursuits, and living on their own property, without the torment of trying for more", the halcyon leisure of the privileged: and concludes with the splendid compliment, "it is only *their* lot, I say, to hold the blessings of health and a good appearance to the utmost". Could her words be other than music to the vain Sir Walter's ears?

A lively and spirited personality is before us. It does not give evidence of the wit and brilliancy of, say, a Mary Crawford, but shows itself possessed of intellect as powerful as hers. And also, in the processes of conversation, an elegance. If to a degree the speech is an indication of the person, then in the style of the words just quoted, or

44

in her observation that "even in the quieter professions, there is a toil and labour of the mind, if not of the body, which seldom leaves a man's looks to the natural effect of time", rings evidence of Mrs. Clay's being someone worthy of note. But what greater proof can there be, than the fact of her having gained the friendship of the haughty Elizabeth Elliot, and suspicion of arousing the ardour of Sir Walter himself – who, in urging her to prolong her stay in his house, can so surprisingly yet deservedly pay tribute to her "fine mind" (20-1)?

This application was the very last thing his neighbour Lady Russell would have approved. Mrs. Clay's association with the Kellynch family was, for her, "an intimacy, which she wished to see interrupted", a friendship "quite out of place". Due allowance must be made for the "prejudices on the side of ancestry" which, Jane Austen informs us, could have the effect of narrowing her sympathies. Whether the estimate of Mrs. Clay as "a clever young woman, who understood the art of pleasing; the art of pleasing, at least, at Kellynch Hall" is that of Lady Russell or the author herself is impossible to determine; but in the sight of the former, the lady is "a very unequal, and in character she believed a very dangerous companion" for Elizabeth who ought to have been "nothing to her but the object of distant civility" (15-6).

However, in the scope of the novel as a whole, this judgment, or the thinking which leads to it, cannot be sound: for, eight years before, Lady Russell had made a similar objection, for pretty much the same reasons, to the man Anne Elliott finally marries. Wentworth she had seen as an unequal companion in his being entirely lacking in wealth; and the very self-confidence through which he was thereafter to amass a fortune "added a dangerous character to himself". In short, "She deprecated the connexion in every light", and prevailed on Anne to end it (27). Wrong as she has proved about him, can she now be right about Mrs. Clay?

Nevertheless, Lady Russell's opinion is one Anne shares and maintains, unyieldingly, to the last. She feels "quite as keenly" as the older woman the inappropriateness of the plan for Mrs. Clay to accompany her father and sister to Bath, especially in view of Sir

Walter's susceptibility, and is moved by the threat to his family to warn Elizabeth of it; and her immediate concern upon coming to Bath is to ascertain whether he was by now in love with Mrs. Clay. She is naturally more knowledgeable than Lady Russell, and also more observant. She well knew her father's propensity "to be constantly making severe remarks" in her absence upon Mrs. Clay's freckles and projecting tooth and clumsy wrist: but the charm of her being "decidedly altogether well-looking" Anne still does not underestimate. And she has sensed an attribute far more potent, in her possessing "in an acute mind, and assiduous pleasing manners, infinitely more dangerous attractions than any merely personal might have been" (34). Intellectually and socially, Mrs. Clay is a gifted being – a fact which must strongly influence the attitude Anne adopts towards her.

Is there a fear in Anne Elliot of being put in the shade? In a sense, this had already happened, long before Mrs. Clay's advent; and long ago, also, she had "become hardened" to the state. For temperamental and other reasons, Anne was odd man out in that family – was "nobody with either father or sister: her word had no weight; her convenience was always to give way" (5). She is a steady, serious character, in manner gentle and self-effacing; it is typical of her that, much as she is minded to reply upon her father's reproof at her visits in Westgate Buildings, she says nothing.

Whenever she speaks at length, it appears that she does so by effort. She is happier and more herself in making what is best described as minimal comment; though it is worth noting that a quiet remark from her can be unusually forceful. In contrast to Mrs. Clay's long speeches in defence of the Navy, Anne's mild observation that they have "at least an equal claim with any other set of men" not only commands respect, but serves to direct the conversation (19). In the very different setting of the windy Cobb after Louisa's fall, when the party are transfixed with horror, Anne's words, again sparing, are of instant effect, for they proceed from a clear and resolute understanding. "A surgeon!" precipitates action: "Captain Benwick, would it not be better for Captain Benwick?" a change of plan (110). When, at the Harville's, she is obliged to affirm her willingness to stay and look after Louisa, it is done as briefly as courtesy will permit. Rather than springing from any sense of inadequacy, this reserve in Anne Elliot seems the sign of a personal integrity and assurance.

The same may be said concerning that helpfulness of disposition which is as constant in her as it is unaffected. It is not just out of duty, but evidently with pleasure that she has industriously made catalogues of the books and pictures at Kellynch, sorted out the plants to be taken or left, and gone to almost every house in the parish as a take-leave. Again, her instinct when the newly-engaged Henrietta confides her anxieties about her husband's future is a readiness "to do good" by entering interestedly into the subject, acquiescing in Henrietta's sentiments and wishes, and adding kindly encouragement of her own. And, upon her coming to stay at Kellynch Lodge, and hearing Lady Russell discoursing about the Kellynch family's concerns when her own thoughts were engrossed by the people at Lyme, and the friendship of the Harvilles and Captain Benwick, she consciously makes the exertion which courtesy demands, to be able "to meet Lady Russell with any thing like the appearance of equal solicitude, on topics which had by nature the first claim on her" (124). All this is simple good manners, of course, but it is also genuine good will: the two are not very much dissimilar.

In the ordinary course of events, Anne Elliot's reactions always tend to be natural and right, often even laudable. Upon her visiting the Crofts at Kellynch after they have taken possession, no thought of her own family's loss afflicts her: she "could but in conscience feel, that they were gone who deserved not to stay" (125). The Admiral's wayward and sometimes brusque manners do not obscure for her that "goodness of heart" in which she takes such delight; though his perplexity at the number of mirrors in her father's room, and their declaring him "a rather dressy man for his time of life", leaves her, while amused in spite of herself, apprehensively "at a loss for an answer". The barely suppressed grief of Captain Harville, as he speaks of the sister so recently lost, is met with her suggestion, comforting though it be commonplace, "but in time, perhaps – we know what time does in every case of affliction" (108). By the thought, when first she is in Westgate Buildings, of the instances of selflessness and fortitude in human nature at its noblest which must pass before those who nurse the sick, Anne is moved; and in the crippled Mrs. Smith's cheerfulness, her power of transforming an evil into good, she reverently finds "the choicest gift of Heaven".

Such sentiments, while not novel, have nothing of the pretentious about them, but are entirely befitting. And the same holds true of her responses in encounters with the opposite sex: while they are properly modest, there is nothing missish about them. Finding herself being very directly complimented by Mr. Elliot during the interval of the concert, she reacts blushingly with an attempt to change the conversation: "'For shame, for shame! – this is too much of flattery. I forget what we are to have next,' turning to the bill" (187). But she will restrain neither her pleasure nor her inquiries at Charles Musgrove's news of Captain Benwick's admiring her exceedingly, despite Mary's graceless disparagement of the idea; and from that time her head is full of the thought of meeting or seeing him again. And why not?

*   *   *

What, however, distinguishes Anne's behaviour from that of a Catherine Morland in her inexperience, and of an Elizabeth Bennet in her capacity to be misled by her spirits, is the implicit conformity to standards which never fails her: standards of decorum, needless to say, and also of morality. The briefest of chance meetings with a stranger at a seaside inn reveal him, "by the readiness and propriety of his apologies" (104), to be a suitable object for her approval and interest. But the excellent manners of this person prove insufficient seriously to recommend him. In themselves they are pleasing to her, as they are commendable by the precepts of her day; but beyond them, she cannot be satisfied that she really knows his character. Hints of bad habits, of a past carelessness on serious matters, have arisen from further acquaintance with him; and though in mature years he might have come to think differently, what, she asks herself, were now his sentiments – and "How could it ever be ascertained that his mind was truly cleansed?" (161)

We are dealing here with an engaging severity, not unlike that sometimes displayed by Fanny Price, but wider-ranging and better informed: with a conceptual kind of thinking, in fact, of sufficient depth to be able, when occasion demands, to capture the essence of that age's outlook, and state it with admirable conciseness. Consider the advice she gives to young Captain Benwick, impassioned as he allows himself to become, that evening at the Harville's, under the influence of a broken heart and the tenderest outpourings of Scott and Byron: that she considers it poetry's misfortune "to be seldom safely enjoyed by those who enjoy it completely", and that "the strong feelings which alone could estimate it truly, were the very feelings which ought to taste it but sparingly". Is it not the voice of the eighteenth century itself that we are hearing in her dictum – or in the recommendation that Benwick apply himself instead to the study of works of morality and memoirs "calculated to arouse and fortify the mind by the highest precepts, and the strongest of moral and religious endurances" (100)? Unlike Fanny Price, whose reflections, dedicated conformist though she is, show her as standing almost on the brink of romanticism, Anne Elliot reveals herself in these speeches to be a thoroughgoing conventionalist.

And she is declared so by a further and yet more formidable constituent of her nature – whose presence there is most pronounced upon occasions when it might be expected to be least in evidence. One comes as she and Wentworth, restored to each other at last, are pacing the quiet and retired gravel-walk in Bath, oblivious of the bustling life around them, explaining to each other through those precious moments their past actions and feelings. Wentworth is eloquent upon his despair during the concert at seeing her in the company of the same Lady Russell who had before persuaded her to reject him. Anne is genuinely surprised that he should have so misjudged. Previously, she had yielded to persuasion on the side of safety, as was her duty; but could he not have seen that in Bath she was not duty-bound; indeed, that in marrying a man "indifferent" to her she would have violated duty through the risk she was taking? Quite how Wentworth was to recognise and be sure of this indifference she does not explain, and probably would be unable to say: but what is transparently clear to her – and, she feels, ought to be as obvious to him – is duty as a moving principle where she is concerned. Diplomatically enough, Wentworth answers, "Perhaps I ought to have reasoned thus, but I could not" (245). We can only sympathise.

Anne Elliott appears to be on remarkably good terms with the "Stern daughter of the voice of God"; so much so, that she dedicates the ensuing opportunity of tender communication to a further exposition. It is after the drawing rooms at Camden Place have been lighted up, the company at Miss Elliot's card party assembled, and the two have stolen away in pretended admiration of a display of greenhouse plants. She has been trying, she tells Wentworth, to judge her own action in obeying Lady Russell – "whom", she confides, "you will love better than you do now". And she had been right to do so, despite the eight and a half years of separation, since otherwise, "I should have suffered in my conscience". And, as emphatically, she concludes:

> "I have now, as far as such a sentiment is allowable in human nature, nothing to reproach myself with; and if I mistake not, a strong sense of duty is no bad part of a woman's portion." (246)

Wentworth replies only by referring to the point of his future relationship with Lady Russell: the disquisition itself is studiously, and one may think advisedly, ignored. If Anne expected concurrence with the final remark, or with the incipient self-congratulation which had gone before, none was to be forthcoming. One is possibly entitled to infer from Wentworth's silence, as well as some suppressed alarm, the disinclination any lover would feel to encourage the beloved in such flights into the moralistic sublime. The notion that she would have suffered greater disquiet in being with him than the pain she had endured in being without him is not one likely to recommend itself to the hero, whatever satisfaction it might afford the heroine.

Perhaps our best resort for adjudging this idiosyncrasy in Anne Elliot is to Jane Austen herself, who, in mentioning *Persuasion* to her niece Fanny Knight, wrote, "You will not like it, so you need not be impatient. You may *perhaps* like the Heroine, as she is almost too good for me"[27]. Such a confession from such a source is not do be disregarded. It gains credence from the apt comment of her biographer Elizabeth Jenkins, that, after her initial blunder in breaking off her engagement with the man she truly loved, Anne "never makes a single error in morality, judgement or taste"; but she points out that her character nonetheless remains neither priggish nor unreal, finding the reason to lie in her clear-sightedness as to her family's failings, and the tremulous experience of emotion's depths and heights, which combine to "keep her altogether vulnerable and human"[28].

Anne's sensitivity to the "thousand natural shocks" life has for us does to an extent moderate, or rather reconcile us to, the goodness in question. But there is a further ingredient of her personality, no less human and humbling, which may however properly lead us to speculate whether the "goodness" Jane Austen comes near to reprehending in Anne Elliot is not to be regarded as somewhat more social than moral, though pertaining to both sorts of virtues: as being rather a correctness, in keeping with the age's delineations, as to what was ideal and so appropriate for admiration and imitation in a young woman, while yet with respect to the former incurring some tincture of that society's austerities.

At the risk of slight injustice to Anne, the suggestion can be made that it might be detected in a wholly inconsequential remark of hers to Mrs. Smith, who had asked whether she had noticed the woman who opened the door to her the previous day. Anne's reply is, "No. Was it Mrs. Speed, as usual, or the maid? I observed no one in particular" (197). The omission had been innocent: it is not incumbent upon, or in the habit of, young ladies like herself to pay any special attention to servants. Nor to the lower orders in general. For this reason, the pleasure which Mrs. Smith confesses she has derived from listening to Nurse Rooke strikes Anne as somewhat singular; but, "far from wishing to cavil at" it she responds with the thought that, "Women of that class have great opportunity, and if they are intelligent may be worth listening to" (155). Harmless truism though this be, it is at the same time in the nature of a concession – and one from which it may be safely conjectured that Anne has done little listening of that variety. These are incidental touches, and in themselves carry little weight; but they are germane to the far more definite comment later on in the session, provoked by Mrs. Smith's inability, during the years of her early acquaintance with Mr. Elliot, to see much wrong in his marrying for money, when this was so common a preoccupation amongst the young men they then knew. "But was she not a very low woman?" Anne asks. There is an incredulity and near expostulation in the remark, which imparts a note of finality. It is not insignificant that Mrs. Smith wholly accords with the sentiment.

In this attitude, both are being correct. Even for the rich and seemingly less fastidious Emma Woodhouse, the evident "indifference to a confusion of rank" in Frank Churchill's recommending a fortnightly ball at the Crown Inn, despite the objection urged upon him of "the want of proper families" in the neighbourhood, "bordered upon inelegance of mind" unacceptable in someone of his station (E 198). Is Anne Elliot to be blamed for sharing views so universally held?

That she has them is certain; but in a curious way she is made to profess a discrepant freedom with regard to rank at variance with the otherwise instinctive and conventional position she takes. When Mr. Elliot seeks to persuade her of the importance of their accepting Lady Dalrymple's preparedness to welcome them, and enjoying "all the advantages of the connexion as far as possible", she makes the almost heretical assertion, in intimating, "I suppose (smiling) I have more pride than any of you", that they have been too solicitous in getting the relationship acknowledged, and that she is and must remain "too proud to enjoy a welcome which depends so entirely upon place" (150). Her idea of good company she had already informed him to be that of "clever, well-informed people, who have a great deal of conversation"; and she does, to do her justice, in general show an impatience with society's externalities, like "the usual style of give-and-take invitations, and dinners of formality and display", and the tedious social gatherings which were "but a mixture of those who had never met before, and those who met too often" (245). Not that this tendency, errant though it be, will lead her too far astray. The prospect of becoming the next Lady Elliot through marriage with the heir presumptive, when first put before her by her friend Lady Russell, obliges Anne to turn and walk aside and pretend employment in the attempt to repress the feelings it creates: "For a few moments her imagination and her heart were bewitched" (160). It is realisation of the incapacity of the man in the affair to exercise bewitchment upon her that causes the dream to disperse; rank itself, and properly so, is under no such disqualification.

The effect of this irregularity – or inconsistency, as it might be supposed – in Anne's character is to make her appear to rise above, and so to obscure, her more ordinary attitude to the matter of rank and class. Jane Austen endows her with, as it were, a refreshing incorrectness which, in its humanity, is safe from criticism and beyond reproach, but which yet does not have sufficient hold to divide her from her more normal and conventional self. Thus is fulfilled a need in the heroine, and manifestly in the author, that Anne's condition of being "almost too good" do not develop into excess: that, though granted such impressive endowment of heroic charm, she will remain

> A creature not too bright or good
> For human nature's daily food –

particularly, as regards the social attitudes she was born to.

*   *   *

Hence, for all that it is undoubted and abundant in Anne Elliot, her good will may not extend to Mrs. Clay. Instead, there is a sophisticated watchfulness that is quick to detect a fault, to fathom the pretences she is often put to in her attentions to the family which has so condescendingly welcomed her into their midst. She is only a visitor when we first find her with them, the reason being – as Anne is aware of it – that her father Mr. Shepherd had driven her over, "nothing being of so much use to Mrs. Clay's health as a drive to Kellynch" (18). In the eagerness of her enumerating the depredations upon men's health and looks of professional practice, we are informed – again, it seems, in terms of Anne's recognition – that "she stopt a moment to consider what might do for the clergyman" (20). These contrivances, if they are at all culpable, are trifling; but that they are being viewed with suspicion, or scorn, cannot be denied. Such perceptions in Anne are illustrative of a dislike, or even an antagonism, that is unrelieved to the novel's end. Even the "pleasant and smiling" greeting she receives from Mrs. Clay upon her coming to Bath is contemptuously regarded: "Anne had always thought she would pretend what was proper on her arrival" (137).

Without doubt, it is the danger she constitutes to her own and her sister's prospects which gives rise to this critical spirit; but the reality of the hurt is plain. Anne's early encounters with Mrs. Clay in Camden Place are diversified by Mr. Elliot's frequent visits; and what makes Anne ready to overlook his lenient censure of the notion of good society she puts to him is the intimated disapproval of the lady they both see as outside its bounds: "she was pleased with him for not liking Mrs. Clay; and her conscience admitted that his wishing to promote her father's getting great acquaintance, was more than excusable in the view of defeating her" (151). The being afterwards put on her guard against him by Mrs. Smith's revelation plunges her therefore into a rather diverting state of exasperation.

> It was bad enough that Mrs. Clay should be always before her; but that a deeper hypocrite should be added to their party, seemed the destruction of every thing like peace and comfort. (215)

To be set between a Scylla and a Charybdis in the confines of a drawing room is a fate no one would envy.

Is it pure alarm at "the results the most severe to his family" that would follow from her father's marrying Mrs. Clay which causes Anne to warn the sister "who in the event of such a reverse would be so much more pitied than herself"? Or is there an admixture of fear of the disgrace which Mrs. Clay's "low" condition would bring upon them all? There is nothing about the latter possibility in what she says to Elizabeth; but it is almost entirely in terms of rank that she is answered, inheritance as such being relegated almost to an afterthought. "Mrs. Clay", Elizabeth tells her with warmth, "never forgets who she is"; more strongly than most people, "she reprobates all inequality of condition and rank"; and her sentiments upon marriage are in this respect "particularly nice" (35). The substance of the matter, though unstated in Anne's approach, is asserted by Elizabeth, and understood by both, to be the formidable barrier of social decorum which they know to exist, and behind which, presumably, they should feel themselves secure.

Upon that bulwark, the visit Anne was to make to Mrs. Smith is nothing less than a formal assault: clear defiance of established custom. And not without due deliberation and caution is it undertaken. From the personal viewpoint, Anne was reasonably confident of not being grossly in error. Apart from intervening misfortunes since they had last seen each other, Mrs. Smith had strong claims upon her in her present crippled state, and in that past kindness when Anne had returned to school grieving over her mother's death, "which had considerably lessened her misery, and could never be remembered with indifference" (152). These considerations, however, were in themselves not enough: for an affair of such moment, it was needful to have recourse to an elder's experience and principle, and Lady Russell was applied to. Her judgment was favourable: Anne's youthful friendship, the then Miss Hamilton's comfortable circumstances and her subsequently becoming the wife of a man of fortune, as well as charitable concern for an invalid, sufficiently militated against her present penniless condition for Anne to renew acquaintance with her. But Lady Russell's preparedness to convey her "as near to Mrs. Smith's lodgings in Westgate Buildings as she chose to be taken" betokens the equivocal nature of the proceeding in the minds of both ladies (153). A stern critic – and what is more, a fair and impartial one – might see in it an apprehension lest the coach and its owner should be so sullied by that proximity as to be in need of the month's ablution which Elizabeth irreverently imagined Mr. Darcy would resort to, "in order that he might be cleansed from the impurities of Gracechurch Street were he once to enter it" (PP 141).

But this time Lady Russell's judgment had been sound. Once the awkwardness and emotion of the first moments have faded, Mrs. Smith is, for Anne, as much still the lady of her remembrance, as Mr. Elliot the gentleman when she again sets eyes on him. Yet she has not been without trepidation as to what change intervening years and events might have brought about in her erstwhile friend. Happily, we are informed, as the meeting progressed, Anne finds in Mrs. Smith "the good sense and agreeable manners which she had almost ventured to depend on" (153). The intimation of verb and adverb conjoined surely is testimony to the existence in Anne Elliot of apprehensions concerning the venture she was engaged upon, not so very far removed from Sir Walter's own. But swiftly they have been done away. It cannot be said at this point that she has crossed the Rubicon of social decorum: but she is now at least safely over one of its lesser tributaries.

For what would have been her feelings if Sir Walter had recklessly launched himself across this fateful waterway with regard to Mrs. Clay, and grandly set foot upon the opposite bank? Would they not have amounted to such dismay as afflicted Emma Woodhouse at the thought of Mr. Knightley married to Harriet Smith?

> Such an elevation on her side! Such a debasement on his! – It was horrible to Emma to think how it must sink him in the general opinion, to foresee the smiles, the sneers, the merriment it would prompt at his expense – the mortification and disdain of his brother, the thousand inconveniences to himself. (413)

For any self-respecting gentleman such things would be sufficiently daunting. But for an individual as considerate of his dignity as Sir Walter Elliot, they would assume tragic proportions.

But what of the subject of "elevation" – which also exercises Miss Woodhouse's mind? Who, let the question be asked, being in social terms a nobody, is to be seen in the novels as achieving acceptability and bliss? Addressing it, we find ourselves embarked upon a rather barren quest. There are, for a start, very few persons so identifiable.

*   *   *

Edmund Bertram, humble as his ambitions and his finances are, is not a candidate: the younger son of a baronet, with "a very good living" kept for him thereabouts, as Miss Crawford has not failed to notice, cannot be so described. Nor can the well-born Edward Ferrars, who, after rejecting the choice of a Parliamentary or military career, finds himself arbitrarily disinherited, but is thereafter moderately redeemed through the unexpected gift of a living. A similar calamity had befallen Elinor and Marianne Dashwood, heiresses of a wealthy old country family unfairly cut out through a trick of senility in their grandfather; but by the end they both manage to do quite reasonably well, their establishments, while far from equal in affluence, being fortunately within thirty miles of each other.

Charles Hayter, though, is at first sight a different case, for his family were not people of any consequence. "And, pray, who is Charles Hayter?" Mary Musgrove asks. "Nothing but a country curate. A most improper match for Miss Musgrove, of Uppercross". But Mary is being rather too severe, as her husband points out to her. It would, he admits, "not be a *great* match for Henrietta"; but Mary is overlooking the fact that Charles Hayter has "a very fair chance, through the Spicers, of getting something from the Bishop" in due course, and that, elder son as he is, upon the death of his father "he steps into very pretty property" in the estate at Winthrop and the farm near Taunton. And "with that property", he concludes, "he will never be a contemptible man.

Good, freehold property" (76). However much this assurance may be unwelcome to Mary, her cousin Charles is unlikely to be despised by anyone other than herself.

Nor is his being a mere curate a hindrance. The clergy in that age had the mild distinction of being regarded as a class of sub-gentry, and tolerated as such, so long of course as they did not give themselves unbecoming airs – or otherwise, in the decorous words of Mr. Collins, "provided that a proper humility is at the same time maintained" (PP 97). Catherine Morland by this same standard deserves recognition. True, she is only a clergyman's daughter; but her father is the possessor not only of two livings, but of landed property which is to be his eldest son's future inheritance; and Catherine's dowry of three thousand pounds, while not great, is respectable.

Catherine's portion is three times the amount of Elizabeth Bennet's, however; and this sober truth brings into sharp question the matter of Elizabeth's status. Mrs. Bennet being left out of the reckoning, she has the indubitable claim of being a gentleman's daughter. But since her father's estate of two thousand per annum is entailed from the female line, she is in practical terms all but dowerless: a consideration which, as Mr. Collins hatefully but correctly advises her, will "in all likelihood undo the effects of your loveliness and amiable qualifications", and make it "by no means certain that another offer of marriage may ever be made you" (PP 108). The inferiority of her social position not only calls forth Lady Catherine de Bourgh's unmitigated horror, but creates those "scruples" and provokes those "struggles" in Mr. Darcy so calculated to nullify the import of his declaration of love, despite his guileless insistence upon their being "natural and just" in a man of his eminence. Neither they nor the reflection they constitute finally prevent her becoming mistress of Pemberley, but that development is a notable elevation; and her claim to social distinction, personable in every other respect though she is, has been only marginally admissible.

Whether it is as strong as that of *Sense & Sensibility*'s Mrs. Jennings is not easily determined. Mrs. Jennings never can have been, as Elizabeth is even in the eyes of Lady Catherine, "a very genteel, pretty kind of girl":

pretty or not, she was and remains incurably vulgar. We learn from John Dashwood that, as we might have guessed, she is "the widow of a man who got all his money in a low way"; but to this material detail must be added Elinor's serious caution to her mother, that "she is not a woman whose society can afford us pleasure, or whose protection will give us consequence" (SS 156). Yet in both respects, Miss Dashwood proves to be mistaken. Since her husband's death, Mrs. Jennings has taken to spending every winter "in a house in one of the streets near Portman Square", which, with her style of living, indicates "an exceedingly good income"; and, of more importance, her decency and warmth of heart so affect Elinor as to promote a highly unlikely but very firm friendship between them. Ill-bred, in her son-in-law's forthright and uncalled-for estimation, and Elinor's unspoken one, Mrs. Jennings may be; but, all things considered, her obvious wealth, and the irrefutable facts that one of her daughters is a Lady Middleton, and the other the wife of a Member of Parliament, will procure for her the complaisance of those she comes in contact with.

Quite who Mr. Smith was, who at his death left his affairs in such confusion, and his wife unprovided for, we are not to learn. His easiness of temper and "not strong understanding" had, as Anne Elliot gathers, between them kept him from retaining his fortune; yet that it had been considerable is evident from his widow's title to property in the West Indies, long "under a sort of sequestration for the payment of its own encumbrances", which Captain Wentworth finally recovers for her. The ensuing "improvement of income", together with some return of health, will, as well as creating in her "a spring of felicity", ensure the justification of any essay on Mrs. Smith's part to resume her former social standing – and discontinuance, it need not be said, of her residence in Westgate Buildings (252).

No such happiness does Willoughby gain or merit. For the wife who has freed him from his "dread of poverty" and conviction of "the necessity of riches", he comes to have unmeasured contempt. The fierce determination in one living above his income to make his fortune by marriage is understandable, though scarcely pardonable by the young woman he has jilted. Success of a kind he attains; bliss most emphatically he does not. But in all his actions, good and bad alike, he is seen to exemplify the manner and style of a gentleman. So also is the cultured Henry Crawford, more fortunate in that money-making need not be one of his preoccupations. With his captivating sister, he is at the centre of happenings at Mansfield Park. Their becoming involved in scandal and failure is the outcome of faults of character, and not related to their assured position in society.

Life, of course, will always have its casualties, even amongst the privileged and advantaged. Within the ranks of Jane Austen's commoners, though, it is a matter of adversity and mischance almost unrelieved. Which of them is not at the end, by social definition, a casualty: can be said to have come to good, to have progressed into status, and the dignified pleasures and eligibilities consequent upon it? Alas, it is not the artless Harriet Smith, who is finally hustled away and finds her proper place as the wife of Farmer Martin – to Emma's infinite relief, and with the dubious distinction of having been in love with three different men in a single year. The ultimate fates of the underbred John and Isabella Thorpe are not vouchsafed to us; but we may be confident that they are of as small concern to ourselves as to the novelist, and will have nothing at all prepossessing about them.

If it were only for the extensive role he plays, George Wickham would appear more fortunately destined. But his have been also the not insignificant benefits of being brought up at Pemberley, educated at Cambridge, and intended for the Church; and in manners and address he is in no way inferior to Pemberley's present owner. His being the son of the late Mr. Darcy's steward is no more disabling to the reader than it is to Elizabeth Bennet when Caroline Bingley laughingly apprises her of it. Nor indeed is it a factor in the estimation of most persons the novel introduces us to, not excluding that of Fitzwilliam Darcy himself, if we accept his explanations. Yet by the end, Wickham is revealed as a liar, slanderer, philanderer and gamester: in the author's words, "one of the most worthless young men in Great Britain" (PP 308).

In descent, Mrs. Clay is Wickham's equal; and her deservings and final repute might seem to be almost a reflection of his own. For her course through events is aided by flattery and artifice, she evokes no good opinion, and contrives eventually to shock and mortify Sir Walter and Elizabeth, having failed in her intention to become the wife of the one, and mother-in-law of the other. What is to lie beyond for her is outside the novel's scope. We last hear of her as being established under Mr. Elliot's protection in London, there abandoned to the unsavoury endeavour of "wheedling and caressing" him into making her the next Lady Elliot. Succeed she may; but the inference through all we have seen of her association with the people of the novel, and particularly that person who is its heroine, is that she does not deserve to.

A distinct success, though one similarly unbeseeming, may be thought to have occurred in Lucy Steele's securing the witless Robert Ferrars as her husband. Certain it is that she gains, with him, both fortune and favour with her mother-in-law and her friends the Dashwoods. But in terms of the ensuing relationships, domestic and other, Lucy's victory is rather to be viewed as of the Pyrrhic sort, and the marriage itself as little other than merited penalty.

*   *   *

Upon a mere two, perhaps three, persons who are nobodies can good fortune and approval by all the standards of Jane Austen's novels be seen to descend. These instances share a vital common element; and in one only is it not obvious.

Fanny Price, at the age of ten transplanted to Mansfield Park, appears to bear the brunt of a social system's severity. Uppermost in her uncle Sir Thomas Bertram's mind is "the distinction proper to be made" between the newcomer and his own daughters as they grow up, the line of conduct which will always impress her lack of claim upon her. So little have her interests been regarded, seemingly, that when she has reached her eighteenth year it is unclear to the Bertrams, and anyone of inquiring disposition, whether or not she is "out"; and she herself has never presumed to consider the subject.

At Mansfield Park there are a number of circumstances helpful to Fanny. She has had at her disposal all the appurtenances of dignified living which a great household can bestow – an immense boon, in comparison with the meagre conditions Emma Watson must compromise with. The behaviour of Maria and Julia Bertram can only confirm Fanny's innate shyness; but upon their departure from Mansfield she is left "the only young woman in the drawing-room", her consequence at home and at the Parsonage increasing to the extent of her having, at the latter, to fulfil the demands of being the principal lady in company. In the resolve constantly to keep before her the fact of her obscurity, her aunt is nothing less than an affliction; but relief comes from Sir Thomas's growing realisation that blood is thicker than water. For, though a commoner, Fanny is a well-connected one – a condition the author herself was not unfamiliar with. Her uncle begins at length to feel proud of his humble relation. He is not under Mrs. Norris's illusion that her beauty is attributable to her upbringing at Mansfield; however, "he was pleased with himself for having supplied everything else – education and manners she owed to him" (276). His protégée differs notably from Harriet Smith in being an excellent recipient of benefits: she possesses that liveliness of mind which, as Anne Elliot so well appreciated, is the height of attraction in a handsome woman.

Yet these not inconsiderable advantages do not of themselves promote the happiness Fanny attains: it is her association with the Navy which is to bring her to distinction. But for midshipman Price's coming, Sir Thomas would never have realised the possibilities in his niece. He encounters in young Price "frank, unstudied, but feeling and respectful manners"; but the effect of their naturalness upon Fanny is a release and joyous flowering "which her uncle could not but observe with complacency". He is moved repeatedly to call upon its occasioner to recount his experiences at sea (233-4), and the qualities manifest in them gain him Sir Thomas's esteem.

Thus, when William asks his uncle a question he cannot answer – "Is not Fanny a very good dancer, sir?" – the outcome, extraordinary for the demesne of sobriety Mansfield Park has been, is that approving determination to satisfy her brother's wish to see her dance which results in the festivity Sir Thomas decrees. To her initial horror, Fanny learns that "*she* was to lead the way and open the ball" as "the Queen of the evening". What in her humility she finds so overpowering is less the situation in the ballroom than the thought of the honour accorded her.

> She could hardly believe it. To be place above so many elegant young women! The distinction was too great. It was treating her like her cousins! (275)

The ball at Mansfield scarcely marks the end of Fanny's trials and anxieties: but it establishes her in full and undisputed possession of those social privileges which will make possible her eventual achievement of a long despaired-of happiness.

*   *   *

Captain Frederick Wentworth is no scion of the Strafford family; and neither he nor his friend Captain Benwick is a gentleman in the strict term which Sir Walter withholds from Wentworth's clergyman brother, Edward. Not surprising are the strong grounds of objection the baronet must entertain towards the Navy: it is an institution by which all proper considerations of social decorum are disregarded, and anomalies of nefarious kind perpetrated. It is a means, he declares, "of bringing persons of obscure birth into undue distinction, and raising men to honours which their fathers and forefathers never dreamt of" – and men, to boot, who have been "all knocked about, and exposed to every climate, and every weather, until they are not fit to be seen" (201). From the latter charge, Wentworth is providentially spared; and as to the former, he may "hug himself". For Jane Austen, the Navy is the realm where the artificialities of her society are blown asunder and scattered, where true merit is revealed: the proving ground of courage, worth, and, yes, nobility. It is a small world in itself – but yet a world apart, removed in concept, as literally by distance, from the outlook and standards of the great and assured social order beneath whose dominance her own life was played out, and to whose enabling impositions she, with all those whom she knew, must ever yield.

*   *   *

In his *Memoir*, written in the year 1870, James Edward Austen-Leigh suggested that the reason for his aunt's laying aside *The Watsons* was that she had

> become aware of the evil of having placed her heroine too
> low, in such a position of poverty and obscurity as, though not
> necessarily connected with vulgarity, has a sad tendency to
> degenerate into it; and therefore, like a singer who has begun
> on too low a note, she discontinued the strain.[29]

The thought comes to us from an epoch much closer to Jane Austen's than ours, and by the hand of a nephew who might with delicacy be presenting as a surmise of his own, intimations from acquaintance with the writer herself. It is therefore deserving of attention.

In citing these words, however, Elizabeth Jenkins admits herself unimpressed by them. "One cannot feel that this reason is a convincing one", she comments, "if only because Emma Watson is shown to such triumphant advantage in the poverty and obscurity of her home"[30]. But, as the evidence of the novels taken together, and particularly of *Persuasion*, may lead us to conjecture, might it not be precisely because of this achievement in Emma Watson, so at variance with the assumptions and mood of those times, that Jane Austen found herself obliged to leave the work unfinished? That, despite all her insights and promptings as to the meretriciousness of "place", and the primacy of human worth, it was not in her nature to become a *bucinator novi temporis*, the herald of change to her contemporaries and her own intimates: to venture into territory untrodden by the polite authors of her day, or admit even to herself such a daunting possibility?

For this same cause (if we are at liberty to apply the phrase she used of herself as an historian) she makes her Anne Elliot resolutely "partial and prejudiced" – not to say "ignorant" – in her treatment of Mrs. Clay. Though never approaching the directness of Edmund Bertram in declaring a commoner's being on equal terms "an evil", Anne is at one with him, and with the restored Emma Woodhouse, in the simple practice of looking down upon those beneath them: in an implicit belief that it is a propensity beyond question, itself a rightness, and, in the social context, a modest but undeniable virtue. This tenet Emma has painfully to learn after her escapade with Harriet Smith; but Anne Elliot, as the very pattern of the ladylike – of feminine "goodness", as the age understood, and Jane Austen acknowledged, it – is incapable of a lapse of the sort.

In the character of Emma Woodhouse, and that of Emma Watson, and in the fortunes of such as Harriet Smith and Penelope Clay, we may see the externalisation of a conflict deep in the author's being: a contention between an instinctive revolt against the pretensions and oppressiveness of "place", and a compulsive adherence to it as the basis of decorum, agreeableness and elegance – in other words, of such goodness in the wide sense as human society is able to afford. And since, for her, these opposites must remain always locked in combat, so their struggle can find vigorous expression, but not resolution, in the novels' world. Mrs. Clay's presence at Camden Place can but prompt in Jane Austen the certitude aroused in Hamlet by a Claudius enthroned in Denmark, that "It is not nor it cannot come to good" [31]. Like the usurper, Mrs. Clay can appear to her only as a threatening intruder into a previously settled milieu – as much so, perhaps, as was the social upstart Wickham beneath Caroline Bingley's contemptuous gaze.

*   *   *

Thus it comes about that, despite her constant observation, Anne Elliot is poorly placed for a true judgment of Mrs. Clay. The latter's recognition of the knock on the door at ten o'clock being Mr. Elliot's gains her notice: but it might have told her more. Mrs. Clay's encouraging the notion of a liking in Mr. Elliot for Elizabeth is picked up through the look the women exchange when the frequency of his visits is under discussion; nor does it elude Anne that Mrs. Clay should steal a glance at her sister and herself when being so very earnestly complimented by Sir Walter upon her "fine mind". But what escapes her is at least as much as what does not – and more remarkably so. While Sir Walter is delivering his vilification of the proletarian Smiths, the fact that Mrs. Clay "thought it advisable to leave the room" is obvious to the rest of them; but Anne "left it to himself to recollect, that Mrs. Smith was not the only widow in Bath between thirty and forty, with little to live on, and no sirname of dignity". This awareness, evidently absent from the other two, is strongly present in her. But its not bringing her to realise the blow his aspersion must have constituted to Mrs. Clay's hopes of the baronet, and the acuteness of the resulting distress which will have accompanied her departure, is more than strange.

It might be held that literary necessity has demanded her imperception here: that an Anne Elliot at this early stage perceiving Mrs. Clay's purpose to have been thwarted, or as unlikely to succeed, would mean a heightening of the coming competition between the two for Mr. Elliot's favour which would give Mrs. Clay greater prominence, as well as taking from the novel what it gains from the manoeuvring with respect to Sir Walter that she and Mr. Elliot are later presumed to be engaged in. And Mrs. Clay herself might have reason to think that her design upon Sir Walter is still not hopeless. But that she has greater cause to revise her policy at Camden Place may be deduced from a feature of her subsequent conduct which Anne becomes conscious of, but whose significance, once more, escapes her. She identifies as suspect in Mr. Elliot his contriving to please all in that house, despite the tempers of its inhabitants being so various. He had, she notes, "appeared completely to see what Mrs. Clay was about, and to hold her in contempt; and yet Mrs. Clay found him as agreeable as any body" (161). This is sound enough where the gentleman's motives are concerned; but it leaves aside any inclination in the lady which the circumstance may denote. She does, indeed, not seem to dislike the man.

The next instance of the kind comes about with a suddenness that leaves Anne in the thick of the fray with scarcely a moment to reflect on what is happening. It is occasioned by nothing more than a slight drizzle of rain in Milsom Street; but the consequence could not be more marked. Shelter in Lady Dalrymple's carriage being the undoubted privilege of Miss Elliot, the remaining seat is at the disposal of one of the other two ladies of the party. Correctly, and politely as ever, Mrs. Clay offers Anne the place: "her civility", as Jane Austen writes with meaning, "rendered her as anxious to be left to walk with Mr. Elliot, as Anne could be". The point is disputed between them with "a generosity so polite, and so determined", in fact – the rain to each being only a trifle, and Mrs. Clay affirming her boots to be "much thicker than Miss Anne's" – that it can only be settled by outside agency, Miss Elliot maintaining that Mrs. Clay has a little cold already, and Mr. Elliot "deciding on appeal, that his cousin Anne's boots were rather the thickest" (174-5). What is evident to the reader from this skirmish, and can only be so to Anne, is the strong desire in Mrs. Clay to be with Mr. Elliot; yet from this open rivalry Anne appears to make no inference as to the state of the other's emotions. – Is it because she is assured of Elliot's preference, reflected in his decision? Or because she regards Mrs. Clay as too far beneath them to be worth considering? Or is the entire incident driven from her mind the next instant, by the sight of Captain Wentworth walking down the street?

Two things at least are clear. Jane Austen will not use what has happened in Milsom Street to do anything that would put Mrs. Clay on a level with Anne, romantically speaking. And Mrs. Clay has learned from Mr. Elliot's action that at this moment he has more interest in Anne than herself.

Needless to say, Mrs. Clay is together with Sir Walter and his two daughters when, the earliest of their party for the concert, they take their position by one of the fires in the Octagon Room. Presently

Captain Wentworth enters alone. Anne boldly steps towards him; and there follows between them a conversation which, despite the door's slam and the "ceaseless buzz of persons walking through" (183), could not fail to impress the others by its length and particularity. It is enough indeed to gain for Wentworth the "simple acknowledgement of acquaintance" formally bestowed on him by Sir Walter and Elizabeth; but it develops into that near-declaration from him which renders Anne "struck, gratified, confused, and beginning to breathe very quick, and feel a hundred things in a moment". Throughout the whole, Anne is too engrossed to have a thought for Mrs. Clay: but the reverse is not true. Mrs. Clay will have seen enough to give her a far stronger hint than that which was soon to suffice for Mrs. Smith, that it is not Mr. Elliot who holds the key to Anne's heart.

The impression will have been confirmed almost immediately afterwards – though, sitting close to them on the "contiguous benches" of the concert room, she is first to see Mr. Elliot talking to Anne with almost equal particularity: confusing her with his flattery, professing in low tones an acquaintance with her character long before their meeting, and gaining her curiosity and eager questioning, until a rearrangement of the party separates them. For, upon a hesitant Captain Wentworth then once more approaching, he is determinedly engaged in conversation by Anne for a second time, only to walk off with abruptness at the moment she is touched on the shoulder by Mr. Elliot making a request. Mrs. Clay now is sufficiently in the secret of Anne's affections to know, with gratification, that Mr. Elliot's chance with her is slight: and conscious that Anne is perfectly unaware, amidst the excitements and intimations the evening has brought her, of having betrayed her innermost feelings.

It is but a matter of hours before Anne, discoursing with her friend in Westgate Buildings, is in receipt of information as decisive about the heart of Mr. Elliot, and his business in Bath. The mystery of his eagerness to be reconciled to Sir Walter, and of his constant attendance in Camden Place, is resolved: all has been brought about through the "very material change in Mr. Elliot's opinion as to the value of a baronetcy", and what has become for him the vital need to head off from its present possessor the advances of the "clever, insinuating, handsome woman, poor and plausible" (206), who, according to Mrs. Smith, is laying siege to its honours. But this estimate of Mrs. Clay is from externalities only, based on information gleaned from hearsay and report; and so is the opinion that the threat is lessening because of the lady's awareness that Elliot "sees through her, and not daring to do as she might do in his absence". The bulk of what Mrs. Smith affirms having been proved accurate, it is not surprising that Anne, in her wider ignorance, should take that part appertaining to Mrs. Clay as comprising the extent of her ambition. The design upon Sir Walter is all that she has managed, and, perhaps, cares, to grasp. Thus she will proceed to dismiss simply as good acting the pleasure now so evident in Mrs. Clay at knowledge that Mr. Elliot will be in the house the same evening. She even can admit herself perplexed by the thought that, while "Mrs. Clay must hate the thought of Mr. Elliot", she could yet "assume a most placid, obliging look, and appear quite satisfied with the curtailed license of devoting herself only half as much to Sir Walter as she would have done otherwise" (213-4). The possibility of another, and a deeper, explanation never crosses her mind.

Is it credible that an Anne Elliot, with her intelligence, reflectiveness, and principle, can have been so deceived as to the conduct of one within her circle, and blind in matters of dearest concern? For answer, we have only to look at ourselves. Making wrong inferences from appearances is a common enough pursuit; and Jane Austen's heroines are industriously engaged upon it. We have for example but to think of Emma's surmisings about Jane Fairfax's pianoforte, or Frank Churchill's rescuing Harriet from the gipsies; of Elizabeth Bennet, who before has prided herself upon her discernment, "wretchedly blind" to Darcy's character; or poor Catherine's deduction from General Tilney's having discarded the portrait of his late wife. Were a calculation to be made, it might well appear that, in terms of their more important suppositions, the heroines are nearly as often mistaken as not. Perhaps for them all, the explanation is that which may credibly be given for Anne Elliot:

that she has been too much governed by preconception, and too full of her own affairs and feelings, to be able to discern the reality.

*　　　*　　　*

But at least she has learned the truth about Mr. Elliot. It is distressing for her now even to see him, painful to have him speak to her, and be finding insincerity in his every word and gesture. Only one course of action is open to her once she is convinced she has found him out. It is, while avoiding any marked alteration of manners, "to be as decidedly cool to him as might be compatible with their relationship, and to retrace, as quietly as she could, the few steps of unnecessary intimacy she had been gradually led along" (214). For, as she knew from the moment of her leaving Westgate Buildings, there was no longer "any thing of tenderness" due to him – nothing, in fact, of the least concern, politeness apart. But however delicately Anne may have conveyed this disfavour, a "sensible, discerning mind" like Elliot's will be conscious of having experienced a rebuff. He might scarcely have noticed Captain Wentworth at Lyme, or in Milsom Street, and have paid little heed to him at the concert; perhaps he would not yet suspect some new disposition on Anne's part. But the change in her attitude to himself, and his sense of the clouding of his prospect of success with her, will be unmistakable: and will give him reason, and put him at liberty, to pursue a long-developing preference of his own.

This apparently is the cause of his absenting himself for a day or two from Sir Walter's house and its constraints, for a visit to Thornbury, as he lets it be known. Part of the outcome is visible to the entire company at the White Hart, in the phenomenon of his being observed under the colonnade by the corner with Bath Street, "deep in talk" with Mrs. Clay, and then shaking hands with her (the sign of cordiality itself) as they turn from each other in different directions. On moving to the window at Mary Musgrove's insistence, Anne, predictably, is put to "checking the surprise which she could not but feel at such appearance of friendly conference between two persons of totally opposite interests"

(223). She is moved by no very generous impulse that evening to let Mrs. Clay know of her having been seen in Elliot's company three hours after his supposedly leaving Bath. All the satisfaction she gains is the impression of a flash of guilt instantly cleared away, an over-long protestation from the lady of having forgotten their meeting, and a supposition thereupon that, "by some complication of mutual trick, or some overbearing authority of his", she had been obliged to listen to his "lectures and restriction on her designs on Sir Walter" (228). It is this entirely mistaken notion of hers that we are left with. Enlightenment at what has been going on between Mr. Elliot and Mrs. Clay, and about the real state of the lady's affections, Anne Elliot is unable, and Jane Austen has been unwilling, to provide for us.

Anything further concerning the pair is conveyed through narration. We are told that Anne's engagement to Wentworth frustrated any design Mr. Elliot had on Elizabeth, and his plan to resume the watch upon Sir Walter which "a son-in-law's rights would have given him"; but that his "double game" in establishing Mrs. Clay in London reveals a determination "to save himself from being cut out by one woman at least" (250). Succinct as it is, the account is just: but can the same be said of Jane Austen's final words upon Mrs. Clay? That "she had sacrificed, for the younger man's sake, the possibility of scheming longer for Sir Walter", as far as it goes, is correct. But the prefatory statement that "Mrs. Clay's affections had overpowered her interest" begs the question of how much of an interest the baronet still remained for her, after the revelation of his aristocratic fastidiousness, and of the next Sir Walter's amorous inclination towards herself. The concluding comment, perhaps fittingly, leaves her prospects with Mr. Elliot as a subject for conjecture; but the laconic admission that Mrs. Clay "has abilities, however, as well as affections" may be regarded as testimony to whatever, in her enforced reluctance, the author has left unexplored or undivulged regarding this character.

For her attitude throughout – only half-acknowledged, doubtless, even to herself – is that the penniless daughter of a lawyer, however otherwise gifted in mind and manners, is not to be viewed as acceptable by society's norms, as they are embodied in the novels, and were present by and large in the minds of contemporary readers. Jane Austen has been anything but lavish in depicting Mrs. Clay; has presented her to us mainly through the critical eyes of her rival, and minimally, even so. But the meeting by the Pump Room shows that the lady had inspired in Mr. Elliot an attachment more certain and real than that he entertained for Anne Elliot – which he had not reached the stage of professing, despite his manifold attentions to her. And from the little we do know of Mrs. Clay – from an appreciation we come at length to share with her literary creator – we are assured she is by no means so common as her name might suggest: and will display more elegance and true personableness in her future role as Lady Elliot, than a Lady Dalrymple, or a Lady Catherine de Bourgh, or a Lady Bertram, is able to bring to her respective position in society. Not to mention Mrs. Ferrars.

Perhaps this is what the disadvantaged rebel within Jane Austen was wanting to say as part of the unwritten story in *Persuasion*. How much of it would have been revealed, one wonders, if the first reference to the novel in her Letters, on March 13th, 1817 – "I have something ready for Publication, which may perhaps appear about a twelvemonth hence"[32] – was a hint of intended revision?

iii

Elizabeth and Mr. Bennet

"They have none of them much to recommend them", declares Mr. Bennet of his five daughters; "they are all silly and ignorant like other girls; but Lizzy has something more of quickness than her sisters". With this reflection upon his own flesh and blood he assails the susceptibilities of his wife, with predictable success. What in particular will incense Mrs. Bennet is the preference openly affirmed in this remark, and in the "good word for my little Lizzy" that he has made so bold as to "throw in".

Elizabeth, as she and her father are well aware, is the "least dear" to her mother of all her children, as the author states it. Who is to say that Mrs. Bennet's resort, in her befuddled consciousness of being the butt of her husband's ridicule, is not to take it out of the sibling who is most like him in critical propensity? But equally involuntary, we may also infer, is Mr. Bennet's confession of regard, indeed, affection, for his second daughter: yet one more instance of a truth being spoken in jest, even by a person customarily as undemonstrative as he.

That roundness in the creation of characters which is the hallmark of dramatic and literary achievement extends, in Jane Austen's writing, to the whole families from which they spring, attributes of the elders being present or reflected in varying proportion in the children: a fact often noted and intriguingly explored. Certainly, Elizabeth displays a decided likeness to her mother in her tendency to indignant expostulation, and, if not ignorance of them, momentary forgetfulness of the demands of the polite conventions. But this is little more than a trick of temperament, in comparison with the substantial qualities of personality which show her so evidently to be her father's daughter.

One respect in which she seems not at all to resemble Mr. Bennet is in his aloofness and imperturbability both as to persons and events. What we soon learn about the lesser detail of his everyday dealings is indication enough. He takes little if any interest in his neighbours, is with a book regardless of time, and pays social functions the compliment of absenting himself from them. The invitation from the newcomers, the Bingleys, to the ball at Netherfield Park must perforce be accepted; but the diversion it affords him is not of the kind that such gatherings would normally be thought to promote. It consists in watching with silent enjoyment, and entire absence of embarrassment, the gaucheries and discomfiture of his own family, from Mr. Collins's bizarre address to the company on the duties of a cleric, and Mary's distressing endeavours at the pianoforte, to Lydia's all too natural yawnings, and the repulse by their disdainful and wearied hosts of his wife's obtuse civilities.

His manner at Longbourn House during the uproar which follows Elizabeth's rejection of Mr. Collins differs not a whit from that he has displayed at Netherfield. When the distrait Mrs. Bennet bursts into his library, he fixes his eyes on her "with a calm unconcern which was not in the least altered by her communication", and expresses itself in the remote and ironic courtesy of, "I have not the pleasure of understanding you. Of what are you talking?" (111) And his first instinct, when the state of affairs is spelled out to him, is to detach himself from it, despite its consequence for the family: "And what am I to do on the occasion? – It seems an hopeless business". His words here belie his intention, which, as it turns out, is most purposeful; but the coolness with which they are delivered aptly denotes a man whose relationship to his own wife is one of being "very little otherwise indebted, than as her ignorance and folly had contributed to his amusement" (236).

No such distance from people and happenings close at hand is observable in his daughter. It is on the contrary only natural in a young woman of Elizabeth's vivacity that she should be intimately involved in her immediate world. Yet she does display a capacity for detachment amidst its impressions and demands which must be seen as estimable, and notably contributes to making her the person she is. Nowhere is it more evident than after she has looked in vain for Wickham at the Netherfield ball, and learned that his absence is due indirectly to Darcy's influence. For a moment her disappointment, and its accompanying anger, is extreme. But, we are told, she was not formed for ill-humour: this destruction of her own pleasure for the evening "could not dwell long on her spirits", and was soon deliberately made to yield place to the recreation of pointing out Mr. Collins's oddities to Charlotte Lucas. Another vexation closer to home is similarly assuaged. Though her appeal to Mr. Bennet concerning Lydia's unbridled behaviour scarcely gains a hearing, she departs from the interview with equanimity. A consciousness of having done her duty helps to sustain her; but more flows from the fact that "to fret over unavoidable evils, or augment them by anxiety, was no part of her disposition" (232). Her aunt Mrs. Gardiner is right in judging that it would have been better if Jane's being jilted had happened to Elizabeth, since she would have laughed herself out of it sooner.

The same attribute enables her to be relaxed in the unfamiliar surroundings at Rosings. As the little party draws near to it, she is troubled by none of those apprehensions which afflict two of her companions, from a certainty alike that Lady Catherine has nothing extraordinary about her, and that "the mere stateliness of money and rank" was something she herself "could witness without trepidation". She is, in consequence, equal to the scene within. That at Hunsford Parsonage when Darcy is making his declaration is more threatening. There, Elizabeth is beset with emotions, strong and conflicting – with shock and embarrassment, with dislike, gratitude and resentment – but she is by no means overwhelmed by them while he remains, or in any degree deprived of her usual ability to see and think clearly. The inflexibility of her opinion of Darcy, true enough, might well have enabled her to retain a proper perspective; but it is not insignificant nevertheless that, despite the surprise, the lover's urgency, the greatness of the offer and the tumult of her own feelings, "she could easily see that he had no doubt of a favourable answer", despite his professions of anxiety (189).

*   *   *

A capacity to distance oneself from the immediacy of event and the threat of emotion's dominance, necessarily an individual trait, is most often the distinguishing feature of a very able mind. Ability, Mr. Bennet and Elizabeth possess in plenty; and in both of them it manifests itself in a certain formality or methodicalness of approach in matters of judgment and within their own mental processes: what might be termed a precision, or a principled way of thinking. Thus, for all his laxity and indolence of disposition, and his straightened means, we would never be tempted to doubt Mr. Bennet's declaration that, had the financial settlement with Wickham been Elizabeth's uncle's doing, "I must and *would* have paid him". This same punctiliousness might be thought to inform his estimate of Mr. Collins as a suitor, and his manner of conveying it to Elizabeth after Mrs. Bennet's ultimatum. "From this day you must be a stranger to one of your parents. – Your mother will never see you again if you do *not* marry Mr. Collins, and I will never see you again if you *do*". And it is surely to be detected in the more serious circumstance of his trying to dissuade her from yoking herself to the "proud, unpleasant" Mr. Darcy. After the initial astonishment he is as deeply moved in the endeavour as father can be; but he has first, with what may be regarded as a laudable paternal rectitude, given his daughter his consent upon her tearful assurance of her affection for the man she has chosen (376-7).

The principled approach is more evident in Elizabeth, if only for the reason that we see more of her than her father. Even in so very personal a discussion as that between Jane and herself on the conduct of Charlotte Lucas in accepting Mr. Collins, Elizabeth's eloquence is engaged not so much in presenting the attitude she has formed as upon defining the concepts it embodies.

> "You shall not defend her, though it is Charlotte Lucas. You shall not, for the sake of one individual, change the meaning of principle and integrity, nor endeavour to persuade yourself

or me, that selfishness is prudence, and insensibility to danger, security for happiness" (135-6).

And though such severity of emphasis might be imagined to have no place in episodes of laughter and happiness, there is a rare delightfulness in the question to Darcy after their betrothal as to the seemliness of her disclosing to him her knowledge of what he had done for Lydia, in the hope that it would bring on his proposal.

> "My resolution of thanking you for your kindness to Lydia had certainly great effect. *Too much,* I am afraid; for what becomes of the moral, if our comfort springs from a breach of promise, for I ought not to have mentioned the subject?" (381)

This propensity to detach the significance from the happening, and to view it in its abstraction as perhaps the greater reality, is present in the lightest instances of Elizabeth's conversation and reflection. Jane's deploring the disappointment Darcy must have suffered upon being so unceremoniously rejected provokes from her the mock-assertion that its effect is to render her correspondingly indifferent and unconcerned. "Your profusion makes me saving; and if you lament over him much longer, my heart will be as light as a feather". After this conversation she is left thinking about the disclosure in Darcy's letter of Bingley's affection for her sister, which she cannot mention to her until there is perfect understanding between the parties: in which presumptive event Bingley is far better suited to be the informant. Between frustration and mirth, she tells herself, "The liberty of communication cannot be mine until it has lost all its value!" – ending, characteristically, with a syllogism (225-7).

For it is in much the same way upon the logic, or lack of it, in the position taken by Mrs. Gardiner with respect to Wickham's new-found interest in Miss King since her acquisition of £10,000, that Elizabeth has pronounced with such peremptory frankness. Her aunt had suggested a venal motive in Wickham, and frowned upon Miss King's acceptance of his hasty attentions. Elizabeth, struck by Mrs. Gardiner's past warning her against an imprudent match with him, and present condemnation of his seeking a fortune upon which to marry, is moved to defend both persons. An impoverished young man, she argues, has not time for the "elegant decorums"; and if the lady herself is content, none can reasonably make objection. But the continuance of her aunt's disapproval provokes her to impatience with inconsistency, even in someone she is so fond of. "Well," she cries, "have it as you choose. *He* shall be mercenary, and *she* shall be foolish" (153).

*   *   *

Elizabeth Bennet is shown to be as susceptible to her feelings as are any of us. But she is unusual in that their very potency can quicken her thinking into new orderliness. The last place where one would expect to find this aptitude is in her angry dialogue with Darcy, but it is most evident there. The final affront – indeed, insult – of his passionate reference to her family's social inferiority induces only the contrasting reserve of her stating that the mode of his declaration merely spares her the concern she would have felt had his behaviour been more gentlemanlike. What follows is like nothing so much as the stages of a reasoned case. In no way could she have been tempted to accept him; the arrogance of his disposition noted on early acquaintance had formed a "ground-work of disapprobation"; and upon this basis succeeding knowledge of him had built an "immovable" dislike. It is only when the successive charges reach their unequivocal conclusion that emotion finds scope in the rather less controlled affirmation of his being "the last man in the world whom I could ever be prevailed on to marry" (193).

An innate tendency to consider the behaviour of others and oneself in terms of the principles underlying it will present rather starkly to its possessor the strange contrarieties and anomalies that subsist in social norms and in the human lot generally. To this kind of awareness Elizabeth is at all times prone; and it accounts for a charmingly philosophical element in her make-up which guards against any waywardness on her part, while endearing her to the reader. When, for example, the object they have all longed for is secured in the arrangements for Wickham's marriage to Lydia, Elizabeth rejoices; but in an instant her mood has changed to a near-horror at the implications: "And they *must* marry! Yet he is *such* a man" (304). She is astonished by the strangeness of their present joy, and need for thankfulness, at the prospect of a union which will afford no chance of happiness, and in which the profligate inclination of the husband is a certainty. But the vagaries of her own dealings can come under as critical a scrutiny; for, with such thinking, there is no room for evasion or dissimulation in one's contemplation of them. It will exact the penalty of always "Doubting sad end to principle unsound", wherever such principle may reside. How ruefully Elizabeth considers her past rashness with respect to Darcy after he has taken his leave at Lambton, as she throws "a retrospective glance over their whole acquaintance, so full of contradictions and varieties, and sighed at the perverseness of those feelings which would now have promoted its continuance, and would formerly have rejoiced at its termination" (279).

*   *   *

What, we might wonder, is the quality of Mr. Bennet's brooding thoughts? He may be as well equipped for introspection as his daughter, though, one suspects, less given to the practice from the consequences of an unsuitable marriage. Happily for them both, however, it is the external sphere which commands their main interest, and provides their greatest pleasure; and it is for the outward aspect of things, further, that their keenly analytical powers of mind make them both suited. In Mr. Bennet they are elsewhere directed while, tiring of his family, he devotes himself to his books; but his ability quickly to grasp and see through a situation when occasion demands it is impressive. Talking with Elizabeth about Jane's disappointment, and offering only the dubious consolation that, next to being married, "a girl likes to be crossed in love a little now and then", he asks her when her turn is to come, and with prophetic insight urges, "Let Wickham be *your* man. He is a pleasant fellow, and would jilt you creditably" (137). The same perceptiveness determines that the provisions set out in Mr. Gardiner's letter for Wickham and Lydia's marriage conceal the chief fact of money having been put down. "Wickham's a fool, if he takes her with a farthing less than ten thousand pounds", he affirms; with contemptuous solicitude then adding, "I should be sorry to think so ill of him, in the very beginning of our relationship" (304).

Such mental achievement Elizabeth can readily equal. Had she not straight away seen from the pompous style and needless apology in the letter from Mr. Collins read out to the family that their clerical cousin must be an oddity? And does she not, contradicting her uncle's hopes of an intention in the eloping couple to marry in London, deduce the worst from the secrecy, and fear of detection in their disappearance, and from the one's need of money and the other's inability to supply it, and unreservedly affirm, "Oh! No, no, this is not likely"? As swift, and correct, is her judgment that in the Bingley sisters' estimation the Bennets are "not rich enough, or grand enough for them"; or, when once shut in her room at the Parsonage, that Col. Fitzwilliam must have been referring to Bingley as the friend Darcy had recently saved from making an imprudent marriage, since "There could not exist in the world *two* men, over whom Mr. Darcy could have such boundless influence" (186).

There is nothing remarkable in Elizabeth's crediting, despite strong initial reservations, the whole of the studied and detailed account of his actions that Darcy had set out in the communication he puts into her hand in the park at Rosings. That the affair of his relation with Wickham "was capable of a turn which must make him entirely blameless throughout the whole" would have been evident in any careful perusal. But what is worthy of note is the rapidity with which she ranges through their entire acquaintance and applies this possibility to her own previous suppositions. The impropriety of Wickham's confidences at a first encounter; the unreliability of subsequent professions; the insincerities detectable in his attentions to Miss King, and to herself; the confidence of a man like Bingley in Darcy's being blameless; the lack of any sign of the unprincipled or the unjust in Darcy, for all his repellent manners: all these contrary tokens are immediately before her. Though unable to overcome her fixed disapproval of the man who has made it, the revelation heightens her chagrin at the indecorum of her family, and acquaints her with a novel and demoralizing dissatisfaction with her own conduct.

Her humiliation is the more profound because she had herself anticipated and all but reached the assessment of Wickham that Darcy puts before her. But for the charm of first liking and the flattery of his attentions, the flaws she had detected in Wickham's intimations would have been further dwelt on, and probably led to disbelief; puzzlement, at least, they do bring about in her. Again and again during their discussion at the Phillipses, she exclaims in surprise and wonder at what she is being required to accept as truth. "Good heavens! but how could *that* be?" is her justified reaction to the idea of so definite an intention as the gift of a living being set aside at Darcy's instigation. The plea of his jealousy and dislike of the companion of his youth, Elizabeth can doubt from her own limited experience. "I had supposed him to be despising his fellow-creatures in general, but did not suspect him of descending to such malicious revenge, such injustice, such inhumanity as this!" The known fact of Darcy's pride is here not persuasive. She has found it insufferable, and levelled scorn at it while a guest at Netherfield; but she speaks her incomprehension that pride itself had not constrained him to be just – "If from no better motive, that he should not have been too proud to be dishonest, – for dishonesty I must call it". And, pondering the question while other subjects are being reviewed, she suddenly ventures upon it once more, in surprise that an assured relationship should subsist between Darcy and Bingley. "How can Mr. Bingley, who seems good humour itself", she asks, "and is, I really believe, truly amiable, be in friendship with such a man? How can they suit each other?" Her queries gain answers from Wickham that are sufficiently plausible; but the whole conversation testifies to

Elizabeth's perspicacity. She has come close to detecting Wickham for what he is in the very process of his gaining her affections (79-82).

Analysis of her own feelings, not surprisingly, she finds much more difficult; and, indeed, is entirely capable of being at a loss when it is essential she should be clear. The change in Darcy's manner, when they meet by accident at Pemberley for the first time since their stormy interview in Hunsford Parsonage, is something the reader might think she should at once understand; but, amazed as she is at the striking alteration in him, she has no idea what to attribute it to: "She knew not what to think, nor how to account for it" (252). The principled nature of her thinking is perhaps the reason for her failure, the assured grounds of her past aversion to the man and estimate of the effect upon him of her denunciation combining to preclude the possibility of affection as a cause. And, after the visit in Derbyshire from the Pemberley party, Elizabeth is so unsure of her feelings respecting him that "she lay awake two whole hours, endeavouring to make them out": methodically dismissing hatred and dislike, admitting respect, allowing esteem, and venturing at last to contemplate the presence of gratitude. But nothing at all hinders her capacity later on to see through the complexities of their earlier acquaintance, and determine exactly what it was that had made Darcy admire and fall in love with her.

> "The fact is, that you were sick of civility, of deference, of officious attention. You were disgusted with the women who were always speaking and looking, and thinking for *your* approbation alone. I roused, and interested you, because I was so unlike *them*." (380)

Is she not perfectly right?

* * *

When, in the throes of her nervous discontent at the thought of being denied formal introduction to the new owner of Netherfield Park, Mrs. Bennet falls to berating her next-youngest daughter, Mr. Bennet comments to the assembled family on Kitty's lack of discretion in her coughs: "she times them ill", he declares. But upon his wife's recovering composure and good humour through his announcement of having paid the necessary visit, he gravely advises, as if the paroxysm were voluntary, "Now, Kitty, you may cough as much as you chuse". The novel shows him a master of laconic and sardonic utterance; but it conveys also the reason for his being so, in his vigour of mind and instant apprehension, the "quick parts" whimsically demonstrated in the opening discourse with Mrs. Bennet. This degree of mental capacity itself accounts for that strongly developed sense of the inconsistent and incongruous in human relationships which makes for and gives force to the well-judged terse remark, expressive as it is of an underlying mirth. Thus his wife's detestation of the man who is next in the entail of the estate, and dispossessor of the mother and daughters she is incapable of seeing as any other than its rightful beneficiaries, brings from him the unstinted concurrence of, "It certainly is a most iniquitous affair, and nothing can clear Mr. Collins from the guilt of inheriting Longbourn" (62). In the act of diplomatically putting an end to Mary's endeavours at the pianoforte he cannot forbear the briefest hint as to their significance, in his, "That will do extremely well, child. You have delighted us long enough. Let the other young ladies have time to exhibit". And his method of bringing solace to Mrs. Bennet, in her wilful desolation at the notion of living to see Charlotte Lucas become mistress of Longbourn, is to put before her a neglected contingency which would spare her such distress. "My dear, do not give way to such gloomy thoughts. Let us hope for better things. Let us flatter ourselves that I may be the survivor" (130).

It is the same suppressed laughter which prompts an equally ceremonious rejoinder from Elizabeth when Lady Catherine de Bourgh, sweeping aside its mistress's prerogatives, insists that she stay longer at Hunsford Parsonage. "I am much obliged to your ladyship for your kind invitation, but it is not in my power to accept it". As toneless and proper a response is forthcoming from her when Mrs. Bennet, in her indignation at the report of Darcy's having deemed her daughter

"Not handsome enough to dance with!" seriously advises, "Another time, Lizzy, I would not dance with *him*, if I were you". Darcy's asking her, and her taking the unheard-of liberty of asking him, being both seemingly precluded, Elizabeth is nothing but correct in solemnly replying, "I believe, Ma'am, I may safely promise you *never* to dance with him" (20).

Darcy and his associates fare no differently when she is in their company. The affront which the former has perhaps unknowingly administered, and Elizabeth's sense of the pretentiousness prevailing amongst them, Bingley alone excepted, contrive if anything to lend her remarks a greater brevity and emphasis. Darcy's unexpectedly offering her his hand as a partner upon Sir William Lucas's over-enthusiastic recommendation, with its accompanying assurance of the gentleman's having no objection to dancing with her, for all his dislike of the amusement in general, draws from her the astringent compliment of, "Mr. Darcy is all politeness". As ironic is her amused entry to the conversation at Netherfield about handwriting that arises from Miss Bingley's admiration for Darcy's epistolary skills, and denigration of her brother's. Bingley does not deny the charge that he writes "in the most careless way imaginable", and cheerfully confesses to a flow of thoughts so rapid that his letters sometimes convey no ideas at all to his correspondents. Elizabeth's contribution of the simple, "Your humility, Mr. Bingley, must disarm reproof", dispraising both handwriting and implicit boast, brings Darcy into the fray, and leads to that confrontation between the two keenest minds present whose ending is no less than a relief to the rest of them. But it is one of short duration. The rudeness of the sisters next day, in having Darcy as their escort on a narrow path and leaving Elizabeth to walk by herself, brings from her a succinct pronouncement that is amply critical, but withering in its incorporation of Gilpin's classic commonplace as to the number of cows for an aesthetically pleasing tableau: "No, no; stay where you are. –You are charmingly group'd, and appear to uncommon advantage. The picturesque would be spoilt by admitting a fourth" (48-53).

Darcy had noted, and tried to do away, his friends' incivility; but he is destined, for all his dawning tenderness towards their guest, to be treated to some of the most intelligible of her brief utterances. He himself, by unwisely claiming to have sought to avoid such weaknesses in character as can invite ridicule, creates that demur in Elizabeth which gives rise to her sardonic, "Such as vanity and pride"; and Miss Bingley's disdainful inquiry as to the result of her examination of her idol serves only to inspire the derisive acquiescence of, "I am perfectly convinced by it that Mr. Darcy has no defect. He owns it himself without disguise" (57). And not yet is she finished with him. Any of his failings, as she will designate them to be, is a mark for her to tilt at; and their next encounter, at Rosings, supplies one, in his offering in defence of his having danced only with members of his own party at the ball in Meryton, the plea of not having been acquainted with any other lady in the assembly. "True", Elizabeth replies; "and nobody can ever be introduced in a ball room" (175). Darcy proceeds to explain himself at length; but, with such an opponent, he will not expect to get the better of the exchange. Fortunately, admiration of the lady renders it no issue. What she will have to say to him when he proposes will be as explicit, but more fluent and expansive than the remarks just cited, and so come into another category.

But her greatest triumph in the laconic art is reserved for her former admirer, George Wickham. After her return from Hunsford, he inquires as to her visit; and, learning that she had met Darcy and Col. Fitzwilliam there, observes with some temerity that the latter's manners are very different from those of his cousin. "Yes, very different", Elizabeth agrees composedly. "But I think Mr. Darcy improves on acquaintance". In apprehension as to her meaning, Wickham jocularly suggests that the improvement is in civility, rather than in essentials. Again, there is the terse seeming accord of, "Oh no! In essentials, I believe, he is very much what he ever was". In his disquiet at the drift of her words, Wickham can only look for some clue in her expression, while she amplifies these brief statements in terms of such neutrality as can only intensify his alarm.

"When I said that he improved on acquaintance, I did not mean that either his mind or manners were in a state of improvement, but that from knowing him better, his disposition was better understood."

So has Elizabeth by these minimal remarks paid off scores for past deceptions, that the two of them part at last "with mutual civility, and possibly a mutual desire of never meeting again" (234-5).

*   *   *

"I dearly love a laugh", Elizabeth confides to the company at Netherfield; and, to make matters clearer, adds, "Follies and nonsense, whims and inconsistencies *do* divert me, I own, and I laugh at them whenever I can" (56). Her confession has been prompted by Miss Bingley's certainty of there being nothing in Darcy's disposition capable of giving rise to laughter – a possibility which for Elizabeth is itself a delicious piece of nonsense, as she thereupon gives him to understand. It is this idiosyncrasy which has ensured her not being long dismayed when Darcy declares her no more than "tolerable" at their first meeting. Though harbouring "no very cordial feelings towards him", she is soon with much merriment telling the story among her friends; "for", we then learn, "she had a lively, playful disposition, which delighted in any thing ridiculous" (12). Life clearly provides for her a plenitude of such objects. Caroline Bingley's commendation of Darcy's letter-writing had kept her "sufficiently amused"; the sight of Sir William Lucas stationed in the doorway of the Parsonage in earnest contemplation of the greatness before him in the phaeton at the gate, "and constantly bowing whenever Miss De Bourgh looked that way", sustains Elizabeth in "high diversion"; and she is reduced to such helplessness by the idea of the solemn Mr. Collins being run away with by his feelings as to be incapacitated from halting him in his amorous declaration. Nor is it the more obvious follies, at moments of ease, that charm her. In the very midst of the embarrassment of having to introduce Mr. and

Mrs. Gardiner in the grounds of Pemberley to their owner, she cannot resist "a sly look at him, to see how he bore it" in going through the formidable ritual, and the half expectation "of his decamping as fast as he could from such disgraceful companions" (255).

That this characteristic in Elizabeth is a paternal endowment is beyond doubt; indeed, it is what closely unites the two, as we see for instance from the looks and glances they exchange when first exposed to Mr. Collins's conversation. Mr. Bennet's "resolute composure of countenance" masks "the keenest enjoyment" he finds in the guest who has answered all his hopes of being the very reverse of a sensible man, and thus is, by his own definition, "a valuable acquaintance". Not with dismay, but with the same glee as Elizabeth is to view Sir William's bowings, does he greet Collins's egregious peroration at the Netherfield ball: no-one there "looked more amused than Mr. Bennet himself". Elizabeth, one suspects, cannot evince such reverential delight at follies and nonsense; the very brainlessness of his own spouse is the source of endless pleasure for him. Tenderly he considers her incomprehension of the legalities by which the Collinses are to become the possessors of Longbourn. "If it was not for the entail", she has pronounced to him, "I should not mind it". The gentle question, "What should you not mind?" secures for Mr. Bennet the answer he has ardently hoped for: "I should not mind any thing at all". With profound satisfaction, both intellectual and comical, he serenely concludes, "Let us be thankful that you are preserved from a state of such insensibility" (130).

*   *   *

The fact that his dearest daughter cannot accompany him into the highest flights of humour is explained by Mr. Bennet's having irresponsibly almost withdrawn from family life, as from that of society round about him. His wife's mindlessness in both contexts means for him nothing other than amusement; in the closer concerns she is no real hindrance, being capable of little more bothersome than a querulous compliance. But with Elizabeth it is otherwise. In her situation as the second of five almost dowerless sisters, family affairs are components of her destiny, and the mother presiding over them a force – erratic, and often perverse – to be reckoned with. Mrs. Bennet's excesses cause Elizabeth not only embarrassment but anxiety: as when, blushing for her, she tries in vain to end her attack on Darcy for what she takes to be his contempt for country living; or, at supper during the ball at Netherfield, with "inexpressible vexation" to interrupt the flow of her mother's self-congratulation at the prospect of Jane's engagement from reaching and offending Darcy sitting opposite. "What is Mr. Darcy to me, pray, that I should be afraid of him?" is the very audible response. "I am sure we owe him no such particular civility as to be obliged to say nothing *he* may not like to hear" (99). Not only by Mrs. Bennet's actions is Elizabeth's task made uncomfortable, and occasionally distressing: she has also to endeavour "to forget what she could not overlook" in her father's treatment of her, and so "banish from her thoughts that continual breach of conjugal obligation and decorum" which daily exposed her mother to the contempt of her children. Tested as she is, it is not as easy for her mind as for her father's to register and contemplate the humorous aspects of existence in their purity (236).

She is unable, therefore, to express an unqualified agreement to Mr. Bennet's question, "For what do we live, but to make sport for our neighbours, and laugh at them in our turn?" Nor, what is more, greatly value his comment upon Jane's disappointment over Bingley, "that, whatever of that kind may befal you, you have an affectionate mother who will always make the most of it" (138). Though quite capable in her livelier moments of causing it, she is not free to enjoy social disharmony; nor, with a becoming modesty, is she so given to abandoning scruple as to seek to provoke and expose folly in the way her father does. His method, often enough, is by the type of mocking query Mrs. Bennet correctly terms tiresome or nonsensical: like the, "How so? how can it affect them?" in response to her exclaiming, "What a fine thing for our girls!" at Bingley's coming to Netherfield Park; and the, "Is that his design in settling here?" upon her explanation that she is thinking of his marrying one of them.

Mr. Bennet's questioning is at its most sinister when it has the appearance of being judicially serious; as when Mr. Collins, elaborating upon "those little delicate compliments" he considers ladies to enjoy, and himself to be gifted in presenting, is told that he judges very properly, and politely asked "whether these pleasing attentions proceed from the impulse of the moment, or are the result of previous study?" (68) But the apparently casual and innocent observation can with equal effect serve as prelude to folly's enactment. The assurance that she is as handsome as any of her daughters, producing from Mrs. Bennet an affected disclaimer on the plea of a grown up family, gains for her the knavish speech of, "In such cases, a woman has not often much beauty to think of" that will, mercifully, sleep in her foolish ear. And his mere remarking of the hat Elizabeth is engaged in trimming that he hopes Mr. Bingley will like it, introduces the singular episode of the girls' bewilderment and their mother's expostulation which ends with the latter's, "I am sick of Mr. Bingley", Mr. Bennet's announcement, full of pretended dismay, of acquaintance with him having already been established, and his departure in fatigued contentment at the domestic squall so induced and allayed.

Elizabeth admittedly makes an attempt in this kind, but she is incited thereto by high spirits, and, falling short of the finesse in which her father excels, rather comes to grief. Impelled by the surge of happiness that runs through the family when the invitation to the ball at Netherfield is given, she mischievously inquires of Mr. Collins "whether he intended to accept Mr. Bingley's invitation, and if he did, whether he would think it proper to join in the evening's amusement". The outcome, in combination with a wordy affirmative, is a request for her hand for the first two dances that she has no choice but to accept with as good grace as she can muster (87).

*   *   *

Behind the enjoyment of follies and nonsense lies a developed appreciation of incongruity; and this, in turn, as it relates to character and conduct, necessarily implies the perception of fault. And since the social milieu possesses more meaning for Elizabeth than for her father, it is as natural that she should exhibit a greater readiness than he to direct blame, and in fact to confront an offender. Thus there is to be found in her a type of ready remonstrance to which Mr. Bennet is hardly drawn. It exists in her meaningfully presenting to Mr. Darcy the twin vices of vanity and pride as failings to be guarded against, and in her more vigorous challenge of, "But these, I suppose, are precisely what you are without" (57). She has previously defended Bingley's self-declared easiness of temper, and attacked Darcy's studied disrespect for it, in her cry to the latter, "You have shewn him off now much more than he did himself". Such criticisms, while pointed enough, are the incidental products of discussion; but in her dealings with George Wickham, Elizabeth does not flinch from the strictest confrontation. When he asks concerning the old housekeeper at Pemberley, she is not restrained from reporting her adverse comment upon him, with the sarcastic observation, "At such a distance as *that*, you know, things are strangely misinterpreted". Her aim, be it said, is to silence him; but, not succeeding, she proceeds to put a stop to his reflections on the clerical life he claims has been denied him, with the facts about the forfeited living she has learned from Darcy. And she counters his facetious reference to the making of sermons with the incisive, "I *did* hear, too, that there was a time, when sermon-making was not so palatable to you as it seems to be at present; that you actually declared your resolution of never taking orders, and that the business had been compromised accordingly". Then, as if her moral ascendancy had not been complete, she imposes it with a change of direction as masterly in its way as anything Mr. Bennet has ever accomplished.

> "Come, Mr. Wickham, we are brother and sister, you know. Do not let us quarrel about the past. In future, I hope we shall be always of one mind."

At this, she holds out her hand. Wickham kisses it, the author tells us, "with affectionate gallantry"; but the fact that when so engaged "he hardly knew how to look" can occasion no surprise (327-9).

She has administered – executed is perhaps the better word – a "set down". Of this gentle art, Mr. Bennet is, by his wife's report, and the single example he provides for us, a consummate practitioner. The recommendation he sends Mr. Collins that, while consoling Lady Catherine at the news of Elizabeth's engagement to Darcy, he should stand by the nephew, since "He has more to give", is as potent as his daughter's, but superior in being so much more economical. The disadvantage he is under, of having to conquer a reluctance to exert himself in this or any other way, is not present in Elizabeth. She has been so liberal in these attentions as to set upon a startled Lady Catherine within her own fastness at Rosings on the subject of a daughter's "coming out", with the unheard-of proposition that "The last born has as good a right to the pleasures of youth, as the first"; for better measure appending, on the assumption of the elder's being unwilling or unable to marry, the insufferable, "And to be kept back on *such* a motive!" (165) For his pains in frankly confessing the normal inability of a younger son "to marry without some attention to money", Col. Fitzwilliam is rewarded with the derisive, "And pray, what is the usual price of an Earl's younger son? Unless the elder brother is very sickly, I suppose you would not ask above fifty thousand pounds" (184).

The personal note present here has, naturally enough, already been repeatedly sounded in Elizabeth's acrimonious dealings with Darcy. At Netherfield, her making at first no response to his invitation to dance a reel with him is explained as the confounding of a wish on his part to despise her taste; "but", she tells him, "I always delight in overthrowing those kind of schemes, and cheating a person of their premeditated contempt" (52). His advancing in stately manner at Rosings while she is at the pianoforte earns him a similar rebuff. This time his intention can only be to frighten her, but she will not be alarmed: "My courage always rises with every attempt to intimidate me". These set downs are in fact accusations, though they lack the denunciatory vehemence of her offering while a guest at Netherfield, when, on Darcy's going so far as to concede that every disposition must have some natural and ineradicable defect, she exclaims, "And *your* defect is a propensity to hate every body" (58). But even this is a trifle compared to her charges at Hunsford Parsonage; the substance of what she has to say there, if it is anything, is one extensive and strident set down. She makes atonement for it in due course by accepting Darcy as her husband; but that she has no intention of abandoning this notable expertise is apparent when, calling upon him, with proper feminine curiosity, to account for having fallen in love with her, she reminds him of their initial encounter with, "My beauty you had early withstood" (380). It is a set down of superb quality, the more so for its being spoken in jest.

*　　*　　*

As with so many manifestations in father and daughter, it is the fundamental excellence of their minds that promotes and pervades them. And their quick recognition of failings in others is more than matched by the rigour with which realisation of their own shortcomings affects them. Both are victims of transient moods of bitter self-accusation and depression. Mr. Bennet is transfixed by guilt upon Lydia's infamous elopement. "I never saw any one so shocked", Jane reports of his reaction. "He could not speak a word for full ten minutes". And he so far interrupts the composure he has reassumed by the time of his return from London as to decline Elizabeth's proffer of sympathy for what he has gone through. "Say nothing of that", he declares. "Who should suffer but myself? It has been my own doing, and I ought to feel it"; adding, however, for their mutual comfort, the assurance, born of self-knowledge, that far from the impression's being able to overpower him, "It will pass away soon enough" (299).

Less severe, possibly, at the time, but longer-lasting, has been Elizabeth's self-reproach when awareness comes of how "blind, partial, prejudiced, absurd" she has been in her relation with Darcy and Wickham. What makes worse her suffering at the discovery is recognition that it is in direct proportion to the high esteem in which before she had held herself. "I, who have prided myself on my discernment!" she cries. " – I, who have valued myself on my abilities!" From such comprehension there can be no escape – and relief only in the truth of its being "how just a humiliation!" (208) So also she views her share of responsibility for what has happened with Lydia, upon the news of the elopement. Certainty that she might have prevented it overcomes all that she feels at this moment for herself, and for Darcy who attends her. The compelling thought is of her failure to take action despite the recently-acquired knowledge of Wickham's character: of the "Wretched, wretched mistake!" Like her father, in a different circumstance, she must admit the full force of blame.

*   *   *

What distinguishes the love between Mr. Bennet and his daughter, and makes it as admirable as it is affecting, is its clear-sightedness. There is no vestige of sentimentality in it. Their relationship is founded upon full knowledge – which, on one side at least, is often wished less. However different by kinship and convention their status might be, and unlike their usual employments and concerns, in intellect they are equals: and it is as equals that they respond to each other. When her father, accurately surmising a personal motive, dismisses out of hand her warning to him of "the very great disadvantage to us all", as she puts it, of Lydia's flirtatious behaviour, Elizabeth, too, puts courtesy aside, and gives him without embellishment her opinion of his neglect of paternal duty. "Excuse me – for I must speak plainly. If you, my dear father, will not take the trouble of checking her exuberant spirits, and of teaching her that her present pursuits are not to be the business of her life, she will soon be beyond the reach of amendment" (230-1). Thus is rebuke given, and received, where reciprocal understanding is complete. Roles are reversed when Mr. Bennet, under the impression Elizabeth has consented to marry a man she dislikes for the sake of his wealth, greets her with the greater plainness of, "Are you out of your senses, to be accepting this man?" and answers her faltering assurance of sincere attachment to Mr. Darcy with the scorn of, "Or in other words, you are determined to have him. He is rich, to be sure". The tone and substance of what he has to say to her change dramatically once the reality of the bond between them is apparent to him; but his advice that it be broken, though to a daughter, has the candour of the truest comradeship.

"I know your disposition, Lizzy. I know that you could be neither happy nor respectable, unless you truly esteemed your husband; unless you looked up to him as a superior. Your lively talents would place you in the greatest danger in an unequal marriage. You could scarcely escape discredit and misery. My child, let me not have the grief of seeing *you* unable to respect your partner in life. You know not what you are about." (378)

A congruity of mind and outlook, and respect for each other that is profound, though never blind, is the basis of the fondness apparent here, as in lesser instances through the novel. Elizabeth's devotion to her father is proof against any criticism that can be levelled at him. The "very strong objections against the lady" which Col. Fitzwilliam had given as the cause of Darcy's detaching Bingley from Jane, Elizabeth knows relate to her family; but she cannot herself admit that anything could justifiably be urged against the father "who, though with some peculiarities, has abilities which Mr. Darcy himself need not disdain, and respectability which he will probably never reach" (187). The only pain she experiences when setting off with Sir William Lucas and Maria to Hunsford, we learn, is "in leaving her father, who would certainly miss her"; and his contentment at her return is evidenced by his more than once during dinner saying "voluntarily to Elizabeth, 'I am glad you are come back, Lizzy'". Is it not therefore inevitable that, when marriage has taken her away from Longbourn, "he missed his second daughter exceedingly", and that he should have "delighted in going to Pemberley, especially when he was least expected"? How could he do otherwise, with a kindred spirit?

*   *   *

As to her mother, it is a different story. Elizabeth remarkably manages almost throughout, despite the temptations, to maintain filial duty and reserve. But once, and once only, at an apparently idle moment – it is while Mrs. Bennet is tiresomely lamenting the departure of Lydia and her husband – she slips perfectly into Mr. Bennet's ironic mode of inquiry into his wife's cerebral confusions. "This is the consequence you see, Madam, of marrying a daughter", she tells her. "It must make you better satisfied that your other four are single". This mild onslaught upon Mrs. Bennet's chief preoccupation in life evokes a retort that would have gladdened her father's heart.

> "It is no such thing. Lydia does not leave me because she is married; but only because her husband's regiment happens to be so far off. If that had been nearer, she would not have gone so soon." (331)

iv

The Enigma of Harriet Smith

Our puzzlement over Harriet Smith begins at the first mention of her. She is introduced as "the natural daughter of somebody", who years before had placed her at Mrs. Goddard's school, where her situation is now that of parlour-boarder. And the action of one of the world's great novels is to turn round the girl pursuing this humble existence: upon her capacity to engage the affections successively of an Elton, a Churchill, a Knightley. The story's credibility and effectiveness, no less, depends on its sustaining the reader's impression that she has qualities which can or will overcome her social deficiency. It takes the shock of Harriet's potential power over Mr. Knightley to awaken Emma to her love for him – and the reality of the distress thus aroused to halt in memorable fashion his proposing to her, in terror lest he should be at the point of confessing an attachment to her protégée. Throughout the novel runs an insistent questioning, whether explicit or unspoken: is Harriet a commendable young woman, a lady in the making – or is she not?

Once she has met her, Emma appears to be certain. She wastes no time, we are told, "in inviting, encouraging and telling her to come very often" to Hartfield (26), resolved to give her the needed sophistication. She has not found her to be clever; but while strength of understanding could not be imparted, Harriet's evident appreciation of what was elegant and witty, her ready embracing of a style of living previously unknown to her, showed that she must have good sense and deserve encouragement. In Emma's first estimation, this was a girl "who only wanted a little more knowledge and elegance to be quite perfect" (23).

The term raises more doubt than it settles. Other than providing herself with an acceptable walking companion, is it Emma's intention to create an agreeable though lesser being, or one who will by these attentions graduate to true estimableness?

An answer is surely present in the fact of what Emma is doing. It is on the face of it unlikely that a woman of her accomplishment would select someone unworthy of her friendship and favour. For Emma is if anything distinguished amongst Jane Austen's heroines by a discernment as to persons in terms both general and particular. Take, for instance, her comment upon Churchill's sudden journeying to London for a haircut, that "silly things do cease to be silly if they are done by sensible people in an impudent way": it is a real insight into human conduct (212). And when, earlier, she has countered Churchill's assertion that no one can be attracted by a reserved character with the retort, "Not till the reserve ceases towards oneself; and then the attraction may be the greater", she is as near as may be to divining the secret of his engagement to Jane Fairfax, which his remark was intended to conceal (203).

Amidst the flow of happenings in Highbury, Emma displays a quick apprehension of motive. She recognises the presence of "great fear, great caution, great resolution" in Jane's determining to stay at her aunt's (285); senses a new happiness after her collecting letters from the post office; and detects her embarrassment at the gift of the piano, and "very reprehensible feelings" as she begins to press the keys (243). The notion that Knightley might be the piano's donor, or that he might care romantically about Jane, are as incisively dismissed as is his own professed indifference to whether he arrives at a dinner party on foot, or by coach as properly he should (226, 213). And, despite the force of her initial attraction to Churchill, Emma is soon sure that there can be no building upon "steadiness or constancy" in his disposition, and of her own undoubted preference not amounting to affection for him (265). His engaging manner towards her upon his reappearance in Highbury, further, does not conceal from her a restlessness, "a liveliness that did not satisfy himself", which betokens a lessening of interest in herself – though she is mistaken, and understandably so, in putting it down to a fear of the effect of her personal charms (316).

The same percipient regard plays constantly upon Harriet. It is with an amused, ironic detachment that Emma contemplates "the many vacancies" of her mind (183), and what Sir Thomas Bertram would have described as her "rusticities" of demeanour. Harriet's being nearly recovered from her cold inspires in Emma a wish "that she should have as much time as possible for getting the better of her other complaint", or else "mania", such being her estimate of her young friend's feelings for Mr. Elton. But the emotion as such Emma is far from scorning: she is herself much affected by the artlessness of Harriet's grief when she has disclosed to her the truth of Elton's indifference, and the extent of her own error. But it is not without significance that, in the depth of her conviction at this point "that Harriet was the superior creature of the two – and that to resemble her would be more for her own happiness than all that genius and intelligence could do", Emma can keep her sympathies in check with the wry thought that it was rather too late in the day "to set about being simple-minded and ignorant". The surmise might be held as indication enough that her decision over Harriet will not have been other than clear-sighted (141-2).

*   *   *

However, there is evidence of a very different order regarding Emma: that while discernment in her is plentiful, her judgment is liable on occasion to impulsive aberration. She shows herself capable of both wilfully suppressing better knowledge, and reversing her opinion without the least awareness of having done so. The matter of the haircut provides an excellent example of the first. Troubled by its air of "foppery and nonsense", she finds Churchill guilty of vanity, extravagance and the like, but also more seriously open to the charge of ungentlemanliness in his disregard of the Westons' feelings, and unconcern as to the impression his behaviour might more generally give rise to. Upon hearing, though, of his highly favourable reception in Highbury, as well as at Randalls, and, from Mr. Weston, how "very beautiful and very charming" he considers her to be, Emma finds that "she must not judge him harshly" (205-6). Nor, when the idea of a ball at Randalls is under discussion, is she able to condemn the lack of gallantry in his studiously ignoring her protest against "a crowd in a little room!" while professing admiration of the phrase. Attributing his persistence to a wish not to lose the pleasure of dancing with her, "she took the compliment, and forgave the rest" (249-50).

Emma's dealings with both the Martins and the Coles are tergiversation itself. The former family, she tells herself at the start, must be coarse and unpolished, quite unworthy of their previous association with her little friend; and as for Mr. Martin when she casts eyes upon him, he "looked as if he did not know what manner was", being, as she proceeds to inform the mortified Harriet, "so very clownish, so totally without air". Her considering, at the end, that "It would be a great pleasure to know Robert Martin", reveals her attitude to have been founded on pure prejudice (475). With the Coles it is much the same, except that they do not have to wait so long for the change to come about. Their invitation to the gentry Emma at first strongly reprehends. Such persons "ought to be taught that it was not for them to arrange the terms on which the superior families would visit them" – though the lesson, she very much fears, will come only from herself. Strangely, however, the prospect of aloofness affords her no contentment, the yielding of her peers demolishes her resistance: and recollection of the dinner party next day is graced with the persuasion that by her presence she must have delighted the Coles – "worthy people – who deserved to be made happy! – And left a name behind her that would not soon die away" (207, 231).

These inconsistencies, while perhaps laudable in denoting the softening of positions that were unduly severe, could scarcely be more evident. They are, it should be noted, in part the outcome of an inability in Emma to tolerate "a subjection of the fancy to the understanding", as Knightley has it (37). In the author's terms, she is "an imaginist": one whose lively mind and unacknowledged feelings can construct "a ground-work of anticipation" for what might prove either fact or fantasy, and cause the last to be treated as substantive (335).

More than this. Engaged as she is in influencing Harriet beneath an appearance of neutrality, Emma is herself subject to a powerful impulsion she can have no idea of, since it arises out of her own disposition. It reveals itself in her besetting imperative of how best to exercise her social superiority. Eminence might be the better word, for Highbury "afforded her no equals", the Woodhouses being first in consequence there. And it is not status alone which makes for self-approval: Emma enjoys full awareness of her claims of personality and intellect. She can boast of having from the start planned the match between Miss Taylor and Mr. Weston, and rejoice at the thought of how "such success has blessed me" (12); and in calmer vein can as hostess demonstrate the "real good-will of a mind delighted with its own ideas" (24), and as a daughter contemplate the benefits of such an affection in her father "as could never find fault" (6).

Might it be that these promptings in Emma combine to evoke instant approval for the girl who upon introduction displays "so proper and becoming a deference" to her, and appears "so pleasantly grateful" for her condescension, and "artlessly impressed" with Hartfield's – and its mistress's – grandeur: whose appreciative response is little less than tribute to all that Emma is, or takes herself to be? For from that moment she is afire with the purpose that is to direct her course through the novel, upon which her every instinct appears to be employed.

> *She* would notice her; she would improve her; she would detach her from her bad acquaintance, and introduce her into good society; she would form her opinions and manners. It would be an interesting, and certainly a very kind undertaking; highly becoming her own situation in life, her leisure, and powers. (23-4)

The aim of Harriet's improvement is to be achieved by the simple means of association with her patroness: mere acceptance is seen as conferring an immediate dignity and worth. It is not therefore surprising that Emma's first remark on hearing of Mr. Martin's proposing to Harriet should be upon his evident determination to "connect himself well if he can" (50); or that she should respond to Knightley's vexation later at the young man's being refused with the deprecatory coolness of, "I cannot admit him to be Harriet's equal". And Knightley's counter-claim thereupon of its being a beneficial offer for Harriet is met with the incensed, "a good match for my intimate friend!" (61-2) This is the outcry of someone as entrenched in the concept of her own superiority as Lady Catherine de Bourgh; and it supports the possibility that Emma's appraisal of Harriet has been unconsciously affected by the idea of her own status and capabilities: that she has viewed her protégée through the distorting glass of her estimate of herself.

In one respect, at least, the above cannot apply: Harriet's remarkable prettiness is beyond dispute. It may be "of a sort which Emma particularly admired" (23), but corroboration is forthcoming from many other observers. There is a certain wonder in Knightley's comment to Mrs. Weston that Emma appears very little concerned with her own handsomeness. She in fact seems more preoccupied with the looks of other women: Jane Austen has endowed her with a distinctive regard for feminine beauty. During her welcoming visit to Jane Fairfax, Emma sits looking at her with the "complacency" which Jane's "very pleasing beauty" inspires. Elegance is its predominant feature; and when afterwards Churchill makes so bold as to belittle it, she is astonished to the point of concluding with some scorn that there must be a very distinct sort of elegance in the fashionable world he belongs to if Jane Fairfax is to be thought "only ordinarily gifted with it" (167, 194).

Emma indeed appears most in accord with Churchill, and as it were mentally attuned to him, when he is itemising Jane's charms to her during their reconciliation at the Westons'. The sentiment of Alexander Pope, that

> Fair tresses man's imperial race ensnare,
> And beauty draws us with a single hair

would have gained her enthusiastic approval. Can it be, therefore, that

Harriet's fine bloom, blue eyes, light hair, regular features and look of "great sweetness" are in effect an assault upon Emma's objectivity, and that "those soft blue eyes" (23-4) are all the while leading her into idealising their possessor for graces not present in her: that, through an excessive preoccupation with what is outward in Harriet, to say nothing of other sources of misapprehension, Emma has come to be quite deluded in her regard for her protégée?

*   *   *

Emma's lifelong acquaintance and future husband certainly thinks so. His view of Harriet, imparted even in the civil tones of his address to Mrs. Weston, is unequivocal. Her companionship will be positively harmful to Emma through the "hourly flattery" that a nature so ignorant will render. She herself will gain only a little polish from the proximity; the "strength of mind" which she sorely needs Emma will be unable to bestow (38-9). This assertion is but a prelude, however, to the scathing assessment Knightley delivers upon discovery of Emma's part in Harriet's declining Martin's proposal. She is a girl of little sense and no information, who is totally lacking in experience, "and, with her little wit, is not very likely ever to have any that can avail her". A prospective lover would face the impediments of "illegitimacy and ignorance"; and Harriet's continued association with Emma will only bring about in her the mischief which "Vanity working on a weak head produces" (61-4).

But this somewhat less than favourable judgment undergoes distinct moderation with the passage of time. Upon Emma's being constrained to confess to him how much Mr. Elton has fallen in her estimation, the gratified Knightley is moved to declare that her friend has greatly risen in his, especially through comparison with the woman Elton has lately taken to wife. He has discerned Harriet to possess "some first rate qualities" which the former Augusta Hawkins is without, amongst them a modest, unassuming nature which makes her "infinitely to be preferred" by any man of sense – who would moreover find, as he has done, that she is "more conversable" than at first appears (331).

True, this is not yet praise of the glowing sort; and some further qualification might be assumed in Knightley's suggestion, in accounting for Harriet's prompt acceptance of Martin upon their meeting in Brunswick Square, that a good-tempered, soft-hearted girl such as she was "not likely to be very, very determined against any young man who told her he loved her" (473). But persuadableness in a young woman, even in a matter of such seriousness, was in that age deemed a virtue, a fact strongly impressed upon the reluctant Catherine Morland and Fanny Price: and had not Knightley himself jestingly taunted Mrs. Weston with it, in respect of the schooling which the young Emma had subjected her to? And on this occasion he is overlooking Harriet's early preference. What though is apparent is that, by the end, his initial disapproval of her has vanished.

No such reversal occurs in Emma's thinking. What she asserts about Harriet during the painful interview which followed Martin's being refused is sustained through all that follows; indeed, there is even to be seen in her a heightening of regard for her young charge. Not that she ever comes to imagine Harriet intelligent: but she remains assured that the girl has "better sense" than Knightley is aware of. The same is true of the prettiness and good-nature which he has discounted. These attributes Emma cannot believe to be trivial: the former, she tells him, will hold sway over men until such time as "they do fall in love with well-informed minds instead of handsome faces"; and the latter cannot fail of being a universal recommendation. In her uniting the two, she affirms, Harriet is "exactly what every man delights in": and were he ever to marry, "she is the very woman for you" (63-4).

The last utterance is a riposte, made with jocularity and abandon by an Emma under attack from her formidable opponent. But that it springs from conviction is proved by the manner, later on, in which Harriet's confiding her hopes of Knightley is received. The overpowering sensation in Emma is of course the product of sudden discovery of her own love; but, this set aside – if it may be – her dominant concern at the news is the consequence for himself if he were to marry beneath him: as she pictures it afterwards, "the smiles, the sneers, the merriment it would prompt at his expense". Neither in Harriet herself, nor in the evidence of his fondness she puts forward, does Emma find grounds for dismissing Knightley's attachment as improbable through personal deficiency in its object. The disparity in qualities, as in rank, she is painfully aware of; yet, "Was it a new circumstance for a man of first-rate abilities to be captivated by very inferior powers?" It is very clear that in her own thoughts Emma accords Harriet the full status of a rival: that she sees her in all her attractiveness as little less than the incarnation of her own outlook and philosophy upon womankind (413).

To this conclusion, however, it might be objected that Emma's mind at the time is not capable of any objective assessment. She is in the grip of new and tyrannical emotions: the desire to possess, accompanied by the terror of losing. Love and fear exert their full force; and, were this not enough, she is all the while being afflicted by the bewildering recognition of "The blunders, the blindness of her own head and heart!" The state is one which, in her apprehension, would invest the plainest of plain Janes with the enchantments of a siren (411-2).

When, much later on, assured of the man she loves, and responding to life in the glow of the heart's fulfilment, she expresses to Knightley a wish for the happiness of the betrothed Harriet and Martin, Emma answers his cryptic observation upon the change she has undergone since they last talked on the subject with the self-accusation, "at that time I was a fool". It would be unwise to take the emphatic remark as a confession of disenchantment with Harriet. It is acknowledgement, rather, of Knightley's having been correct in his view of the sphere that life and fortune had marked out for the girl, and of her own lapse in having so romantically departed from the prevailing conventions she is now re-converted to. Here also, therefore, she is not in suitable mood to pronounce upon Harriet's promise. No more, evidently, is Knightley himself, in the indeterminate approval he then voices as to her being "an artless, amiable girl, with very good notions, very seriously good principles, and placing her happiness in the affections and utility of domestic life" (474). If there is apology of a sort in these words, repentance has been present in Emma's little outburst for the presumption she was guilty of in taking it upon herself to direct another's destiny, and the blunders and embarrassments it has involved them in. The matter of Harriet's personableness – her fitness to attach a man of some consequence, and gain respectability in the world Jane Austen's novels reflect – is left still to be determined.

*   *   *

The question arises whether Harriet's moderate mental powers would be a hindrance. Emma sees the want of cleverness as adverse; and our own early impressions are of a thoughtlessness and indecision implicit in the "Oh, dear, no" and "Oh! dear, yes!" of Harriet's hasty assents during their first walk (87), the see-saw response to Emma's inference that Mr. Martin does not read – "Oh, yes! – that is, no – I do not know – but I believe he has read a good deal – but not what you would think anything of" (29) – and the agonising at Ford's as to the destination of the purchased muslin and ribbon.

These are minor issues – but not so the cause which brings Harriet with all speed to ask advice upon her receipt of Martin's letter. Emma, we are told, is even half ashamed of her young friend "for seeming so pleased and so doubtful" upon such a theme. The doubt persists throughout their interview, Emma's approval of the letter on perusing it, and inquiry as to whether the answer is to be favourable, gaining little more than a, "well – and – and what shall I do?" and a, "What would you advise me to do? Pray, dear Miss Woodhouse, tell me what I ought to do?" And when, after being with solemn propriety cautioned that marriage is not a proper state to be entered into "with half a heart", and questioned as to Mr. Martin's being "the most agreeable man" she has ever been in company with, Harriet is propelled to a decision, it is couched in terms which reveal it as a lesser triumph of equivocation: "and I have now quite determined, and really almost made up my mind – to refuse Mr. Martin. Do you think I am right?" (50-3)

But indecision at a first proposal is entirely fitting in Harriet's case. She is scarcely out of school,

> a green girl
> Unsifted in such perilous circumstance;

and one, further, whose origins have precluded the ambience and support of a family, as they have acquaintance with the modes of decorum in the imposing world to which she has been so extraordinarily elevated. What is more natural than that Martin's declaration should enhance the sense of her solitariness, and cause her fearfully to seek counsel and comfort from the greatness that has befriended her?

In whatever context she is finally settled, Harriet will not be renowned for resource and positiveness in reasoning. Her capacities as displayed in the novel are limited, from the instance of her wondering whether the solution of Elton's charade is a "trident? or a mermaid? or a shark?" (73) to its being "very odd" that there should be a fortnight and a day's difference between Mr. Martin's birthday and her own (30), or her finding it almost conclusive that Martin's letter of proposal is mere prose, in comparison to the verse of the charade (76). In the latter instances, though, we are encountering the force of affection – as we are in Harriet's tempering the admission of Jane Fairfax's playing being perhaps superior to Emma's with the consoling irrelevance that "if she does play so very well, you know, it is no more than she is obliged to do, because she will have to teach"; or in her designating, and actually enshrining, Elton's bit of plaster and pencil-end as "*Most precious treasures*". Her distaste for Italian singing upon the plea that "There is no understanding a word of it" can, however, admit no such extenuation (232). And if her logic is more admissible when she reacts to Emma's declared resolution never to marry, it derives from the commonplace notions of its being unusual to hear a young woman say such a thing, and "so dreadful" to end up an old maid.

Be this as it may, amidst society at any level Harriet appears a lively and personable presence, taking a keen interest in all its manifestations.

Possessions as such excite her, whether the Martins' "very handsome summer house, large enough to hold a dozen people", or their "two parlours, two very good parlours indeed" – or even the "beautiful goose" Mrs. Martin presents to Mrs. Goddard. But it is people who truly hold her interest. She can, for example, speak with the same "exultation" of Mrs. Martin's having "an upper maid who had lived five-and-twenty years with her" (27-8); and she is most freely herself when concerned with the sayings and doings of others. In the recital of her being discovered by Miss Nash peeping with the two Abbots through the blind at Mr. Elton, and their being scolded away from the window only for Miss Nash to take their place and then good-naturedly call her back to let her see too, and their confiding to each other "how beautiful we thought he looked!" Harriet is at her liveliest (75). She is so again when repeating to Emma, "with great delight", what Miss Nash had told her about Mr. Perry's meeting with Mr. Elton on the road to London, and being informed he is the bearer of "something exceedingly precious" which Mr. Perry inferred must be to do with "a lady" (68) – or, for that matter, when she is detailing the comments of anyone upon a subject she has at heart.

Harriet is in fact a social creature. Emma notes her gratitude at being first received in the way she is, and the pleasure she evinces at her hostess's affability and parting handshake; and the responsiveness of a different order when, having been driven to the Martins', Harriet looks around "with a sort of fearful curiosity" before her frought resumption of relations with them (186). The account of the meeting she gives afterwards so well conveys the naturalness and delicacy of feelings on both sides as to cause Emma alarm. But there was in truth nothing for her to fear. Harriet's protestation earlier, upon realising that Emma must have dropped acquaintance with her had she married Mr. Martin – "It would have killed me never to come to Hartfield any more!" – had expressed what was for her the true scale of values. She feels as strongly as the other the distinction which admission to that demesne has accorded her (54).

This is to be confirmed in intimate terms as Emma endeavours to check her wistful preoccupation with Mr. Elton by mention of the pain which being reminded of her error brings, and Harriet's need for her own sake to acquire the habit of proper self-command. By this hint of thanklessness on her part, Harriet is plunged into a violence of remorse.

> "You, who have been the best friend I ever had in my life – Want gratitude to you! – Nobody is equal to you! I care for nobody as I do for you! Oh, Miss Woodhouse, how ungrateful I have been!" (268)

Nothing becomes Harriet more than this display of "tenderness of heart", as Emma esteems it; nor is the latter wrong in being tempted at this point to consider the young girl as exceeding her in attractiveness. She recognises the want in herself of the capacity for affection which Harriet possesses in having an instinctive liking for people. It is in fact Harriet's social predisposition which puts an end to her tenderness for Mr. Elton. Her sense of the humiliation she is subjected to at the Crown by his ostentatious declining to dance with her is acute: as is her awareness of its dissipation by Knightley's courtly offer of his hand. The whole is an intense experience for her. "Such a change!" she declares afterwards to Emma; "In one moment such a change! From perfect misery to perfect happiness" (342). From what she had said before they quitted the ball-room Emma has realised that it was as if her eyes were suddenly opened to Elton's character; but she does not appreciate the depth of deliverance socially speaking Knightley's intervention has constituted for Harriet: what must be its significance for a nature as open and sensitive as hers.

*   *   *

For she is naturally drawn to the opposite sex; and though always conducting herself with modesty, is not inhibited by undue reserve. There is an appreciative regard for the gentlemen she encounters at

Hartfield, and a respect, which can amount to near-reverence, for their virtues. Mr. Woodhouse's gentleness she had voluntarily remarked upon with admiration verging upon awe; first acquaintance with Mr. Knightley produces the open admiration of his being "so very fine a man!" (32) and even when Mr. Elton is lost to her, she can aver that it will remain a pleasure to admire him at a distance, and "think of his superiority to all the rest of the world with the gratitude, wonder, and veneration which are so proper, in me especially" (341).

Is this responsiveness to men the explanation of Harriet's extraordinary amatory career? If it were, it would declare her more than a little of a coquette, and betoken an instability or shallowness of disposition making her unworthy of being taken seriously. If, though, it is not, the question must be asked why in the first place Emma should have found it possible to blight her protégée's early but very real affection for young farmer Martin with little apparent difficulty.

The answer surely lies in the influence which Emma is able so cleverly and determinedly to exert. The slightest suggestion of an attachment from Harriet is enough to call forth the assurance of her being a gentleman's daughter, and consequent necessity of supporting her claim to that status "by every thing within your own power", against those intent upon lowering her, to wit, the Martins. Their meeting with Mr. Martin next day on the Donwell road is prelude to deliberate vilification of his appearance and manner, which brings from Harriet the abashed admission that "he is not so genteel as real gentlemen". There follows a series of denigrating comparisons with men of the Hartfield circle, and introduction thereupon of Mr. Elton's charms, with allusion to the recent "additional softness" of address by which, "If he means anything, it must be to please you". By these means is "the very person fixed on by Emma" now flatteringly introduced to Harriet's shaken sensibilities (30-4).

The business of prevailing upon her to reject Martin's proposal is admirably contrived. There is no urging: instead, an assumption as between ladies of a negative in such a case being without question, of course accompanied by "expressions of gratitude and concern for the pain you are inflicting" – succeeded by affected restrained surprise at the possible existence of "doubt as to the *purport* of your answer". Instantly, the intention is understood. "'You think I ought to refuse him then?' said Harriet, looking down". Ensuing protestations of unwillingness to advise or influence are beside the point: the damage has been done. For her now to accept Martin, as Harriet is acutely aware, would mean the sacrifice of a unique friendship, an abandonment of all that Emma prizes in her and is yet to come to fulfilment, and a betrayal of the social convictions and aspirations that are a true component of her being (51-2).

Such loss and harm, at this early stage of her life, Harriet is not able to contemplate. It is all the more remarkable, therefore, that once decision has been reached and letter despatched, she should display residual independence of mind to the extent of contradicting to her face what Emma has so strenuously impressed on her. Certainly, she concedes, with respect to handsomeness and manner he may not equal others; "However, I do really think Mr. Martin a very amiable young man, and have a great opinion of him" (54). This view, here boldly stated, she can never change, under any form of persuasion, or whatever else may betide: and she confirms it the moment she has the chance.

In recommending Mr. Elton to her, Emma exerts influence of an entirely different kind. The method of disparagement with admixture of pretence, which Martin's inferior social position had made requisite, now gives place to an impulsion of the purest friendship and goodwill. Emma "had no scruple with regard to Mr. Elton", convinced as she is of his being "in the fairest way of falling in love, if not in love already" with her young charge; and while she cannot feel any doubt of having given Harriet's fancy "a proper direction" at the earliest moment by assurance of his admiration, she assiduously follows it up "by agreeable hints". She goes about her task with a delighted certainty, with an enthusiasm at the near-realisation of her dream, by which Harriet, in her inexperience, and fresh from her confined upbringing, is impelled to view matters through her benefactress's eyes (42).

Emma's attributing Elton's attentions to a love for Harriet, gratifying though the idea be, is not a product of her active imagination. She cannot conceive of so inordinate a propensity in him as to have designs upon herself. Her action when he has presented his charade is thus fully expressive of her mind. Smilingly, she pushes the paper towards Harriet with the words, "take it, – it is for you. Take your own". The word *courtship* can be no other than "a very good hint" of the desire to pay his addresses; and the poem's application, as Emma construes it, is so pointed and particular a compliment "that I cannot have a moment's doubt as to Mr. Elton's intentions. You are his object – and you will soon receive the completest proof of it". The purpose it denotes is as clear, she assures Harriet, as her own wishes for her have been since she first knew her (70-3).

The interchange that follows is charged with Emma's exclamations and congratulations: upon the naturalness and desirability of the attachment, its being in every sense prudential and advantageous, its acceptability to friends and family, its elevating tendency, its giving every prospect of happiness through Elton's amiable character, its arising between people called together by situation, and belonging to each other "by every circumstance of your respective homes". The list is all but exhaustive: and the certainty is complete.

As far as Harriet is concerned, Emma speaks with a womanly and social authority that is irresistible; and yet, in the very act of yielding to it, she gives voice to intimations of a contrary sort. "Whatever you say is always right", she cries; "and therefore I suppose, and believe, and hope it must be so; but otherwise I could not have imagined it". The gradations of her acquiescence are significant – as are the reasons she puts forward for her misgiving. Elton in his eligibility is "so much beyond anything I deserve"; his interest in her "is a sort of thing which nobody could have expected"; and she "did not know him, to speak to him, at Michaelmas!" These considerations are commonsense. From their perspective what Emma is urging is most unlikely: but Harriet is without means of resisting it. And soon she is reduced to, "How nicely you talk; I love to hear you. You understand every thing" (74-6).

That she is without defence is the fault, not of herself, but of the usages of social life that directed relations between the sexes.

Attachment and wooing was on both sides a matter of suggestion – delicate, as in the bestowal of compliment, or more explicit, by such gesture or token as the conferring of Harriet's portrait on Elton, or his ceremonious presentation of the charade. By her generous invitations to Hartfield, and the easy sociability she favours him with on Harriet's account, Emma is unwittingly guilty of a liberality that Elton, and even the disinterested Mr. John Knightley, can understand only as encouragement (112). Ordinarily, however, a heedfulness alike in behaviour and in its interpretation is rigorously observed. The Eltons and Knightleys, the Wentworths and Bertrams, agonise over having their discreet inferences "understood" by the beloved: and Harriet is not the least credulous, fanciful or foolish in being guided by Emma's appraisal of the indications in Mr. Elton's conduct. There is for her, in addition, the flattering thought that, just as greatness in Emma's person has lifted her out of obscurity into distinction, so it is now coming more wonderfully to her aid, in Mr. Elton, "who might marry any body!" succumbing to her charms. Could someone as innocent and trusting as she be expected to oppose so felicitous a development, guarded and instructed as she is by an Emma Woodhouse? Harriet is no simpleton in believing herself beloved by this respected gentleman, but reacts to the unusual circumstance as would any well-conducted lady of her tender years.

*   *   *

For Emma, strolling on Hartfield's lawns the morning after the Westons' ball, her head full of gratified musings upon Knightley's gallantry to Harriet, to be confronted with the sight of the sweep gates opening to admit the same Harriet in swooning state on Frank Churchill's arm, after his rescuing her from the gipsies, is a masterpiece of literary construction. No manner of person whatsoever, as Jane Austen mischievously affirms thereupon, would have been dead to the happening's romantic possibilities. Certainly Emma's mind is not proof against them; and afterwards it seems to her the most natural thing in the world that Harriet should be confessing an utter devotion to her champion, though with hopelessness as to the likelihood of his stooping to her. Influence, therefore, is not called for here; and Emma, chastened now as she is by recollection of the confusion and distress she had involved Harriet and herself in over Elton, is resolved against the slightest interference, even to the mention of a name. Her advice is therefore what might properly be given to any young woman in this predicament: that matches of such disparity are not altogether without precedent, and that she should observe with the closest attention the beloved's attitude towards her (342).

Harriet is of course talking about Mr. Knightley. The service he had rendered her the previous evening, in its moral and social implication, is for her infinitely greater than the physical deliverance Churchill has just effected. For the latter she is naturally obliged: but by the former she has been captivated. It would have reduced to insignificance any allure that Churchill's forthright conduct might have conferred on him; but in fact Harriet has never even thought of Churchill, except to be conscious of his lacking the distinction, the true gentlemanliness, she had recognised in Knightley. In this she has shown herself possessed of a measure of discrimination which Emma, distracted possibly by romantic schemings, is yet to attain; and at the tense moment when misunderstanding is finally rectified, it is with indignation that Harriet rejects the idea of her having been predisposed as Emma had imagined.

> "Mr. Frank Churchill, indeed! I do not know who would ever look at him in the company of the other. I hope I have a better taste than to think of Mr. Frank Churchill, who is like nobody by his side." (405)

This outspokenness is in part due to the pressure of wounded feelings; but it tends, amid much else, to demonstrate that Harriet is far from being the sentimentalist, the innate romantic, that her dealings might at first suggest.

Falling in love with Mr. Knightley is something she does entirely of her own accord. It is a love born of admiration and esteem; but it arises also from immense gratitude. Knightley's inviting her to dance upon her being scorned by Elton was more than rescue from social affront. It had in truth been a healing in emotional terms, for a nature simple and sincere, shocked and dismayed at sudden perfidy in the man for whom she had entertained a genuine affection. The restoration brought about in her manifested itself outwardly in her bounding "higher than ever" in the dance, and being "in a continual course of smiles": but its effect upon the heart has been far more dramatic, though unseen (328).

It is the greater for what is not present in Harriet's awareness. She has no means of comprehending Elton's ill-treatment to have been a revenge upon Emma for the insult she had administered in specifying his social inferiority, both in the match she had sought to contrive, and that to which he had himself aspired. Quite what sense she might have gained of Knightley's acting to quell a flagrant discourtesy, and in preservation of social decorum, would be hard to determine. But his deepest motive – a wish to remedy the injury to Emma in this public slighting of her friend, an impulse of love itself, which escaped Emma's own recognition – Harriet could not begin to fathom.

As any young woman might, she views what has happened from a personal perspective: sees herself singled out, honoured, redeemed by the man she has throughout identified as in a class apart from the others. His asking for her hand in that situation was the highest compliment that could be paid within the sphere of her experience. With this certainty, enhanced as it is by powerful feelings of thankfulness, she cannot doubt herself as being the woman preferred – and as yet again distinguished by a benign suzerainty seemingly intent on claiming her as its own.

That his inviting her to the dance might be liable to such interpretation would not occur to Knightley. From his social altitude he would, like Emma, never expect persons admitted to a modicum of familiarity to venture above their condition, presuming upon an invulnerability which, however, in the nature of things, a moment's inadvertence might dispel. What preoccupies him is a desire to defend his Emma against affront, and thereby perhaps re-establish himself in her goodwill by graciousness towards a girl he has without doubt judged too severely in the past. The particularity implicit in his so doing can but be regarded, by Harriet and onlookers alike, as a marked attention. The incident, with all that subsequently flows from it in Knightley's seeking with the same determination to cultivate further acquaintance with her, has the appearance in ordinary social terms – as ultimately to Emma's own understanding – of plain romantic attachment.

Harriet is therefore justified in the hopes of Knightley which, in discourse somewhat hesitant and by no means "Methodical, or well arranged" (409), she is later to confide to her sponsor. Bearing in mind the vulnerability with which she is beset by reason of her few years and scant experience, and the pressures social and emotional so arbitrarily brought to bear upon her at Hartfield, her having been or fancied herself in love with him, as with Elton, is in the light of events not at all as remarkable as would appear. And when, freed at last from the affliction of Emma's tutelage, she chances to re-encounter Martin in London, she gives evidence of a praiseworthy maturity, both in the constancy of her first love despite the onslaught made against it, and in the decisiveness she demonstrates in there and then accepting him.

*   *   *

When Fanny Price comes to live at Mansfield Park, the Bertram girls are unremitting in their disparagement of their poor cousin for her inferiority. The one respect in which they will allow her any equality with them is disclosed in the grudging admission that "Fanny is good-natured enough". This attribute is largely to be seen in Fanny's compliance with the obligations of her dependent situation at Mansfield, and a readiness to be generally helpful: but with Harriet Smith, it is evident in a variety of relationships in Highbury and at Hartfield. It is perhaps at its most moving in her reception of the news of Emma's having been in error as to Elton's feelings and intentions. There is no blame, no recrimination; instead, a "lowly opinion of herself" which acquits the other of accountability. The affection of such a man, she protests amidst her tears, would have been "too great a distinction". She never could have merited it; indeed, "nobody but so partial and kind a friend as Miss Woodhouse would have thought it possible" (141-2). Both he and the as yet unknown Miss Hawkins are held in high regard: and merely to reflect that he had not thrown himself away is for Harriet "such a comfort!" (272)

Almost as affecting is the sensitivity and tenderness that is demonstrated during her accidental encounter with Mr. Martin and his sister at Ford's, after relationship with them has been abruptly ended. She is near fainting, knowing that she will have turned as white as her gown. In the sister's coming forward and seeming ready to shake hands, Harriet is sorely conscious of the reluctance Elizabeth has contrived to overcome. Her state is not so much embarrassment, as misery at the couple's struggling to hide their pain in complaisance; and Elizabeth's expression of regret at their not meeting now is "almost too kind" for her to bear (179).

But it is surely in her unfailing amiability towards Emma that Harriet's good nature is most apparent. Not only has she repeatedly been led into disappointment and grief, but the friend whose self-centred enthusiasms have been responsible is unmasked at the close as an enemy. Yet so unassuming, gentle and mannerly has she been in all, that not the least semblance of reproach has passed her lips or appeared in her reactions. After she is banished from Hartfield to the John Knightleys in London, Emma can fancy there being present in her letters "something of resentment, a something bordering on it in her style", which, she realises, "might be only her own consciousness" – or in other words, the trick of a merited self-reproach. But even if the former, as she goes on to tell herself, "it seemed as if an angel only could have been quite without resentment under such a stroke" as her appropriation of Knightley. Having, in short, consistently been made a fool of in concerns close to the heart, Harriet reveals, in disposition and in conduct, qualities which by any standard must be seen as admirable (451).

* * *

Amongst them is one which her naiveté and want of cultivation might lead us not to expect. It is to be detected in the conversation with Emma that follows their encountering Mr. Martin. When the mistress of Hartfield, describing him as awkward and abrupt, asks with rhetorical emphasis what he will be at Mr. Weston's time of life, Harriet responds with a solemn, "There is no saying, indeed!"; and the answer of Emma's own providing, that he will have become "a completely gross, vulgar farmer", receives the quiet accord of, "Will he, indeed, that will be very bad" (33). Even allowing for Harriet's inclination and habit of respectfulness, there is, in her demeanour as she meets this slander of the man in whose company she had experienced much pleasure, a deliberative reticence that merits the name of composure.

It is evident also when, under Emma's reproof as to her being "overpowered" by so small a token of admiration as Mr. Elton's charade, she replies with the brevity and self-possession of, "Oh! no – I hope I shall not be ridiculous about it. Do as you please" (77-78). The same tones accompany her appearance before Emma one morning with the Tunbridge-ware box, and confession of having treasured Elton's relics therein. Now professedly an altered creature, she declares a duty and wish to have no reserves from Emma on the subject; and continues, "it is very fit that you should have the satisfaction of knowing it. I do not want to say any more than is necessary – I am too much ashamed of having given way as I have done, and I dare say you understand me". The matter itself is trivial: but the language by which it is conveyed, in its simplicity, has an elegance of its own (337).

More often than not, the mode of address mirrors the mind of the speaker. What, therefore, are we to make of Harriet's words at the moment when realisation has dawned upon Emma that it is Mr. Knightley, and not Frank Churchill, for whom her friend has been nurturing so passionate a regard? "I am sure, but for believing that you entirely approved and meant to encourage me in my attachment", she protests, "I should have considered it at first too great a presumption almost, to dare to think of him". That a degree of sophistication rings through these accents is borne out by the style and content of what ensues. Emma, exclaiming at the "most unfortunate – most deplorable mistake!" she has made, is reduced to a silence. Its significance is not lost upon Harriet, and she responds with an injunction whose mild terms in no way belie its directness. The possibility of such a match has been Emma's own urging: and "if Mr. Knightley should really – if *he* does not mind the disparity, I hope, dear Miss Woodhouse, you will not set yourself against it, and try to put difficulties in the way. But you are too good for that, I am sure" (405-7).

Her meaning could hardly be more plain, yet it is not offensive. Perhaps its very clarity takes any hurtfulness from it: but this can only be when the disposition behind the utterance is innocent and engaging. Of its being so with Harriet, if it were not evident from her previous attitudes, there would be confirmation in her final remark. Until this point, she declares, she had as instructed gone by outward indications of regard in Knightley: "But now I seem to feel that I may deserve him; and that if he does choose me, it will not be any thing so very wonderful". In this speech there is a confidence and womanliness which impresses – and conveys the truth that Harriet has about her at this testing juncture an innate dignity, which others, of more years and greater claim, might well envy (411).

*   *   *

But does she have the stature which might make some future Austen heroine? The comparison suggests itself with Catherine Morland, who is also at the stage between girl and woman, and certainly not a giant of intellect – but who displays an adherence to principle, a resolution in the face of difficulties, and an ability to think something through which can unsettle even a Henry Tilney. But Catherine has not been subjected to another's authority – save that of Mrs. Allen, which for all practical purposes can be safely discounted. She is obliged almost throughout to stand on her own feet, whereas Harriet, confined to a subordinate role, has small scope for initiative; were she placed in a similar situation, indications are that she would acquit herself creditably. In Fanny Price, by contrast, we observe a profoundly moral nature and contingent strength of personality that can slowly impress itself upon wholly adverse circumstances. But the demands of everyday living oblige her to withdraw into a diffidence which masks her superiority from all who do not know her well; and the hesitation and solemnity of manner which results robs her, in the opinion of many, of heroic pretension.

How different is Harriet's refreshing spontaneity and naturalness. Certainly there is little in her outlook of a detached and speculative kind: her thoughts are a process of responses to events around her, and the hopes, joys and sorrows they give rise to. But the same can largely be said of all Jane Austen's young women: none of them is the stuff philosophers are made of. They are in love with the present as they encounter it, with the men they will marry, when they have found them; and do not seem at the point we know them to be seeking much beyond.

However, there is an exception to what has just been said that concerns Harriet. It has to do with a remark she makes at the end of her account of the distressing meeting with Martin and his sister at Ford's, from which the rain permitted no escape. She would rather have done anything, she tells Emma, than have had it happen: "and yet, you know, there was a sort of satisfaction in seeing him behave so pleasantly and kindly. And Elizabeth, too" (179). In the midst of her anguish at such close contact after the estrangement, she has been struck by the rightness of conduct and delicacy of sentiment in those now permanently distanced from her. Her being so is a piece of wonderment and true reflection. But it is more.

If what defines a gentleman is his predominant desire to set others at their ease, may it not be that a corresponding pleasure in fineness of comportment, and the decencies of social interplay, is what distinguishes a lady? If this be allowed – and who would pronounce otherwise? – it suggests, with much else, that, deceived though Emma may sometimes have been as to character and conduct in the unfolding of events, she made no mistake in her choice of Harriet Smith.

Mr. Darcy in Love

As all critics well know, they will get to the truth of a work of literature only if their mind is attuned to that of its author. In Alexander Pope's words, "A perfect judge will read each work of wit / With the same spirit that its author writ".[33] They address themselves to the task with unquenchable optimism, but they labour on difficult, if not enchanted, terrain. The very means they bring to it – their personal gifts and outlooks – can, if they are unwary, prove a source of insensibility. And even if not, the author of the piece, though it be Jane Austen herself, may at times be less than sure about motivation: for fictional character readily tends to have a life of its own in the creative mind. Indeed, the persons of her novels are constantly endeavouring, and as often as not failing, to make out one another's promptings.

Naturally enough, where the emotions are involved, unsureness prevails most; and fortunately we have in Elizabeth Bennet an example of a character insistently demanding of another at the novel's close to account for behaviour that has been puzzling her through half of it. Her spirits "rising to playfulness" after getting her father's consent to her marrying the man for whom she had long professed aversion, she inquires of Mr. Darcy when he fell in love with her (380). "How could you begin?" she asks. She can comprehend his going on charmingly once he had started; "but what could start you off in the first place?" What he has to say for himself does not amount to much.

> "I cannot fix on the hour, or the spot, or the look, or the words, which laid the foundation. It is too long ago. I was in the middle before I knew I had begun."

His situation is the same as that of Henry Crawford, who on declaring his attachment to Fanny Price, and being asked by his sister Mary when his love for her had begun, protests a similar ignorance. "Nothing can be more agreeable," remarks Jane Austen, "than to be asked such a question, though nothing can be more impossible than to answer it". Whether or not Elizabeth expects a positive reply from Darcy, she is prepared for any doubt by having an answer of her own.

> "The fact is, you were sick of civility, of deference, of officious attention. You were disgusted with women who were always speaking, and looking, and thinking for *your* approbation alone. I roused, and interested you, because I was so unlike *them*."

As she puts it, he had in his heart despised the women who in this way had been courting him; and though he knew no actual good of her, such considerations were not present in people falling in love.

Elizabeth had quickly sensed the impression her disinterestedness and naturalness, and the very direct manner of their operation, had made upon Darcy, and much also of the attraction she exercised thereby. Is she right? Can the contrast between herself, and the women who had flattered and fawned upon him, have heralded, or invoked, love itself? Or was it, rather, no more than a realisation that awoke his first interest in her? Only the evidence Darcy shows of being stirred by it can determine the issue. What is clear, though, and in this respect surely important, is that Elizabeth assigns Darcy's falling in love with her to an early stage in their acquaintance.

But what would have been the moment? By way of prelude to her assertion, she has reminded her fiancé of their first casting eyes upon each other at the Meryton ball, when love would decidedly not have been present in him, and his scornful rejection of her as a partner for the dance, as being "tolerable, but not handsome enough to tempt me" – doing so with the withering, and almost wifely, observation, "My beauty you had early withstood". He soon enough had, despite himself, found this critical attitude unsustainable in the presence of such a woman as Elizabeth Bennet; nor would the reader have imagined that he could long persist in it.

*   *   *

Relations between the two of them are largely determined by the series of debates, or contentions, which occur during the Bennet sisters' stay at Netherfield Park. Soon after her arrival there, Elizabeth, momentarily free from attending Jane, had come amongst the others, and taken up a book, till diverted by a discussion raised by Bingley of accomplishment in ladies (37-40). All ladies, pretty well, are according to him very accomplished; Darcy, with his "faithful assistant" Miss Bingley, insists on the comparative rarity of accomplishment amongst them; and Elizabeth, intrigued, asserts its almost complete absence in women, if the attainments being insisted upon really apply. "I never saw such a woman. I never saw such capacity, and taste, and application, and elegance, as you describe, united".

This is a tense little skirmish; and it is noticeable that, despite their views being entirely opposed, Darcy contrives to be complaisant towards Elizabeth, and a determined defender of her character after she has left them. On hearing Miss Bingley's impressive list, he advises that a woman "must add something yet more substantial, in the improvement of her mind by extensive reading". And to Caroline's indignant exclamation, once the door is closed upon Elizabeth, that she is one of those young ladies who try to appeal to the other sex by the paltry device of undervaluing their own, Darcy's rejoinder is that there is meanness in all arts so employed amongst women: that "Whatever bears affinity to cunning is despicable". This is no mere fair-minded comment; there is too much purpose in it – a calculated irony, which instantly achieves its object of silencing Caroline in her attack on the girl she has so quickly seen as a rival. "Miss Bingley was not so entirely satisfied with this reply as to continue the subject", we learn. We observe here the action of a man who surely feels a strong regard for Elizabeth.

Darcy's comportment during the quieter little social episode next day, before Mrs. Bennet's departure with her younger daughters, may be thought to indicate the same thing (41-6). He plays a correct and if anything helpful role, in the desultory conversation which provides scope for Elizabeth's liveliness. Bingley having been somewhat dismayed by her professed ability perfectly to see through his character, and no less by her assurance that a more complex character need be no more estimable than one such as his, Darcy tactfully intervenes with the reflection, albeit to Mrs. Bennet's witless displeasure, that subjects for character study are fewer in a country neighbourhood. That lady's mention of Jane's once having had affectionate verses written to her brings Elizabeth's impatient pronouncement on the efficacy of poetry in driving away love, and from Darcy the contribution of poetry's conventionally being regarded as the food of love. For his pains he is rewarded with the assertion that, if the love in question is "only a slight, thin inclination… one good sonnet will starve it entirely away". At this, we hear, Darcy only smiled; but who could do otherwise, at such a delightful paradox? In these relaxed moments, one would say that Darcy is favourably disposed towards Elizabeth for a man of his reserve, and seemingly encouraging her to speak.

That evening, after dinner, Miss Bingley's comparison between Darcy's handwriting and her brother's causes the latter to return to his disclosure of the morning, and admit to having a flow of ideas so rapid that his letters often "convey no ideas at all" to his correspondents. This development is ominous (47-52). Elizabeth ventures the mildly sarcastic, "Your humility, Mr. Bingley, must disarm reproof" – a touch which Darcy seizes upon for actual dispraise. They dominate from this point a discussion which becomes a clash of two attitudes – solemn from Darcy, sceptical and jocular from Elizabeth and Bingley – and a conflict also between two dissimilar concepts which Darcy himself introduces, perhaps without his being conscious of it.

The case Darcy puts forward is that Bingley's seeming humility is deceitful. He is, though indirectly, boasting and complimenting himself on the quickness of mind that allows him to make decisions immediately. But the self-congratulation is spurious: for if he were by chance to be asked by a friend not to leave his house in a hurry, as he might have resolved to, Bingley would, to Darcy's knowledge, probably not rush off as intended, but stay for a month.

The last point does not prove the first, and is incompatible with it, as being of a different order. Personality does not exist by virtue of a single characteristic, but comprises many: someone can be both hasty of temperament, and at the same time friendly and persuadable. Elizabeth at once perceives the error; and upon Bingley's affirming that his critic would think better of him if he were to give the supposed friend a flat denial, and ride off as fast as he could, brings the inconsistency into prominence with the searching question, "Would Mr. Darcy then consider the rashness of your original intention as atoned for by your obstinacy in adhering to it?" Bingley is now at a loss; Darcy, while not acknowledging the stated opinion as his own, points out that no reason had been given for the persuasion; and the argument reaches the impasse of two opposite yet complementary statements of possibility: the one,

"To yield readily – easily – to the persuasion of a friend is no merit with you";

and the other,

"To yield without conviction is no compliment to either."

The matter in effect is concluded, having become one of speculation. Darcy's unwise attempt to prolong it, by urging that all facts relating to the situation between the mythical friends must be known, leads to his discomfiture. For Bingley's comic demand that Darcy's height, and its awesome influence on those around him, also be taken into account, topples the verbal edifice, to the company's diversion.

How is Darcy affected? He shows obvious annoyance at the ridicule he has incurred – but not for long. His mind evidently is preoccupied with other thoughts. In due course he requests some music; and Miss Bingley obliging him, Elizabeth becomes aware "how frequently Mr. Darcy's eyes were fixed upon her". Unable to suppose she can be "an object of admiration to so great a man", she concludes it is not amorous intent, but something incorrect in herself, that is the cause – only to find that, taking advantage of a lively Scotch air, he is asking her to dance a reel with him. She has pleasure now in returning the compliment of Meryton, and rejecting him both as partner and critic with a defiant, "and now despise me if you dare". She is totally unprepared for, and amazed at, his gallant, "Indeed I do not dare".

This singular step in Darcy might lead to a lingering surmise. Is it possible, human nature being what it is, that the preceding diatribe against Bingley, arising as it does from Elizabeth's initiative in a critical mock compliment to him, had been part of an endeavour by Darcy to win her agreement, or otherwise to impress her? Were that indeed the case, he could not have known that Elizabeth's sympathies would be at once on Bingley's side.

For a man of his social eminence to invite her to dance, not at a ball, but in a private residence where dancing is not part of the proceedings, is a distinguishing courtesy. Far from there being in him a sign of resentment at Elizabeth's part in his late rebuff, or, for that matter, at her incivility, Darcy is now displaying a hitherto unseen spontaneity and eagerness at the prospect of being in her close company. Are not these the actions of a man in love? As Jane Austen herself states here,

> Darcy had never before been so bewitched by any woman as he was by her. He really believed, that were it not for the inferiority of her connections he should have been in some danger.

The words 'bewitched' and 'danger', while not unambiguous, do indicate the operation in Darcy of that conflict between the forces of love and social status which he has to resolve before he can offer Elizabeth his hand; and from this fact it might reasonably be inferred that by now he is in love.

But the inference will need modifying, if we are to judge from the argument impending at Netherfield next day. It is what Bingley would call a "dispute" – and the worse for being highly personal. For Darcy's holding forth on the subject of his own dignity, and the proper direction of what he believes to be an allowable pride, proves too much for restraint in Elizabeth (56-8).

The preliminary is Miss Bingley's proclaimed horror at Darcy's less than proper remark that she and Elizabeth may have taken to walking about the room the better to display their figures, which instantly she transforms into the assertion that he is not to be teased for making it, as Elizabeth suggests, since such "calmness of temper and presence of mind" as he possesses preclude his being laughed at. The passage of arms that follows seems to bode ill for the evolving relationship. It might be described as a succession of strategic withdrawals in face of determined attack. To Elizabeth's assertion of the necessity of laughter in social intercourse, Darcy protests that all are vulnerable to those "whose first object in life is a joke". Her distinguishing "what is wise or good" from risible "Follies and nonsense, whims and inconsistencies" is accompanied by the derisive supposition of his being devoid of the latter. Darcy's affirming that it has always been his purpose to avoid those "weaknesses which often expose a strong understanding to ridicule" provokes Elizabeth's delicate suggestion of "pride and vanity" being amongst them. Under the onslaught Darcy's last line of resistance is the rather dubious proposition that "where there is a real superiority of mind, pride will be always under good regulation". Thereupon he is outflanked: for Elizabeth is able solemnly to assure the fretting Caroline that Darcy indeed has no defect, since "He admits it himself without disguise".

The final assault necessarily follows: what has been veiled mockery from Elizabeth now becomes open recrimination. Darcy's honest self-appraisal in admitting to a temper that is "too little yielding", an unreadiness to restore a good opinion once lost, is scathingly dubbed "implacable resentment"; and his gesture in defeat of pleading the commonplace of all having some ineradicable natural defect is swept aside by the intended *coup de grâce*, "And your defect is to hate every body".

Few would draw from this interchange the impression of the two involved to be enjoying mutual understanding and goodwill. Socially speaking, it is deadly stuff: apart from whatever emotions might be in play, Darcy is being soundly beaten and made to look small. But he has found in Elizabeth a foeman worthy of his steel, and he does not appear apprehensive; if anything, he seems to be enjoying the intellectual challenge – as appears from his parrying her ultimate thrust with his smiling, "And yours is wilfully to misunderstand them". This is the sort of encounter where the combatants, however embroiled, come increasingly to respect and admire each other – though here, only one is in a state of mind to do so, Elizabeth being a little carried away by her enduring resentment. But, while displaying neither ire nor indignation, Darcy is beginning to feel what Jane Austen terms, "the danger of paying Elizabeth too much attention". The threat might be to the social distinctiveness he is so zealous always to protect. It might on the other hand lie in the romantic charm of an acute mind in a prepossessing young woman. Significantly, however, the danger could only come about through love itself.

When the Bennet sisters' departure from Netherfield Park is imminent, Darcy for reasons of his own welcomes it – one being that Elizabeth "attracted him more than he liked". Is this love at work? However defined, the emotion is such as to force upon him a degree of caution one would think unprecedented in a man like himself.

> He wisely resolved to be particularly careful that no sign of admiration should *now* escape him, nothing that could elevate [Elizabeth] with the hope of influencing his felicity; sensible that if such an idea had been suggested, his behaviour in the last day must have material weight in confirming or crushing it (60).

Accordingly, he scarcely looks at or speaks to her in the remaining hours.

If it is not love which so prompts Darcy, it must be something fairly close to it; and perhaps that is just what it is. We might well bear in mind the impressions of *Persuasion*'s Anne Elliot, as she wonders about the apparent devotion of the two Musgrove girls to Capt. Wentworth. She dares to judge that Wentworth was not in love with either: that

> They were more in love with him; yet there it was not love. It was a little fever of admiration; but it might, probably must, end in love with some. (P. 82)

*   *   *

The discussion so far has not identified "the hour, or the spot, or the look, or the words" which mark the beginning of Darcy's love for Elizabeth: for the very reason, it may be, that love and admiration are not easy to tell apart. They are of course related. Darcy himself distinguishes between them, when Miss Bingley teases him on his confession to pleasure in beholding Elizabeth's "fine eyes". "A lady's imagination", he counters, "is very rapid; it jumps from admiration to love, from love to matrimony, in a moment". Elizabeth is less specific in asking him, later on, "did you admire me for my impudence? (380)" This, though a complicating consideration, is important, since neither Darcy nor the reader can be sure what he is responding to in Elizabeth throughout the novel; whether, that is, it is less the individual than the attitude that has been captivating him – a situation not altogether unknown in human affairs.

For Elizabeth is something of an anomaly: a free spirit, within a formal and mannered society, not always restrained by the modes which limit a young woman to a modest and guarded reticence in men's presence. Being very much a person, and a mind, she is ready to address those of the other sex boldly as equals, and to take up a subject as keenly as it merits, whatever be the company, or the occasion. That the discussion may easily become disparaging is manifest in her telling Bingley that his admission of a customary readiness to resolve on matters in five minutes is exactly what she would have expected of him. His distress at this imputed transparency moves even the obtuse Mrs. Bennet to expostulation: "Lizzy, remember where you are, and do not run on in the wild manner that you are suffered to do at home"; the reproof, needless to say, being more unmannerly than the offence.

But here we are dealing with an exception that proves the rule. A man in those times could only receive as compliment a fair young lady's interest in his ideas and in himself: a compliment, moreover, more substantial than the kind convention restricted Caroline Bingley to in her dealings with Darcy. 'Compliment', in this context, is hardly the word. Such unreserve in a young lady could normally denote only one thing: a bestowing of favour upon a gentleman – or, in the term that would commonly be employed, encouragement.

It had been as encouragement that Darcy had interpreted Elizabeth's forwardness of behaviour towards him. When, later, they recall her amazed reception of his proposal at Hunsford Parsonage, and his consternation at her reprimand, Darcy tells her, "I believed you to be wishing, expecting my addresses". Her own astonishment at his declaration of love arose from her having made her dislike, as she thought – indeed, hostility – perfectly obvious throughout. As she admits, "I never spoke to you without rather wishing to give you pain than not". What Elizabeth had never understood, Jane Austen makes clear:

> there was a mixture of sweetness and archness in her manner which made it difficult for her to affront any body (52).

The endeavour to annoy had served only to endow her with appeal. Without realising it, she had been engaged in self-recommendation, in encouragement: and the likelihood exists that Darcy might all the time have been "drawn in", enchanted by the appearance Elizabeth presented to him, not by the reality. The alarming reflection is both acknowledged and apologised for:

"My manners must have been in fault, but not intentionally I assure you. I never meant to deceive you, but my spirits might often lead me wrong" (369).

Before the stormy interview at Hunsford, Darcy had done no less than take for granted something which Henry Tilney was assured of with respect to Catherine Morland: that in proposing to her, he was soliciting a heart "which, perhaps, they pretty equally knew was already entirely his own" (N.A. 243). Otherwise he would not have presumed to address her as he did; a precipitancy in that situation would have been unworthy of a gentleman. And, as Mr. Knightley asserts to Emma Woodhouse, upon her protesting that Harriet had rejected Robert Martin because of not liking him enough, Martin had

"too much of real feeling to address any woman on the haphazard of selfish passion. And as to conceit he is the farthest from it of any man I know. Depend upon it he had encouragement" (E. 63).

How potent had been that certainty in Darcy that Elizabeth was encouraging him? There having been encouragement does not rule out love. We would all presumably assent to Charlotte Lucas's dictum that, while a slight preference for someone is natural, few amongst us would have heart enough to be really in love without encouragement – though we might not agree with her conclusion that in most cases a woman had better show more affection than she feels. Elizabeth does not altogether reject her friend's recommendation: and she seems unknowingly to have adopted it in plenty towards the man who, with encouragement real or imagined, finds himself helplessly in love with her, and naturally not knowing the moment of its beginning.

*   *   *

The prospect of his love becoming evident at the Netherfield ball, the occasion of their last being together before Darcy's leaving Hertfordshire, appears small (91-4). The meeting is the sternest test of whatever kind or degree of affection Darcy felt then or had entertained previously. By nature it is a sustained quarrel, which Elizabeth mischievously and doubtless vindictively provokes. Before the start the omens are unfavourable. She had dressed with more than usual care, we are told, in the highest of spirits prepared "for the conquest of all that remained unsubdued" of the heart of her favourite, Wickham. The shock of his absence, and learning of its being indirectly due to Darcy, now in attendance, creates in her almost insurmountable ill-humour. Any attention, forbearance or patience towards Darcy is "injury to Wickham", and she resolves against any conversation with him. But in vain.

Very soon, in a moment of thoughtlessness, "without knowing what she did", she is accepting Darcy's unexpected application for her hand. Her vexation at the error will not bear the hint from Charlotte that he might prove very agreeable: "To find a man agreeable whom one is determined to hate! – Do not wish me such an evil". It is in this spirit that her dancing begins, the initial silence between them inviting her mocking approval, and the near insult of their both being of "an unsocial, taciturn disposition". But his seemingly random question whether she and her sisters often walked to Meryton, where he had lately glimpsed her in Wickham's company, is a temptation too strong to resist. Conscious of the enmity between the two men, she adds to her affirmative the hostile, "When you met us there the other day, we had just been forming a new acquaintance".

The result in Darcy is "a deeper shade of hauteur", a resumed silence, and a measured word of caution respecting Wickham; and from herself a bitter accusation of inhumanity towards that gentleman. As if this were not enough, she is soon to challenge Darcy on the most contentious point of their last encounter, his unreadiness to forgive a past injury, in a pretended investigation into his character; and her determination to persist, in spite of his advice to take her inquiry no further for the present, extorts from him at last the barely civil, "I would by no means suspend any pleasure of yours".

Their parting in mutual displeasure is only to be expected: but we are left with Jane Austen's comment at the fraught episode's conclusion, that

> in Darcy's breast there was a tolerable powerful feeling towards her, which soon procured her pardon, and directed all his anger against another.

Can this tolerable powerful feeling, that will so readily forgive after so vehement an affront, be other than love? If not, the phrase, if perhaps typical, is also necessary, understatement. The author cannot at this stage name the motive for what it is, since the outcome would be to deprive the story, the reader, and more important, Elizabeth herself, of all mystification and surprise at Darcy's subsequent conduct.

For the rest of the novel, uncertainty about him abounds. It comes thick and fast upon Elizabeth while she is at Hunsford. She and Charlotte do not know what to make of his indeterminate looks and minimal speech during courtesy calls at the Parsonage. The episode at Rosings where, with Fitzwilliam's assistance, Elizabeth demolishes with ease Darcy's excuses for not dancing with her at Meryton, has a sequel whose purport is obvious, but whose purpose she could not guess at (174-6). Accepting her charge that his inability to converse easily with a partner, like her own falling short of excellence at the pianoforte, is due to lack of practice, he strangely and smilingly turns defeat into graceful compliment with the words,

> "You are perfectly right. You have employed your time much better. No one admitted to the privilege of hearing you, can think any thing wanting. We neither of us perform to strangers" –

performance here relating to what Sir William Lucas would term "converse", and the whole implying a confidential bond between the two of them which we can be sure Elizabeth would strenuously have denied, had not Lady Catherine thereupon called out to know what they were talking of.

The very next morning brings astonishment and embarrassment to her through his appearance in the absence of the other ladies at the Parsonage, with apparently little to say; until, the rather forced discussion turning upon her maintaining a distance of fifty miles to be a long journey in visiting, Darcy draws his chair towards her and declares,

> "*You* cannot have a right to such a very strong local attachment. You cannot always have been at Longbourn" (179).

His intention is to introduce intimacy into their talk; but it merely causes Elizabeth to display the surprise she feels at the attempt. She cannot know he is in love with her; and when, within days, he formally proposes in that house, can only give expression to the store of bitterness and resentment she has been amassing during their acquaintance, at the prompting of his initial disdain. From now on, it will be Elizabeth's emotions that naturally come under scrutiny as the story proceeds: for Darcy's state is clear. The very subscription of his letter of explanation to her the following morning – "God bless you" – is another way of saying, "I love you".

*   *   *

The development of Darcy's love has been followed through interest and attraction, and the possible effect of Elizabeth's unconscious encouragement; but no instant of his falling in love has appeared. It remains only to see what if anything is revealed in those brief moments of their early acquaintance where, in the absence of speech, there seems no possibility of his having been influenced by her: the first at the Meryton ball, the other at the Lucas's a little later. At Meryton we have nothing but Darcy's professed indifference; upon his viewing her at the Lucas's, however, there occurs a quite extraordinary reversal

(23-4). He had come critically inclined – only to make the "mortifying" discovery of features "rendered uncommonly intelligent by the beautiful expression of her dark eyes", of a light and pleasing figure, and of manners which, while not those of the fashionable world, are of an "easy playfulness". His stationing himself near Elizabeth involves him in the conversation he seeks, but he gains from it what he does not wish to hear: the advice, implied in her regaling him as she prepares to sing with the unbeseeming proverb, "Keep your breath to cool your porridge", that she is otherwise disposed than to wish to talk with him. But she has exchanged words with a Fitzwilliam Darcy whose attitude to her has, within minutes, undergone a complete change.

This transformation, occurring as it does at the beginning of the novel, would be easy for any reader to underestimate or overlook; is it not after all a natural thing that he should later or sooner be attracted by a pretty girl? It is, indeed: but not so, that an impression should be made upon him in those few minutes strong enough to oblige him, with unaccustomed frankness, to let Miss Bingley know of his having been "meditating on the very great pleasure which a pair of fine eyes in the face of a pretty woman can bestow" – and then, "with great intrepidity", confess them to be those of "Miss Elizabeth Bennet" (27). He, from then on, is the object of Caroline's envious teasing; she, the recipient of his impassive rebuffs; and the "fine eyes" themselves something of a theme in the novel, not occurring in any other. Elizabeth's "adventure" in walking to Netherfield, far from lessening his admiration of them, increases it by their "being brightened by the exercise"; it would certainly be difficult, as Caroline points out, for a painter to do justice to them: but "their colour and shape, and the eye-lashes, so remarkably fine, might be copied" (53). Their praise is even sung by the unlikely person of Sir William Lucas, who, having interrupted the partners in the dance at Netherfield, apologises to Darcy for detaining him from "the bewitching converse of that young lady, whose bright eyes are also upbraiding me" (92).

Jane Austen will have known the phrase to have originated in Milton's dreams of festivities in fabled cities,

With store of ladies, whose bright eyes
Rain influence, and judge the prize
Of wit or arms;[34]

gained from Shakespeare the concept of "love, first learned in a lady's eyes";[35] and smiled at Pope's hyperbolical praise of his Belinda in depicting her awakening, when through the curtains a timorous ray of the rising sun "ope'd those eyes that must eclipse the day".[36] These, and the multitudes extant of such tributes, are not there for nothing; and it cannot be for nothing that Jane Austen dwells so much in *Pride & Prejudice* upon the eyes of Elizabeth, and their appeal to the susceptibilities of its hero. Is this accumulation of reference to them in any way a hint of Darcy's being a lost man from the start?

*   *   *

To ascertain the possibility, the first words Darcy speaks in the novel must be considered – the substance of his refusal to dance with Elizabeth (11-12). The foremost concern his disinclination to dance with a near-stranger:

"You know how I detest it, unless I am particularly acquainted with my partner";

then follows an insistence upon the lady's beauty:

"*You* are dancing with the only handsome woman in the room";

and finally, on Bingley's urging him to dance with Jane's sister "sitting down just behind you, who is very pretty, and I dare say, very agreeable", Darcy's, "Which do you mean?" in turning round and "catching her eye", to be followed by the cold and insufferable,

"She is tolerable, but not handsome enough to tempt me; and I am in no humour at present to give consequence to young ladies who are slighted by other men".

The pronouncement could be simply a symptom of male arrogance, an awareness of looks and worldly means. More particularly, it might represent Darcy's characteristic attitude of pride at his social eminence, and the self-esteem devolving from it. But there is also present, in the initial remark, a diffidence resulting from a customary aloofness of manner – a real disinclination for the small talk requisite in dancing. Above all, though, there are the tones of an acute consciousness of rank and class, which has kept and continues to keep Darcy amongst his own party at the ball: something that is no fad or pretence, but a matter of clear, and in his day justifiable, principle, and a dominant concept in his outlook to which full weight must be allowed. We may recall that incident at Netherfield when, upon the Bingley sisters laughing at the Miss Bennets having an uncle who lived near Cheapside, and their brother's expostulation that, "If they had uncles enough to fill *all* Cheapside, it would not make them a jot less agreeable", Darcy silences his friend and settles the affair with his steely observation, "But it must materially lessen their chance of marrying men of any consideration in the world" (37). Darcy has that to think of by which Bingley would be unaffected.

There is however a further element that merits close attention, in Darcy's desire not "to give consequence to young ladies who are slighted by other men". He has a sense of bestowing enormous social elevation – or of himself shamefully losing social status – in at all showing favour to a partner-less girl. The question arises whether he is taking a somewhat extreme view, even allowing for a particular sensitivity in a person of his position. An indication to the contrary might be claimed from the feelings of Elizabeth herself at the Netherfield ball, when she

took her place in the set, amazed at the dignity to which she was arrived in being allowed to stand opposite to Mr. Darcy, and reading in her neighbours' looks their equal amazement in beholding it (90).

Here, her hand has been solicited in the ordinary way, before the dancing began; but the matter of "bestowing consequence" on a girl seated during the dance is not as absolute as it might appear, since handsomeness in the lady concerned, from Darcy's own words, was able to release a gentleman from any such apprehension.

The expression Darcy uses in declining to dance with Elizabeth – "not handsome enough to tempt me" – contains a verb of great power in relation to human conduct. Is his thought essentially that of being tempted by any consideration whatsoever out of his attitude of splendid social isolation? Or is it that he has sensed an immediate temptation in the person of Elizabeth, in that instant of "catching her eye"?

Should it be the latter, his words take on a profounder meaning. Even if he is not aware that she might be hearing him, there is a hint of an excessive presumption in the notion of Elizabeth's being "slighted by other men", the want of a partner being a happening frequent enough at a public ball, though admittedly less likely to befall a pretty woman. From whatever cause, or combination of causes, it may arise, Darcy's declared position is somewhat rash and tendentious, with a trace of artificiality. At worst, it is silly – a fact which Elizabeth's reaction confirms. For, despite her remaining "with no very cordial feelings" towards the stranger at being thus disdained, she is prompted spiritedly to tell the story amongst her friends, by a lively, playful disposition "which delighted in any thing ridiculous" (12). We should be justified in taking Elizabeth's immediate assessment to be conclusive. For it is apparently the judgment of both herself and Jane Austen that Darcy's posture indicates a degree of self-regard beyond what is admissible, and sufficiently out of the normal to be absurd.

But there is more to the incident. Should Darcy have been conscious that his remarks might reach the lady, and yet proceeded to make this statement, he cannot escape the charge of culpable indifference to the feelings of another: of a readiness to hurt that is nothing other than reprehensible, and out of character in himself. It would be one of those failings which, according to Elizabeth later on, merit her being spared the concern she might have felt in refusing his proposal, had he behaved "in a more gentleman-like manner". But Darcy's utterance at Meryton might not have been purely casual and unfortunate: neither might it have been at all a considered comment. Close to an insult as it is, it may convey a note of involuntary defiance. The beautiful expression of Elizabeth's dark eyes, the elegance of the slender figure turned to catch his words, could have been making their timeless challenge, and administered the bewildering shock of attraction which the normally self-possessed Darcy finds himself there and then having to overcome and repel. His manner retains the appearance of calmness; but the speech itself may well denote the impact upon him of the phenomenon which Jane Austen in her sophistication might view with disfavour and distrust, but which, as a student of human dealings, she could not bring herself entirely to dismiss: that of love at first sight.

*   *   *

Her heroine, at least, appears subject to no such thing. Not love, but hate at first sight, rather, is what Elizabeth typifies. The determination to hate Darcy, which she vows at an early stage, is given full freedom in the accusation of "your arrogance, your conceit, your disdain of the feelings of others" upon his declaration in Hunsford Parsonage: the language of utter denunciation. The outburst is understandable. Elizabeth had been gratuitously insulted, with respect to her personal attractiveness: she is a woman scorned, no less. That anger has not been the feeling of days and weeks, but persists through the novel, blinding her to qualities in Darcy which otherwise, with her quickness, she would soon have discerned. The condition of her mind is at variance with her own philosophy, which, to the same Darcy, she afterwards declares to be, "Think only of the past as its remembrance gives you pleasure" (369). On this basis – despite having previously made her feelings abundantly plain to him – Elizabeth has been ready to forgive her errant first love with a, "Come, Mr. Wickham, we are brother and sister, you know. Do not let us quarrel about the past. In future, I hope, we shall always be of one mind" (329).

Towards Darcy, however, there has been no such relenting: the unyielding dislike, the preparedness to accuse, continue to dominate. We might say that any young woman, and especially one of vigorous mind, could have been so affected. But is it not well within the realm of human experience for a young man and woman to have responded to each other with an intensity of dislike, the cause of which is found ultimately to have been a similarity of sentiment, a degree of mental kinship, which had first magnified any disagreement between them, only in the end to ensure their lasting affection? And could we not say that if Darcy, from the very first moment of her beholding him, had not, colloquially speaking, meant a great deal to Elizabeth, his words would not have infuriated her and distorted her thinking to the extent they did: that a less prepossessing man – or any other man than he – might have provoked anger in her, but never caused her to be so unlike herself until that moment when, receiving Darcy's letter, she came to realise how "blind, partial, prejudiced, absurd" she has been, and in self-condemnation cries, "How despicably have I acted!" (208).

It is with herself, and her inconsistency, though, not with Darcy, that she is at this point concerned; and awareness of her love for him comes gradually, and only after much self-questioning. Having recovered from the agonies she went through in accidentally meeting him with her uncle and aunt at Pemberley, she lay awake, we are informed, "two whole hours" endeavouring to make out what her feelings with respect to him were, successively ruling out hatred, and admitting respect and esteem for his qualities, and gratitude for his loving her (265).

Jane Austen is at pains to tell us towards the novel's end that, having tried, in her partiality for Wickham, the method of love coming into existence "even before two words have been exchanged", Elizabeth was thereafter prompted "to seek the other, less interesting mode of attachment" founded upon gratitude and esteem (279). – But is this quite so? With the greatest trepidation, might it be suggested there are one or two indications that love for Darcy had an earlier beginning than her heroine – to say no more – has imagined? There was the time, for instance, when Bingley's jocular reference to Darcy as being a "tall, great fellow" who awed him into deference, and on occasion an ogre, created a moment of triumph for Elizabeth amidst the general amusement. Mr. Darcy had smiled:

> but Elizabeth thought she could perceive that he was offended; and therefore checked her laugh –

with a concern on his behalf, a considerateness for his feelings, which had not before appeared in her, and was entirely at variance with her ruling disposition. It is as if in her deeper self she does not want to hurt him: to be giving him offence would be to cause her pain (51).

The frustration, amounting almost to horror, that she manifested when Darcy, at the Netherfield ball,

> took her so much by surprise in his application for her hand, that, without knowing what she did, she accepted him (90),

we have all sympathised with: but have we equally reflected that she might have been acting by instinct, before her conscious mind (for the unconscious will have existed in Regency times) could discipline her impulsion? Should this indeed explain her action, it would have been a Freudian slip before Freud – and an especially revealing one, at that. The question arising is whether it is reasonable, in the light of the novel as a whole, so to interpret Elizabeth's coming to be dancing with Darcy then.

There is a further instance in support, which the author herself puts before us half-way through the novel. We learn that once or twice, when Mrs. Collins hinted to Elizabeth at the possibility of Darcy's being partial to her, Elizabeth had laughed at the idea. Delicacy prevented her from pressing the subject:

for in her opinion it admitted not of a doubt that all her friend's dislike would vanish, if she could suppose him to be in her power (181).

The judgment proves to be a true prophesy. Is Charlotte here being the "intimate friend" she has long been, who understands the other very well, and better than she knows herself? It may well be that Jane Austen was only obeying literary necessity in foreshadowing the resolution of the story, to give it the proper air of inevitability. Free as she was, though, to fulfil a number of objects with a single detail, might not her wish to register the truth, in anticipation of many misleading appearances to come, have been one of them?

But what of Charlotte's opinion itself? Why, it might be asked, would the author come to see it as right, and needful, that this settled conviction should be present in such "a sensible, intelligent young woman" (18)? Must not the explanation be that Charlotte had opportunity for observing Elizabeth's variations of inclination and mood in her relation to Darcy from the very beginning, sufficient to recognise love's presence and working within her, despite – and, here and there, because of – her protestations?

If she is to be so regarded, Elizabeth has been an exceptionally bad exemplifier of love at first sight, and in consequence given Darcy a great deal of trouble. Like the gentleman he is, he has no thought of returning the compliment of asking when and where her love for him began. It is enough, and more than enough for him, as for any man, that it exists. For, if this estimate is correct, he has, like many another man, been in love with the girl from the minute he clapped eyes on her.

vi

The Prisoner of Mansfield Park

So great is the impression created in the mind of Edmund Bertram by the festive spirit prevailing in Mansfield Park during his father's absence in Antigua, that he can scarcely conceive of life there ever having been different. Despite the drastic restrictions that marked the latter's return, it takes some moments for Fanny Price's gentle reminders of the unvarying soberness of their former state – the rarity of such a thing as laughter in Sir Thomas Bertram's presence – to register in his awareness. Fanny's own years at Mansfield have rendered her incapable of such illusion. Though not without some measure of happiness, they have been largely a time of oppression for her sensitive being.

A nameless fear created at first by the huge scale of the house, and the magnificence of objects within it, was accompanied by humiliation at the offence noticeably caused to the Bertrams by her uncouthness and lack of manner. It was however the way she was treated by the family that most often mortified her; yet, child as she was, an intuitive sense of its inevitability saved her from despair: "she thought too lowly of her own claims to feel injured by it" (20). She was helped, too, by an obligingness of disposition that made her useful to her betters in running errands and carrying messages: but her celerity in so doing was matched by quickness in comprehending those she served. "She began at least to know their ways, and to catch the best manner of conforming to them" (17).

In this word Jane Austen uses to denote Fanny's response to the surrounding attitudes lies the secret of her development as a person. Throughout much of the novel she can appear merely as a timid, and, for some, insipid conformist: but those who so classify her misread her nature in taking little cognizance of the constraints, domestic and social, to which she is day by day subject, and of the expedient to which they drive her. She has no choice but submission, if she is to attain to any tolerable mode of living within a context which, for all the comforts it is empowered to offer her, is – from the moment of her being deposited within it till she reaches maturity – inimical to her deepest instincts through its constant reminders of her inferiority and helplessness.

One happening after another shows the completeness of Fanny's subjugation. She performs without murmur the drudge's task of gathering roses in the heat, not daring to give the least hint afterwards of its effect upon her health. Sir Thomas's offering her the coach for the first dinner-party she has ever been invited to causes a degree of astonishment which makes it impossible for her to speak, reducing her to tears of gratitude. His yielding to her unthinking appeal to be allowed to breakfast early with William before his departure moves Fanny to wonderment and rejoicing at having carried her point: "she was so totally unused to have her pleasure consulted, or to have any thing take place at all in the way she could desire" (280). And, long after the indulgence of the ball at Mansfield, her habits of compliance make her instantly rise and lead the way to her room, upon Mary Crawford's request for the interview she has anticipated with such loathing.

But it is in the person of Sir Thomas Bertram that her servitude is concentrated. Upon his unheralded reappearance among them, Fanny, though herself innocent of indecorum as they are not, is at the point of fainting; and it is "with desperation" that she at last turns the lock and enters the room. Misgiving at his stern disapprobation is always with her; even her brother William's casual inquiry of him as to whether she is a good dancer produces in Fanny expectation of a cutting reproof, or otherwise a remark of contemptuous unconcern (250). And the heavy step, recognised as her uncle's, and as familiar to her as his voice, outside the East Room consequent upon Henry Crawford's being in the house, provokes again in Fanny the trembling it has often occasioned in the past.

Such, until almost the last, is the condition of Fanny Price at Mansfield Park. The few spells of respite and relative freedom which she enjoys there originate in a manner which would be amusing if it were not pitiable: when, naturally excluded from the privileges of seasonal socialising, she has been left with the dubious consolation of Lady Bertram's vacuous companionship; and

> the tranquillity of such evenings, her perfect security in such a *tête-à-tête* from any sound of unkindness, was unspeakably welcome to a mind which had seldom known a pause in its alarms and embarrassments. (35)

In their progress to adulthood, Sir Thomas's children go through quite the reverse of Fanny's experience. The buoyancy of youth and consciousness of privilege join to produce in them a kind of delighted ease; the girls especially, handsome, accomplished, and outwardly unassuming, regale in assurance of universal favour. There was however in their upbringing a deficiency whose seriousness had been absent from their thoughts: the lack of affection for a father whose authority had largely determined both its method and content. This truth, which became apparent at the time of his leaving for the voyage to Antigua, is conveyed in a characteristic triple-sentence of Austenian emphasis: "Their father was no object of love to them, he had never seemed the friend of their pleasures, and his absence was unhappily most welcome" (32). Not surprisingly, Fanny shared their relief at his going – but, being herself, is affected nonetheless by her inability to grieve.

It is not until Sir Thomas's homecoming, almost two years later, that his children reach a just appreciation of what his custodianship and dominance at Mansfield has meant for them. Julia's appearing at the door with blanched countenance to announce, "My father is come! He is in the hall at this moment", produces amongst the cast of 'Lovers' Vows' not simply consternation, but "a moment of absolute horror". Uppermost in nearly every mind, certainly in those of his sons and daughters, is the conviction of its being "a stroke the most unwelcome, most ill-timed, most appalling!" (172-5) If, by the right of a disposition prone to disquiet, Fanny's agitation exceeds theirs, they are equal in recognition of that moment's significance. It takes the obvious form of apprehension at what might be the outcome of their error in having indulged in theatricals: but their alarm more truly arises from resumption of Sir Thomas's rule at Mansfield. The fact constrained the children to view past years with new eyes; and what they saw was not only an encroachment upon the blissful freedom of latter months, but a threat to their very existence as persons.

All Maria's hopes had been centred upon her love for Henry Crawford, and expectation that he would declare himself. Disappointment in him brought her to recognise her predicament, and the means of relief afforded by her engagement to the blockish and unloved James Rushworth.

> Independence was more needful than ever; the want of it at Mansfield more sensibly felt. She was less and less able to endure the restraint which her father imposed. The liberty which his absence had given was now become absolutely necessary. She must escape from him and Mansfield as soon as possible, and find consolation in fortune and consequence, bustle and the world, for a wounded spirit. (202)

Ironically enough, it is this decision of Maria's, known to her sister for the desperate remedy it was, which ensures the success of the unlikely Mr. Yates with Julia. She was, we are informed, all but indifferent; what strongly affected her was nothing in herself, but dismay at the tenor life would assume upon Maria's becoming Mrs. Rushworth: "her increased dread of her father and home, on that event". Foreseeing that its consequence to herself would be "greater severity and restraint" caused her without delay to "resolve on avoiding such immediate horrors at all risks", and endowed John Yates with attractions by which he would scarcely have been flattered, had he known them to be the product of his object's "selfish alarm" (466-7).

With the sons it seems otherwise. In different ways they already have considerable independence, Tom being able to draw readily enough on Newmarket's resources at appropriate seasons. He always appears relaxed and confident; yet in both his habitual expansiveness and jocularity might be detected some trace of reaction to the irksomeness he finds in his father's regimen, heir apparent though he be. Amongst the Bertram children as adults, only Edmund is naturally and unaffectedly himself at Mansfield, untroubled by any notion of distancing himself from it – and, let it be said, unawed by its master's bearing.

*   *   *

What above all makes Sir Thomas formidable is that distinguishing demeanour which social eminence confers on those born to it, or comes mystically to devolve upon the newly-elevated. Though always adapted to the person, it is invariably recognisable as a feature, and indeed a force, in human affairs; and, for an observer of the comedy of life such as Jane Austen, it has an interest bordering upon fascination, as is evident in so many of her characters.

In Lady Russell it is a settled formality allied with seriousness of disposition; in Lady Catherine de Bourgh, a self-regarding imperiousness which treats inferiors and equals alike with audacity. Mr. Darcy has inherited more than a little of his aunt's hauteur. Upon first acquaintance, Mrs. Gardiner finds "something a little stately in him", confined to his air, however and "not unbecoming"(257); but the author herself is not able to dismiss it so lightly, attributing it (with all the inhabitants of Meryton) to the deeper cause of a nature "haughty, reserved, and fastidious" (16). While Lady Catherine constantly affronts, her nephew contrives as often to offend.

With General Tilney, appearances are almost the opposite. His prevailing mien – the random outbursts of military irascibility apart – is courtesy itself; and, until enlightenment somewhat drastically supervenes, Catherine Morland is set wondering how so charming a man should seem always a check upon his children's spirits. *Persuasion* affords us an example of a potency in Sir Walter Elliot perhaps at once more refined and more sinister. Though in Admiral Croft's opinion and the reader's he appears harmless enough, and not destined to set the Thames on fire, he has the capacity to cast "instant oppression" upon a roomful of vivacious people at the White Hart, reducing them to "cold composure, determined silence, or insipid talk" by his own and his daughter's "heartless elegance" (226), as his creator defines it. All these instances point to manner in itself being the outward token of that transmutation which consciousness of birth, rank, possession and power may work in the human psyche. If the phenomenon can convert the silly and spendthrift baronet of Kellynch Hall into a "formidable" presence in the environs of the Octagon Room (181), it is small wonder that his fellow of Mansfield Park should be the potentate there that he is.

In this regard, Sir Thomas's distance of manner and deliberateness of speech are ominous. His grave looks cause fearfulness in the child Fanny from the moment of her arrival, rendering vain his well-intended condescensions. The accompanying slowness of utterance is also unpropitious, but has its amusing aspect, as Jane Austen is well content to demonstrate through the agency of his spouse. Lady Bertram will long since have come to terms with it, by habitude or stark oblivion; but when, at the Grants', Sir Thomas twice inquires into her enjoyment and success at the game of Speculation, "no pause was long enough for the time his measured manner needed" (240). And not entirely void of humour is his perplexity at Tom's sick-bed, where he "knew not how to bring down his conversation or his voice to the level of irritation and feebleness" (429).

Like the Duke of Wellington after him, the baronet has no small-talk, nor either the capability of indulging it: as Mary Crawford sagely remarks on hearing of the brevity of Edmund's letter to his father, "Who could write chat to Sir Thomas" (288). And Edmund is himself concerned at the impression his father might in their few encounters have made upon the same Mary: "his reserve", he confides to Fanny, "may be a little repulsive" (119). This is no idle supposition. That Edmund's sisters, for all their erudition, were deficient in generous and modest aptitudes, is the result precisely of the barrier of estrangement existing between them and the supervisor of their instruction. Sir Thomas had been unaware of what was wanting in the girls,

> because, though a truly anxious father, he was not outwardly affectionate, and the reserve of his manner repressed all the flow of their spirits before him. (19)

The same can be said respecting highly personable guests who are vouchsafed welcome at Mansfield Park. The Honourable John Yates, despite his financial adequacy being suspect, positively abounds with self-confidence. Acutely frustrated at the demise of 'Lovers' Vows', and at the irrationality responsible for it, he is strongly disposed on the way back from Mansfield Wood to argue his host into some sense; but when they are sitting round the same table, he begins uncomfortably to distinguish a something in Sir Thomas which makes him "think it wiser to let him pursue his own way, and feel the folly of it without opposition" (191). Similarly, while the whole party, including Henry Crawford and William Price, is entertained to dinner at the Grants', Mary Crawford in her turn has endured the destruction of her hopes by Sir Thomas's insistence that evening upon Edmund's being Thornton Lacey's resident clergyman. She sits considering him with decided ill-will – and suffering the more from not daring to ridicule his position by one of her witty diatribes, through "that involuntary forbearance which his character and manner commanded" (248). If it could still the promptings and enforce the compliance of such free-born sophisticates as these, what chance was there of a Fanny Price prevailing?

Although Sir Thomas's ascendancy arose out of intrinsic merits, it was enhanced by the strength of principle: the concept of what is befitting, in all circumstances, in relation to a person of his degree. It can be summed up in words like pride, and decorum. It is pride of family that makes him solicitous for the advancement of the Price sons in their careers, and evokes the "unanswerable dignity" with which Mrs. Norris is rebuffed when she opposes the carriage being ordered for Fanny: " – My niece walk to a dinner engagement at this time of the year!" (221) These gestures of his are laudable enough; but they should be understood in the light of the specific condition attached to Fanny's being brought to live under that roof at the beginning. She was always to be kept from the illusion, never be allowed to lapse into the gratification, of imagining herself a Miss Bertram. The imperative of rank was to be obeyed, the "distinction proper to be made between the girls as they grow up" (10) inflexibly enforced, the claimless newcomer kept in her place through all her formative years.

Exactly the same resolve directs Edmund's conduct at the prospect of Charles Maddox being invited to play the role of Anhalt in 'Lover's Vows' which he has himself declined. According to Tom, Maddox is as gentlemanly a man as is to be seen anywhere, and Edmund knows no harm of him: but the problem lies not in his endowments, but in his birth. For he is not a Mr. Bertram; and his admission into the intimacy of a family group, and, indeed, the familiarity which acting must promote, would constitute such a betrayal of aristocratic obligation, so great a sin against the dues of precedence, as only the word evil can convey. Hence Edmund's decision to take the part after all, despite the shame of inconsistency, and the testimony of his own conscience (153-6).

There must ever be something admirable in devotion to principle, for it both requires, and confers, fortitude. But it may also exact penalties, through the dulling of sympathies and vision it can effect. The necessity of wealth in persons of social eminence is for Sir Thomas an absolute. Thus it comes about that, though he is struck with puzzlement at Mrs. Norris's refusal to do anything for Fanny, after having been so urgent for her adoption, the germ of discernment so born is quelled by his sister-in-law's assurance that the whole of her possessions is destined for his family. His far stronger sense of Mr. Rushworth's being an inferior young man is for long held in check by the gratification he had felt, on news of the engagement reaching him when abroad, that this was "a connexion exactly of the right sort; in the same county, and the same interest", an alliance "unquestionably advantageous" (40). Upon coming to realise later that, far from loving Rushworth,

Maria did not even like him, he is ready to act for her and release her; but, though unpersuaded by his daughter's assurance of esteem for her betrothed, he will not urge the ending of "an alliance which he could not have relinquished without pain". Instead, he reasons with himself that Rushworth might yet improve; that Maria's declared confidence of happiness should be believed; that a woman not marrying for love would be the more likely to find solace and enjoyments amongst her family; and so on. His own profound satisfaction at the prospect of a connexion "which would bring him such an addition of respectability and influence" makes him, in Jane Austen's observation, "very happy to think any thing of his daughter's disposition that was most favourable for the purpose" (201).

Sir Thomas's perceptions and judgment concerning persons, even in respect of a daughter, have been blinded and distorted by social dogma – as they had, by implication, in the limitations he had decreed for the growing Fanny Price. For many years he regards her, not as she is, but in terms of the situation these preconceptions have assigned her. Whatever of kindness there might be in his invitation, on the last morning before his departure, for William to visit Mansfield when his squadron comes home, it is dissipated by his coldly imparting to her his fear that "he must find his sister at sixteen in some respects too much like his sister at ten" (33). Fanny is timid and shy still; but her uncle speaks largely in ignorance, as Edmund was in a position to have informed him. It is not insignificant that what first brings her truly to his notice is the being struck on his return by "her equal improvement in health and beauty" (178): in other words, by her looks – to which considerations of social standing do not apply.

*   *   *

Unlike Sir William Lucas in his contentment at Lucas Lodge, the baronet has more to do than think with pleasure of his own importance. As an ancestral landowner he takes very seriously his traditional duties, not only to tenants, but to the nation at large, by supporting its institutions and the upholding of its moral standards. His readiness to pursue without compromise the latter obligation is clearly to be seen in the doom of 'Lovers' Vows'. Not content with proscribing the theatricals and dismantling the theatre, his determination impels him to "wipe away every outward memento" of a play noted for its indelicacy by consigning to the flames, with the ardour of a zealot, every unbound copy that meets his eye (191).

No less emphatic is the response he makes to Henry Crawford's polite expression of a wish for tenancy at the Thornton Lacey parsonage. In declaring pleasure at the prospect of Crawford's becoming a neighbour in any house but this, and affirming the naturalness of the young man's not having thought much on the subject, Sir Thomas's rejoinder is equally polite, even excessively so. But in his assertion that he would be "deeply mortified" if Edmund were to become an absentee parson, and the insistence that only a resident clergyman can know a parish's needs, there lies a severity which cannot be mistaken – and, in the remark that ensues, finality itself. Edmund will be aware

"that if he does not live among his parishioners and prove himself by constant attention their well-wisher and friend, he does very little either for their good or his own."

By this "little harangue", as the author names it, Crawford is reduced to silence, and successive bows; and in the gathered company activity is likewise thwarted for its duration. The sentiment is impeccable: but its statement and mode of delivery, coming as it does in the midst of after-dinner talk, is at least unfortunate. The party is being treated to somewhat of a lecture; and – if such comparison dare be made – there is in its ponderousness more than a slight similarity (absurdity apart) to the address on the duties of the rector of a parish with which Mr. Collins favours guests at the Netherfield ball (PP247-8).

The position taken regarding Maria's adultery with Crawford is still more rigid, yet by the standards of that day, admissible. Sir Thomas will not offer "so great an insult to the neighbourhood" as to allow her to appear at Mansfield Park: so to do would be "affording his sanction to vice" (465). The same estimate and purpose at first moves Mr. Bennet with regard to Lydia; but the having attained the status of matrimony enables the manner of her securing a husband to be seen as an *étourderie*, so justifying her reception at Longbourn.

There is no doubting the correctness, and uprightness, of Sir Thomas's promptings and actions in these respects. They are morally founded, and abundantly well-meant: but they are enforced with a stringency which tends all but to nullify their essential worth. That the style of their application is involuntary, and the effect almost certainly uncomprehended, should however always be borne in mind in relation to the person from whom it emanates. This is what Fanny Price may well have been trying to tell herself when, at the sounds denoting Sir Thomas's approach, "The terror of his former visits to that room seemed all renewed, and she felt as if he were going to examine her again in French and English".

Nothing in the novel is more indicative of the extent to which Fanny is in subjection than the treatment she receives from her uncle upon his coming to tell her of Henry Crawford's application for her hand. What will be the outcome of the message he bears is for him certain, and he derives happiness from the conviction that in imparting it, "he must be gratifying her far more than himself". His astonishment on hearing his niece's exclamation that it is out of her power to return Mr. Crawford's good opinion is such that he is reduced to echoing her words – as he does again, with Lear-like disbelief, after asking directly whether it is Fanny's intention to refuse the offer of marriage.

What he had seen of relations between the two convinced him of the contrary. Her cool, seemingly unaffected reception of his advances had by the accepted standards been entirely proper. From it he was confident that she had given her lover "as much encouragement to proceed as a well-judging young woman could permit herself to give": where her deportment was concerned he has "no accusation to make". Beyond this observation he is initially aware of nothing that could or should have led her to an adverse decision. The reason his questioning extorts from her – "I – I cannot like him, sir, well enough to marry him" – moves Sir Thomas to comment "in a voice of calm displeasure" on its strangeness: of there being "something in this which my comprehension does not reach".

He sets out thereupon conscientiously to understand, with searching inquiries on the state of her affections, and – watching her intently – her estimate of his son Edmund's tenderness toward Mary Crawford. Satisfied in these respects, he is left only with the question whether she has cause "to think ill of Mr. Crawford's temper?" The possibility of there being objections of a more serious kind is beyond his calculation; and Fanny is inhibited by loyalty and fear from referring to Crawford's unprincipled conduct with Maria and Julia.

As the interrogation has proceeded, and Fanny's unaccountableness become more pronounced, so her uncle's displeasure is more evident; and at its end, in a tone of "cold sternness", he impresses upon her the grounds of its being so. The conduct which, he asserts, has "disappointed every expectation I had formed", is simply an incompliance with the conventions and norms of society for a young woman of any pretension. Fanny has, in effect, shown an independence of spirit "which in young women is offensive and disgusting beyond all common offence" – the unpersuadableness incompatible with womanliness itself – in respect of deference to the wishes and wisdom of her elders, and thought for the social elevation an advantageous match would bring her family. But she is more culpable still in the requirement of love, which has apparently brought this obduracy about: her not feeling for Crawford "what a young, heated fancy imagines to be necessary for happiness". For this inordinate longing has impelled her to the ultimate failing in a female: the sin against wealth, property and station, the intolerable affront to the expectations of the whole social order. Had either of his daughters, Sir Thomas declares, at the tirade's logical conclusion, declined a proposal with only half the eligibility of Crawford's, he "should have thought it a gross violation of duty and respect". – This, however, does not end it. His final utterance is of another nature, and left incomplete.

"You do not owe me the duty of a child. But, Fanny, if your heart can acquit you of *ingratitude* –" (312-9)

It is understandable, especially in terms of the reigning conventions, that Sir Thomas should regard Fanny's refusal as a defiance of his overriding will as master of Mansfield, so identifying himself with the demands of the system that has made him what he is. But the sudden change of tone, the new note, amidst reproof, of urgency and tenderness, is striking. It may be attributed to a final and calculated invoking of known susceptibilities, rather than be thought evidence of an unguessed-at sensitivity in the speaker. To think that the baronet might have seen himself as another Lear, protesting to a lesser Regan, "I gave you all –", only to receive the chilling answer, "And in good time you gave it", would be to picture him as more deserving of sympathy at this point than his sobbing, afflicted niece.

In the same way, were we not, like the astonished Fanny earlier, to ascribe to the momentary workings of time and distance the change of manner in her uncle upon his unannounced return from Antigua – the unexampled kindness, the voice "quick from the agitation of joy" (178), the dissipation of former severity by a new-found affectionateness – we should incur the notion of Sir Thomas being a quite different person from him whose harshness was soon to reduce to misery the girl who declined to take his approved Henry Crawford for husband.

*   *   *

The crisis point of the novel is not the painful interview between them in the East Room, despite appearances, but a slighting comment upon Fanny which Mrs. Norris makes to her brother-in-law at dinner that evening, after the girl had at his suggestion taken to walking in the shrubbery to regain her calm. There are, she tells him, and all present, faults in Fanny which she has often observed:

"she likes to go her own way to work; she does not like to be dictated to; she takes her own independent walk whenever she can; she certainly has a little spirit of secrecy, and independence, and nonsense, about her, which I would advise her to get the better of."

Sir Thomas's reaction comprehends more than the walking in question. It is that as a general reflection on Fanny, "nothing could be more unjust, though he had been so lately expressing the same sentiments himself"; and he tries repeatedly, as well he might, to turn the conversation, but without any success until half through dinner (323-4). At an earlier stage, he would certainly have disapproved of Mrs. Norris's acquiescence in Maria and Julia's scorn for Fanny's lack of learning; and he would doubtless have deemed ill-advised her inculcating in the girls' minds the doctrine that it was unnecessary for their cousin to be as accomplished as they, and "much more desirable that there should be a difference" (19). But Fanny's being constantly at her relations' beck and call, the exclusion from their social round and pretensions – the life in fact of subservience – has been entirely in accord with Sir Thomas's expectations for her, and, be it said, with Fanny's own. If he had then been present, he would have shared the startlement of the hearers, and the indignation of some, at his sister-in-law's accusation, when Fanny declines the others' united wish for her to act in 'Lovers' Vows', that she was showing herself "very ungrateful indeed, considering who and what she is" (147). But had it not been his requirement throughout that "who and what she is" should always be impressed upon her: that the "dependence of her situation", as Jane Austen puts it, ought as was proper to be part of her everyday consciousness? (150)

Nor can it be denied that the same spirit and logic in her aunt Norris which would grudge Fanny a horse of her own, or set her cutting and carrying roses in the sun, or evoke wrath upon her being offered the carriage, is at work in the deploring the Grants' lavish meals – "And round their enormous great wide table too, which fills up the room so dreadfully!" – as in the denying little Dick Jackson the casual hospitality of the servants' hall. After pausing for breath, preparatory to urging Fanny not to be putting herself forward during the dinner visit, she gives unambiguous voice to the doctrine in the ample phrase, "The nonsense and folly of people's stepping out of their rank and trying to appear above themselves" (220-1).

With the affirmation *per se*, Sir Thomas is perfectly in agreement. But it is a very different spirit within him which soon thereafter is asking Fanny what time she wishes the carriage to come round for her, and crushing so disdainfully her aunt's objection. As decisive is his remark, when she is swift to assure William of the impossibility of there being a dance at Mansfield when Julia and "dearest Mrs. Rushworth" are not present, that "the absence of some is not to debar the others of amusement". It requires some minutes' silence for the lady's vexed surprise to abate (252-3).

The surprise in Sir Thomas exceeds this when he comes into Fanny's room to find no fire burning in the grate on a day when snow is on the ground. His repetitions of, "here must be some mistake", and, "Here is some great misapprehension which must be rectified", and the shortness of sentence in, "You are not strong. You are chilly. Your aunt cannot be aware of this", are indications of a mind momentarily shocked. Customary utterance is resumed in the address which follows in defence of what he now comprehends to have been Mrs. Norris's prohibition. Influenced perhaps by her own hardiness, she has been a constant advocate, "and very judiciously", of young people's being brought up without undue leniency. The principle is good in itself, but had in Fanny's case been carried rather too far. It has not escaped his notice that, in the worthy attempt to prepare Fanny for the "mediocrity of condition" which appeared to be her lot, there was "sometimes, in some points, a misplaced distinction". Professed confidence that she will harbour no resentment does not hinder him from urging his niece never to fail in treating her aunt Norris "with the respect and attention that are due to her" (312-3).

The pointedness of this homily, its meticulous excusing of his sister-in-law, and cautioning Fanny against ill-will, shows the degree of Sir Thomas's own reprehension of her conduct, in truth his dismay at her measures. For Mrs. Norris has been made the representation of the precepts, customs and values, in their negative aspect, which motivate him: by Jane Austen's art, she is the embodiment of his own social persona. Herself of no status, fortuitously raised to the dignity she now exults in, she imposes upon her hapless niece the aristocratic code, without the compensating graciousness by which at its best aristocracy is always accompanied. And in the process of so doing she has been revealing gradually to her brother-in-law the realities of the system that operates around and within him: significances which nurture, habit and elements of character have combined to withhold from his ordinary consciousness. She is in effect the glass in which, as life proceeds, he finds himself mirrored.

Hence the gathering annoyance, amounting to detestation, which he comes to feel respecting her. His opinion of her, we are told, has been sinking from the day of his return from Antigua.

> He had felt her an hourly evil, which was so much the worse, as there seemed no chance of its ceasing but with life; she seemed a part of himself, that must be borne for ever.

The sentiment appertains to the tragic. It is one which makes memorable appearance in the impassioned King Lear, when he addresses his daughter Goneril as, "my flesh, my blood, my daughter; / Or rather, a disease that's in my flesh, / Which I must needs call mine" (II. iv. 224-6). Strictly, Mrs. Norris is not Sir Thomas's flesh and blood: here are not matters of regality and statehood, or even of life and death, but of mere domestic disquietude. But when subsequent events procure the banishment of his sister-in-law from Mansfield Park, the relief is "so great a felicity" to its master that, but for the bitterness of memories connected with her departure, he might almost have been tempted "to approve the evil which produced such a good" (465-6). The presence of feelings like these suggests that, as with Lear himself, so with Sir Thomas Bertram: typical of them as their attitudes and policies of rule, national or domestic may be, they are in neither case expressive of the underlying self.

Nevertheless, the baronet has been guilty of deliberately propelling Fanny Price into a known evil, in compliance with those same principles which, as put into practice by Mrs. Norris, were becoming, seemingly, ever more displeasing to him. The scheme he devises, to his unsuspecting niece's delight, for her to spend some months in Portsmouth, "had very little to do with the propriety of her seeing her parents again, and nothing at all to do with any idea of making her happy". His wish was that she should be "heartily sick of home before her visit ended"; that, brought into "a sober state" through deprivation of Mansfield's luxuries, she should form a "juster estimate" of the establishment at Everingham which Henry Crawford was offering her; that, in short, his purpose of disposing her fitly in marriage by Mansfield's concepts should be achieved.

The shortcomings, even vices, of an order of society, and of those upholding it, ought not to be allowed to obscure its virtues from us. This, Jane Austen profoundly believed; and the latter part of the thought we may be sure was present to Sir Thomas in his "experiment" (369). A preponderant system's injustices and wrongs having been exposed to the reader in their effect upon Fanny, and particularly in the person of Mrs. Norris, so the Prices' household and its inhabitants are made to bring painfully into view the consequences of incompliance and exclusion. Miss Frances Ward had married to disoblige her family, and incurred a debilitating penalty. For, as Fanny is grieved to discover, in that context of deprivation life itself is crudified, and the values even of kinship can be brought almost to nothing.

It is less the smallness of rooms and thinness of walls that is disconcerting on her arrival than the house's being "the abode of noise, disorder, and impropriety" (388): a bewildering impression of nobody in the right place, and nothing being done as it ought to be. Her father, upon encounter, was in his uncouthness and vulgarity a figure of repugnance; having observed that she was grown and would

159

be wanting a husband soon, he "seemed very much inclined to forget her again" (380). That the mother, bearing a faded likeness to her sister at Mansfield, was "a dawdle, a slattern", incapable of any kind of domestic management, was harrowing enough; but more wounding to Fanny was her seeking in vain for the appearance in Mrs. Price of a will to know her better, or inclination for her company: absence of the benison of affection itself (390). And the neighbourhood and its people came to afford much the same demoralising apprehension: "The men appeared to her all coarse, the women all pert, every body underbred" (395). Such was the impact upon a privileged upbringing of poverty's endless attrition.

Eagerly did Fanny recall the peace, elegance and tranquillity of Mansfield Park, as they were brought to her remembrance by their very opposites; and with fondness did she now reflect upon a habitation where each person's importance was recognised, and everyone's feelings consulted: where, "If tenderness could ever be supposed wanting, good sense and good breeding supplied its place" (392). Her present abode was, however, not entirely without such propensities: to her surprise Fanny discovers their existence in the "proper opinions of what ought to be" (397), and "an innate taste for the genteel and well-appointed" (419) in her sister Susan, and wonders at this evidence of natural light of the mind amidst such an environment. But it was her just conviction nonetheless that, outside the pale of social privilege, those finer sensibilities which gladden human interrelationship are endangered, if in the end they are not entirely overcome.

The truth of her belonging now is inescapably upon her. Mansfield is her home. Delicacy towards her parents causes her not to betray it in speech, but to talk of returning to Mansfield, or going back into Northamptonshire – until longing defeats caution, and the word home interposes itself. She knows to the full the implication of this change. It means that the house, the style, the system, which had for long years tyrannised over her, is now claiming her as its own: that (to employ the idiom of Mammon to the fallen angels in their infernal dwelling) Fanny's former tortures have become the very elements of her being: that her uncle's stratagem to engender within her proof of her conditioning has beyond measure succeeded. That Sir Thomas has finally triumphed, and his niece's durance is complete.

*   *   *

The novel's ending does allow itself to be construed in these terms: but only figuratively so. To apply them in any realistic sense would be to belie the nature of both principals concerned. Time's mutations have affected all at Mansfield Park; and Fanny Price by now is an attractive and cultivated person. Edmund's friendship and Lady Bertram's dependence have established her position there; and the Bertram girls' departure accords her the distinction of social recognition and invitation, of Mary Crawford's favour, and of Henry's proposal; and the Crawfords' disgrace opens the way to her heart's desire. What once was discomfiture and suffering in her uncle's house has been subtly transformed into an influence of fulfilment and delight.

As for Sir Thomas, though from his dominance he must appear the spokesman and stern administrator of social rigidities, he has given indication through events of certain characteristics more than a little at variance with what is to be expected – and we have tended to assume – of the occupant of such an office. When considered in their light, the flow of spirits and geniality upon his return to Mansfield, and the fervency of his plea to Fanny respecting ingratitude, are revealed to be, not exceptions, mere tricks of an otherwise austere mind, but rather evidence of a benignity, which a patrician aloofness normally conceals. And it will remain hidden, unless – as with Fanny Price herself – the possibility exists in the reader of coming to terms with a forbidding manner.

*   *   *

In all his dealings Sir Thomas manifests an apparently innate concern and respect for persons. Perhaps the gift of a substantial living to his friend Norris had betokened it; but certainly the ten year-old Fanny is its object while still in her parents' home at Portsmouth. Mrs. Norris's eager proposal that they should undertake the care of the Prices' eldest daughter inclines Sir Thomas to debate and hesitate for more than one reason. Unless what they did for her was entirely adequate, "there would be cruelty instead of kindness in taking her from her parents"; if she were unable, later on, to marry greatly, they must consider themselves engaged to secure to her "the provision of a gentlewoman". But what causes him most apprehension is the matter of the distinction of rank upon Fanny's adoption. That it must be maintained is unquestioned: but his mind is not so much exercised on its preservation, as upon the need for it to be humanely applied, so that there would not be "the smallest degree of arrogance" in his daughters towards their poor relation, and that the latter's inequality should be made clear to her "without depressing her spirits too far". What above all would be called for in her upbringing, he insists, is "delicacy" (6-11).

In specifying this quality, Sir Thomas is not demanding of others something not present within himself. How else could it come about that his stricture upon Tom for his extravagance, which has forced the sale of the valuable living intended for his brother, should amount to no more than the moral reproof of, "I blush for you, Tom" – albeit delivered "in his most dignified manner"? At this point his composure is perfect. It is less so when, upon opening the door of the billiard room, he finds himself on a theatrical stage, and confronted by a ranting young man "who appeared likely to knock him down backwards". Though angered by being affronted in his own house and finding himself part of "a ridiculous exhibition", he is yet able to receive so undesirable a stranger "with all the appearance of cordiality which was due to his own character" (182-3). The demands of baronetal dignity are here incumbent; but in dealings with his offending children and sister-in-law a similar forbearance and gentleness is evident. With the former there is no remonstrance: the sweeping away of their preparations is to be sufficient rebuke. And the hint at lack of sound judgement that he cannot help giving Mrs. Norris at her sanctioning the play is evaded by that lady's instant eloquence on other subjects.

Even his ruthlessness over 'Lovers' Vows', which appears unseemly and dictatorial to present tastes, has sufficient justification in the intellectual climate of the age. The conjunction of fear of Jacobinism and influence of the evangelical revival had made condemnable any example of lavish frivolity or dissipation in the residences of the privileged. The inclinations of Sir Thomas's own temperament are naturally involved; but his action might suggest a responsiveness to the contemporary mood of moral earnestness by which his children, with Edmund's exception, were seemingly unaffected.

In other respects the baronet is admittedly the embodiment of fixed and established notions, no more so than in his preparedness to allow Maria's marriage to go forward upon the prospect of his own advantage, financial and political. But the explicitness of his daughter's assurances ought not to be ignored; nor should the "solemn kindness" with which she had been addressed, and the undertakings made for her release "if she felt herself unhappy in the prospect of it" (200). Though the consent Sir Thomas gives in the end is mistaken, it cannot be attributed to the lack of paternal affection: at the wedding, Jane Austen tells us, he felt as an anxious father must feel, and was "indeed experiencing much of the agitation that his wife had been apprehensive of for herself" (203).

Emotions of this nature are neither exceptional nor remarkable in a man whose thoughts centre upon his children's interests and welfare to the extent Sir Thomas's prove themselves to do. In seeking to ascertain whether Fanny has a liking for either of his sons, he puts to her his judgment from observation that Tom as yet has no thought of marrying, but that Edmund "has seen the woman he could love" (317). Concern for his younger son never lessens. Amidst his "poignant" suffering over the mischance that so suddenly befalls Maria and Julia, he is by perception and conjecture also sentient of what must be Edmund's pain, in the loss to him of Mary Crawford through her brother's turpitude. It is he who, realising how much it must have been increased by the pair's late interview, and anxious on that account "to get him out of town", orders that Edmund should take Fanny back to her aunt, "with a view to his relief and benefit, no less than theirs" (452-3).

The positive gratification he derives from the society and advancement of the young is shown in his treatment of William Price. No sooner had the joyful Fanny received the letter sent into Portsmouth when his ship is at anchor, than her uncle is "most collectedly dictating" a kind invitation in reply. He and his younger son have separately connived to ensure that the meeting of brother and sister should have no witnesses; and with "sympathetic alacrity" the two of them frustrate Mrs. Norris's intended "rushing out into the hall as soon as the noises of the arrival reached them". It is with complacency that Sir Thomas surveys the delight William and Fanny have in each other's company, which every day renews; and, in calling upon his nephew to recount his exploits, his chief object is not their interest in themselves, but "to understand the recitor, to know the young man by his histories"; and he derives great satisfaction from their evidence of his excellent abilities, from "every thing that could deserve or promise well" (232-6).

The same pleasure is conferred by consideration of the growing personableness of William's sister. When the news of Fanny's unprecedented invitation to dinner had been imparted by a troubled Lady Bertram, his reaction, after a short deliberation, was, "Nothing can be more natural" (218). Though his own agreeing, later, to dine with the Grants proceeds from simple good-breeding, it is not unconnected with his having noted, "in a grand and careless way that Mr. Crawford was somewhat distinguishing his niece" (238). The fact has bearing upon his decision "to gratify so amiable a feeling" as William's wish to see Fanny dance – and, as Jane Austen comments, "to gratify any body else who might wish to see Fanny dance" (252). She is, for him, "an interesting object" at the ball. Her informing him that Crawford is to be her partner for the first dance is "exactly what he had intended to hear" (272-5); and it is concern for her exhaustion that decrees, first, that there must be no more dancing, and, thereafter, that she go immediately to bed. A reason for the last, the author implies, is that he might mean to recommend her as a wife to Crawford – who else?

– "by shewing her persuadableness" (281).

Such has been Sir Thomas's regard for his niece, before the denunciation he inflicts on her for rejecting Crawford. Its vehemence has arisen out of concern that is real, if based on devout conviction of the rightness of all he has been urging. Realisation, as it comes, of what the distraught girl has been enduring, with the self-accusation implicit in his inward acknowledgement of her being "very timid, and exceedingly nervous", brings about however a complete change of attitude, which the writer amusedly chooses to describe as, "a little relenting". The idea dawns upon Sir Thomas of an approach quite other than that of blame: that a little time, a little pressing, a little patience, and a little impatience – "a judicious mixture of all on the lover's side" – might work their usual charm on a mind so affected. Not only is Fanny spared the immediate interview he had proposed, and left in quietness for a spell; but her uncle upon return brings comfort in word and manner, speaking only to urge self-control, and to advise her with kindness "to go out, the air will do you good" (320-2).

When they are together some while afterwards, Sir Thomas, having decided against further importunity, contents himself with informing her of his meeting with Crawford, and congratulating her on having inspired "an attachment of no common character" in the suitor's perseverance – something which her being as yet little acquainted with love's "transient, varying, unsteady nature" might have led her to undervalue (330). Agreeably, if belatedly, she is advised that he has no intention to persuade her into marriage against her will; and, having before determined the family should have no knowledge of what had taken place between them, he declares the subject to be closed. Few would disallow that his altered conduct, towards a niece blameable in his eyes, is deserving of words like consideration, courtesy and kindness.

Whether these same terms can be applied to his immediately thereupon sending Fanny to Portsmouth is another matter. But it is done in pursuance of her interests as he views them. Henry Crawford's firmness had impressed him; and, wishing this wealthy aspirant to be a model of constancy, he fancies the best means of ensuring that end will be by not trying him too long. From Edmunds's report – he will no longer trust his own judgment – he finds his hope that Fanny would miss Crawford once he were gone has been dashed; and the plan he contrives for her temporary separation from the elegances she had grown used to is "a medicinal project upon his niece's understanding", to inculcate such moderation of outlook as would make her a wiser and happier woman all her life (369). From social imperative, and ignorance of the character of its owner, he had equated Everingham with her happiness. He was on both counts mistaken: and yet he had not erred. After so hurtful an experience of uprooting, the sampling of underprivilege was what Fanny needed for the attaining of selfhood.

In her case, Sir Thomas's wisdom justifies itself; but in other respects more nearly affecting him, and of disastrous consequence, it is soon revealed to have been flawed. The family of which he is head is plunged in sorrow by the untoward events at the close; each person and life undergoes alteration – but none to the extent Sir Thomas does himself. Horror at the scandalous break-up of Maria's marriage, with Julia's attendant elopement, and dismay at the destruction thereby of his hopes for three of his children, overthrows his confidence in the engrained assumptions that have throughout governed him. And, of all the family, he is the longest to suffer, from consciousness of having been mainly responsible for the calamity which had befallen them. It is with anguish "never to be entirely done away" that he now contemplates having brought up his daughters in a manner that deprived him of acquaintance with their natures, and hindered in them appreciation of what is most laudable in conduct. While their aunt's indulgence had implanted assurance in them, his own severity had prevented their confidences: and it had been to the superficialities of knowledge and deportment, not the disposition itself, that he had given attention. The instruction in religious precept they received had been theoretical only: they were "never required to bring it into daily practice" (463). As with the training of the youthful heir of Pemberley, in fact, they had been "taught what was *right*", but not to correct their disposition; given good principles, "but left to follow them in pride and conceit" (PP369).

Scarcely could Sir Thomas comprehend how so material a fault had been possible; but, bitterly as he now deplored it, there had been an error of still greater magnitude, now all too readily understood. His cognizance of Maria's feelings towards her intended husband should have made him prohibit their union: in allowing it, "he had sacrificed the right to the expedient, and been governed by motives of selfishness and worldly wisdom" (461): by those considerations of affluence and station which so far had been sacrosanct.

Enlightenment had been dearly bought. Now that it was come, however, his one great object must be "to bind by the strongest securities all that remained to him of domestic felicity". In his desolation he has noticed the developing friendship between Edmund and Fanny, and pondered upon the more than possibility of their finding in one another consolation for the disappointment each had undergone. His consent when applied for is given joyfully, by a man now "Sick of ambitious and mercenary connexions", aware of the meretriciousness of rank and wealth in comparison with "the sterling good of principle and temper". It is with eagerness that he has promoted this match between his son and the girl he recognises to be the daughter he wanted. Though his former notions and harshness of bearing had deprived him of her early love, it had been "an error of judgment only"; and their mutual attachment, we are informed, now became very strong (471-2).

Through all her childhood dread of him, Fanny had come to appreciate her uncle's fine qualities; and, even at the height of distress of his causing, can esteem, in him, a man "so discerning, so honourable, so good" (318). Yet almost to the very last he is presented to us as a distant, formal figure lacking in appeal and warmth – as if the concept of degree with which he is identified has chilled and repressed the humanity within him. By displaying, in a personality whose motives are entirely admirable, the severities of his infliction, the warping of his nature from which they had issued, and the ultimate renunciation of his former standards and very being, Jane Austen is engaged in nothing less than implicit censure of the social order beneath which she lives: of the inhumanities and injustices, smaller and greater, which, with all its excellences, it correspondingly nurtures. And, upon the baronet's alliance in kith and in soul with a penniless commoner of his own fostering, the confining bars are sundered, the flinty walls dissolve, and the prisoner of Mansfield Park steps forth, self-liberated, from a life-long captivity.

vii

Jane Austen's Personal Faith

At the very end of the sixth volume, the *Minor Works*, in R. W. Chapman's standard edition of Jane Austen's novels, after the Juvenilia, the Fragments, and the comic verse she would have termed "enigmas, charades and conundrums", come the three known *Prayers* of her composition, with 'Solution of the Charades' placed at the foot.[37] Their humble positioning is doubtless inevitable, in that they cannot be classed as literature; but it is at the same time derisory, since by the nature of things they are of greater significance than anything else she ever wrote.

These brief effusions are perspectives into that realm from which emerge outlook and attitude, which determines principle and motive, and is largely formative of personality itself. To consider them is to find oneself in the midst of forces that helped to make Jane Austen the woman she was, and moreover to impart to the novels their particular savour. In terms of capacity to bring us close to the author's mind, indeed, the novels are themselves little other than comprehensive 'Charades', to which her *Prayers* might well provide some 'Solution'. For prayer is "thinking towards God", in the words of John Baillie:[38] the soul's own eloquence, an outpouring of the most intimate perceptions, fears and wishes of "this pleasing, anxious being", as the poet fittingly describes human life.

The writing of Jane Austen, when compared with the achievement of other major novelists, poses an intriguing question. How does it come about that her heroines and heroes are so distinctly unheroic? Their being presented as continually beset with uncertainties and alarms might be accounted not unreasonable; but, as Richard Simpson declares in his distinguished 'Memoir' of 1870, the author exhibits nothing in them that is ideal. On the contrary, in her persons "She shows strength dashed with feebleness, feebleness braced with some fibres of strength"; and, even where they are conducting themselves with obvious rectitude, can contrive "to see on the face of goodness the impress of weakness and caducity".[39] In them all, seemingly, what is in any respect positive is compounded with failings.

However, the acceptability of the characters is by no means impaired by defects thus exposed. Jane Austen's people are the more endeared to us by their shortcomings: for the reason that their creator, though keenly and unsparingly observant of imperfections, contemplates those who display them with remarkable tolerance and gentleness. If therefore her novels can be said to be devoid of heroes, there is equally no one in the guise of a villain. The humanity they bring before us – as a chastened Catherine Morland, fresh from her reading of Mrs. Radcliffe, comes to realize – embodies nothing so stirring as an angel's spotlessness or the malevolence of a fiend, but merely "a general though unequal mixture of good and bad".

Only an unusually benign disposition could convincingly sustain such a depiction, in featuring forth with credibility the solicitudes and vexations, passions and conflicts of mortal circumstance, even in the mannered and cultured society Jane Austen knew. If such triumphant moderation represented the height of what is set before her readers, it would be laudable enough. But her work is chiefly distinguished by a quality so intrinsic as to incur the notion of uniqueness. It is nothing less than its tendency to create in readers generous and compassionate feelings towards their fellows: to convert them, in fact, to her own charitable regard.

This exceptional characteristic was recognized within a few years of her death by Richard Whately, later Archbishop of Dublin, in a review of 1821. Its derivation he traces simply to the extraordinary extent of her insight: to her being

> a thorough mistress in the knowledge of human character; how it is acted upon by education and circumstance, and how, when

once formed, it shows itself in every hour of every day, and in every speech of every person…….. in Miss Austen's hands we see into their hearts and hopes, their motives, their struggles within themselves; and a sympathy is induced which, if extended into daily life and the world at large, would make the reader a more amiable person; and we must think it that reader's own fault who does not close her pages with more charity in his heart towards unpretending, if prosing worth; with a higher estimation of simple kindness and sincere goodwill; with a quickened sense of the duty of bearing and forbearing in domestic intercourse, and of the pleasure of adding to the little comforts even of persons who are neither wits nor beauties.[40]

It universally applies to the great novelists and dramatists that their writing enhances our appreciation of human potential, and deepens sensibility in us; but rarely can it be possible to say of any of their work that it promotes or inculcates actual benevolence in the beholder or reader. This distinguishing propensity of Jane Austen's novels was without doubt the grounds of an even earlier observation, anticipating Whately's own, that "the temper of her writings" could not have been formed "without a feeling for the spirit of Christianity".[41] The mental and intellectual climate may have changed since these comments were made, but their appositeness is beyond dispute. For is not the framing of her characters, with all their fine attributes, as persistent and irreclaimable defaulters much in need of understanding and forgiveness, and consistently receiving it at the hand of the one who has brought them into being, a reflection – pale as it must be – of the chief proclamation of Christianity's gospel? And a paradigm of the predicament and prayer of every member of its faithful, in relation to the Divine understanding?

What insight, then, is to be sought, or can be afforded, by the three *Prayers* for which she is responsible? They are brief, and in appearance conventional, conforming to the pattern in Anglican liturgy of adoration, confession, supplication, thanksgiving and intercession. The intercessions are, as one would expect, general and varied, ranging from the plight of the sick, the captive, orphan and widow, and the afflicted, the despairing and the faithless, to pleas for the welfare of relations and friends. At an indifferent glance, such requests, and the prayers as a whole, may appear as religious commonplaces, containing little if anything that is unexampled in other like compilations. Many, in fact, will see them as no more than a descant of assent to prevailing assumptions of that era; but by some they may perhaps be better comprehended as relating to truths able to set an ardent soul aflame.

This much at least can be said where Jane Austen herself is concerned: that we have in these prayers concepts which were dominant in her mind, which informed her waking moments – and which in subtle ways must have suffused her creative imagination, without gaining overt expression. Further, there are to be found in them touches, by word, image, or turn of phrase, that are striking, and so indicative of aspects of faith that deeply impressed her. Above all, their choice of themes represents the things in this life which were for her of supreme importance.

For it to be affirmed that the idea of God was uppermost in Jane Austen's devotion may be deemed a statement of the obvious. Its being the first article of belief, and the consideration which must dictate the course of Christian conduct, assures its supremacy. But the manner of its presentation in these *Prayers* – by repeated use in their short space of the image of vision – signifies not mere acceptance, but direct apprehension: that "sense of God on the soul"[42] which is the fountain-head of faith. "We are", she declares, "alike before thee, and under thine eye"; God's pardon is invoked for "what thou hast seen amiss in us": for he is the One who is "everywhere present, from whom no secret can be hid". What are these affirmations but an echo of the Psalmist's cry, 'O Lord, thou hast searched me and known me': his confession of the redeeming God who 'compassest my path and my lying down, and art acquainted with all my ways'?

Awareness of the Divine omnipresence implies an imperative for her and all true believers, in that it impels them to "fix our thought on thee with reverence and devotion, that we pray not in vain". Intensity is an essential in their personal response, and supplication arising from it. Jane Austen would like to see Christians "equally united in faith and fear, in fervent devotion to thee"; and since of ourselves we are impotent in devout undertakings, she asks particularly that God "will dispose our hearts in fervent prayer". Prayer that does not betoken a completeness of self-offering, that partakes of the nature of pious tribute and decorous petition, is without meaning to the possessors of a life which, like her own, is consciously lived in his presence.

For it makes manifest their utter dependence. This world is for them charged with God's sustaining power, subject throughout to his direction: those who inhabit it draw the means of existence, of very being and breath, from his constant provision. Jane Austen's praise is offered with overwhelming feelings of gratitude for all things given, for every benefit experienced, every source of happiness: "for every hour", as she puts it, "of safety, health and peace, of domestic comfort and innocent enjoyment". It is conviction of the totality of our reliance upon God that prompts thankfulness of this order. The close of each day, the coming of night's "darkness and dangers", is for her symbolic of human frailty and need, as it is of the brevity of our life's span. "We are helpless and dependent; graciously preserve us", she pleads.

But man's greater frailty is in the spirit, and his more pressing need is forgiveness. A consequence of her lively faith, to which the novels themselves bear testimony, is heightened sensitivity to wrongdoing. The *Prayers* are notable for the horrified consciousness there disclosed of the assaults of evil within our natures. They are filled with an anxious seeking after the offences for which she will ask pardon: the malicious thought, the neglected duty; the sin unremembered, and that which is unrecognized; the momentary impulse of rebellion by which God is spurned and his commandments wittingly transgressed; the perverse pleasure in deliberate infliction of pain on others. The phenomenon of an innate perversity brings from her the plea that God will grant "a stronger desire of resisting every evil inclination and weakening every habit of sin", and that he will end our capacity for self-deception through the "vanity and pride" so characteristic of fallen condition. But more than all these misgivings is the dread of that sin of the spirit by which faith itself is dissipated in the rejection of God and his truth; and she implores him "to quicken our sense of thy mercy in the redemption of the world, and of the value of the holy religion in which we have been brought up, that we may not, by our own neglect, throw away the salvation thou hast given us". The plainness of the latter wording should not blind us to its purport.

Recognition of sin for what it is, and of ourselves as 'miserable offenders', is normal in Christians; and the absoluteness of our unworthiness in God's sight, if not explicitly stated in their petitions, is invariably assumed. But in Jane Austen's prayer it ushers in a sentiment which is not usually met with:

> We feel we have been blessed far beyond any thing that we have deserved; and though we cannot but pray for a continuance of all these mercies, we acknowledge our unworthiness in them and implore thee to pardon the presumption of our desires.

Such is her sense of the scandal and outrage of the demands we make of God, the benefits we plead for, considering our depravity in the light of the Divine righteousness. Is this not a state of dismay similar in kind, if not in degree, to that of the prophet before the vision of God 'high and lifted up', at being a man of unclean lips, dwelling in the midst of a people of unclean lips?

It is with admission of a profundity of guilt and undeserving that Jane Austen addresses her Maker. The initial thought of the third *Prayer*, at evening, is that "Another day is gone, and added to those, for which we were before accountable"; and early in the first, she is asking not only that he will look mercifully upon sins committed, but, as mercy and blessing, make them deeply felt: that he will teach the supplicants "to understand the sinfulness of our own hearts, and bring to our knowledge every fault of temper and every evil habit we have indulged in to the discomfort of our fellow-creatures, and the danger of our own souls".

This is no impulsion to luxuriate in the fact of sinfulness, a kind of spiritual masochism, but a will of militancy and high endeavour. It is that she may be so fitted and provided for what is to her the most urgent of tasks: to fight for God and his Kingdom against the forces of darkness within the soul, and, armed with this knowledge and self-knowledge, counter and defeat them. Such resolve is in keeping with the instruction, 'If thine eye offend thee, pluck it out, and cast it from thee'. Here is the intimation conferred upon the faithful, that the better they understand what are their besetting sins, the more readily Divine grace and strength will be available to them in the battle for their eradication.

And in one of the battle's sectors, help and initiative thus bestowed is soon evident. This degree of acquaintance with one's own faults, imparting a corresponding appreciation of human deficiency in those we are involved with, produces a sympathy otherwise not readily engendered in us – indeed, barely within the scope of human resource. And the manner of its unfolding is illuminated in Jane Austen's asking grace to attain that "temper of forbearance and patience" exemplified for her and all Christians in the Saviour. She prays that God will grant those who call upon him "to think humbly of ourselves, to be severe only in the examination of our own conduct, to consider our fellow-creatures with kindliness, and to judge of all they say and do with that charity which we would desire from them ourselves". The wish accords with the injunction of love to God and neighbour. Its working in the person whose it is, we may try to assess from what we know of her life and character; but more particularly and surely, from the attitude that is mirrored in the meetings and entreatments of the people of her novels.

But far more effectual in this regard than awareness of imperfection in ourselves as in others is recognition of the Divine goodness which moment by moment we encounter. This is the dynamic that must bring about the transformation: the glow of creaturely gratitude alone can cause the generous and beneficent finally to blossom in such unlikely soil. The 'golden rule', as it has been named, command though it be, is also a corollary, and in its observance a manifestation, of the potential of God's animating bounty upon our natures. To those of faith, the moral and the spiritual are intimately linked, indeed part of one process; whilst the ethical approach, in itself admirable, but lacking provenance and means that are above the human, cannot avail: God ultimately is cause of any good we do. This discernment, with its wealth of implication, Jane Austen conveys in the simplicity of a single petition: "May the comforts of every day, be thankfully felt by us, may they prompt a willing obedience to thy commandments and a benevolent spirit toward every fellow-creature".

A theme is therefore present in these *Prayers* which we would never think of questioning because of its evident rightness and propriety, but whose application might easily escape us. It concerns Jane Austen's assurance of the meaningfulness of ordinary happenings, and of the manner in which they are responded to. Her wish is that by our behaviour we should bring them into accord with the highest purposes. "Teach us, almighty father", she asks, "to consider this solemn truth, as we should do, that we may feel the importance of every day, and of every hour as it passes, and earnestly desire to make a better use of what thy goodness may yet bestow on us, than we have done of time past".

The aim is unexceptionable by any standard; but it is in its religious connotation – and by the sombreness of the note it strikes – that it should be judged. For it bears relation to one of the New Testament's most persistent urgings, that for vigilance in the believer. It is present at all points, but most frequently in the last stages of the Gospel account, and typically in the words from *Mark*,

> Watch ye, therefore: for ye know not when the master of the house cometh, at even, at midnight, or at cockcrowing, or in the morning: lest coming suddenly he find you sleeping. And what I say unto you I say unto all, Watch. (13:37)

The precept is vividly conveyed in the metaphors of lamps kept supplied and burning, and the fastened belt; and usually taken as reference to the nearness of the end. But it is addressed, not towards some unpredictable crisis hour, but rather to the immediate situation, and the work the faithful will be about whenever that hour should come: the conscientious discharge of duties of the present, and especially that of resistance to its manifold temptations. This, according to John Baillie, is "The true state of Christian readiness";[43] and it is so apprehended, as it is demonstrated, by Jane Austen in the prevailing thought of the critical importance of all our allotted moments, and our accountability for every act within them. Far from the sentimentalizing of Divine justice typical of those who are, in her explicit phrase, "Christians only in name", there is acute realisation of its inexorability, and of its operating both within the life of the present, and that which is to come.

In company with devout Christians of every generation, she is in aspiration an inhabitant of two worlds. All have been constantly reminded that while in this world they must walk by faith, trusting in an unseen God, there is another and eternal life to come in which faith will yield place to vision: where, no longer seeing as in a glass darkly, they shall know God even as they are known by him. Amidst all the preoccupations, loves, anxieties and longings of her mortal existence, Jane Austen lived in anticipation of the greater life that would be its fulfilment. It is appropriate therefore, but also infinitely revealing, that the final supplication in the *Prayers* should be, "may we by the assistance of thy holy spirit so conduct ourselves on earth as to secure an eternity of happiness with each other in the heavenly kingdom".

The prospect of heaven which she held in contemplation as a Christian could not but affect her literary intent. As is widely understood by readers and critics, her novels constitute in essence an inquiry as to that which conduces to the maximum of happiness for individuals in their social interrelation. It is seen to exist in the possession and practice of right principle, good manners, and the promptings of kindness –

but derives from the deeper conviction that earthly happiness is of a kin with that of heaven, and the things which make for it here are established in us by the Divine constraining. Thus, though centred in the novels upon the minutiae of domestic happenings, hers could never be a purely mundane quest. Its quality is made clear as, in prayer, she seeks enabling to reach the level of conduct

> which, while it prepares us for the spiritual happiness of the life to come, will secure to us the best enjoyment of what this world can give.

Each of the *Prayers* concludes with the reciting of the Lord's Prayer, invited by the words "Our Father" at its close. The paternal invocation has, however, resounded through them: seven times in their narrow compass, apart from the introductory summons, God is so addressed, with or without accompanying epithets like "heavenly", "almighty" and "gracious". The concept at the heart of Christian faith of God's loving Fatherhood is dominant in these *Prayers*, expressing itself in a reverential awe in face of His immediacy, and an eagerness and warmth of adoration, that testifies to its being a matter of profound personal experience.

viii

Fanny Price's Principles

The exception to the rule, mentioned in the Preface, that in comedy as in tragedy the writer is obliged to keep to the secular, is to be found in *Mansfield Park*. It is part of a further exception, affecting the novel itself, introduced by the author's careful analysis of some unaccustomed feelings in that professed connoisseur of women, Henry Crawford.

As he makes his sister Mary acquainted with his delight at finding himself in love with Fanny Price, Jane Austen comments, Crawford has too much sense not to feel the worth of good principles in a wife, though he was too little accustomed to serious reflection to know them by their "proper names";

> but when he talked of her having a steadiness and regularity of conduct, such a high sense of honour, and such an observance of decorum as might warrant any man in the fullest dependence on her faith and integrity, he expressed what was inspired by knowledge of her being well principled and religious.

Their proper names, conveyed at the close of this cautious observation, lets us know that in Fanny Price we are being presented with a heroine possessed of an assured faith.

By no other token is the fact revealed in Fanny's earlier life at Mansfield Park; nor, it could be said, at any other point through the length of the novel, even in those moments of great agitation by which she is afflicted. The most severe, perhaps, is the interview with Sir Thomas when she informs her uncle of her inability to accept Crawford in marriage. And another, arising out of her frustrated love for Edmund Bertram, shows emotions entirely natural to any woman in such a predicament.

The last occurs after Fanny, in a state of mixed emotions at having been presented by Mary Crawford with a necklace on which to wear her amber cross at the approaching ball, is made the recipient by Edmund himself of a gold chain for this very purpose. His gratification on learning of Mary's action destroys Fanny's pleasure in his gift; and it is with a lover's zeal that he urges her, in her distress, to wear Mary's necklace "For one night, Fanny, for only one night". He goes on, his voice sinking a little, "I would not have the shadow of a coolness arise between the two dearest objects I have upon earth".

For Fanny, these words are nothing less than "a stab". They betoken Edmund's utter ignorance of the woman he loves: he attributes to her merits she does not possess; the faults he had once been so conscious of are now forgotten. Upon his leaving her, Fanny abandons herself to grief.

> Till she had shed many tears over this deception, Fanny could not subdue her agitation; and the dejection which followed could only be relieved by the influence of fervent prayers for his happiness.

Regardless of actual faith, turning to prayer in so desperate a situation might be irresistible in any person of normal sensibilities; indeed, it would be almost strange if it were not. This will be unquestioningly accepted by the sympathetic reader.

The expression "fervent prayer", though, is exceptional in the novels. The word 'prayer' itself, whether or not prayer is present in their heroines, is rigorously avoided. After she has accepted Darcy at Longbourn, Elizabeth Bennet remains burdened in spirit; but upon her father's giving his consent, her mind, we are told, was relieved from a very heavy weight; and, "after half an hour's quiet reflection in her own room, she was able to join the others with tolerable composure". What could be more decorous in a heroine?

The well-conducted Anne Elliot, in this as in all respects conforming to the standards of that age, finds upon reaching Camden Place after her memorable walk with Frederick Wentworth that

> An interval of meditation, serious and grateful, was the best corrective of every thing dangerous in such high-wrought felicity; and she went to her room, and grew steadfast and fearless in the thankfulness of her enjoyment.

Her conduct is entirely in keeping with the gentleness and moral inclination of her disposition. If there is a hint of prayer in this, it has to be inferred.

'Fervent', however, in the "fervent prayers" Fanny Price utters for Edmund's happiness, comes into another category. The word is present on two occasions elsewhere in *Persuasion*. In one it is coupled with prayer, in the "fervent ejaculations of gratitude to Heaven" of the afflicted party at Lyme, Captain Wentworth included, in their rejoicing upon the surgeon's assurance of Louisa's eventual recovery. It occurs again in the impassioned declaration of love for Anne Elliot which Wentworth writes at the White Hart, imploring her to accept a constancy and attachment that is, in him, "most fervent, most undeviating".

But the word, and the concept itself, are prominent in Jane Austen's *Prayers*, of which a leading motif is the vital necessity that prayer addressed by humankind to its Maker should be "fervent". Fervency as such is there pleaded for as a Divine blessing. Her desire is to see Christians "equally united in faith and fear, in fervent devotion to thee"; and, men and women in themselves not having the capacity for achievement in things of the spirit, she prays that God "will dispose our hearts in fervent prayer", as the very means of a life lived in His presence.

Suggestive as it is, a distinct verbal echo of something in a context apart cannot be conclusive. But confirmation may be judged to exist in a lesser but related instance, introduced almost at the novel's end. The illness of Fanny's cousin Tom Bertram, after his excesses at Newmarket, is becoming more severe. His death is apprehended, and Fanny, naturally, is concerned. Jane Austen makes her feelings exceedingly clear.

> Without any particular regard for her eldest cousin, her tenderness of heart made her fear that she could not spare him; and the purity of her principles added yet a keener solicitude, when she considered how little useful, how little self-denying his life had (apparently) been.

The word 'apparently' is very properly inserted so as not to put Fanny in the position of judging a fellow-being; but "her fear that she could not spare him" ushers in a profounder concern. Though acknowledging that it is bound up with her tenderness of heart, Jane Austen nonetheless ascribes the severity of her grief at the prospective demise of a person with no particular claim on her affection to the operation within her of certain "pure principles" in response to Tom Bertram's selfish style of living.

A connection must almost certainly exist with the phrase "well principled and religious", used earlier in the novel to describe Fanny Price. Understandably, the author chooses to be less than explicit upon a delicate issue. Her brevity in itself will not trouble a reader; but the present-day agnostic consciousness will be somewhat bemused as to the cause of Fanny's pained apprehension. A reason is beyond the novel's scope. But it is present, and amply set forth, in Jane Austen's *Prayers*: in the prayer at evening, that "Another day is gone, and added to those for which we were before accountable"; in the desire that our God-bestowed comforts should prompt us to the "highest purposes amongst our fellow-creatures"; and in the plea that God will "bring to our knowledge every fault of temper and any evil habit we have indulged in to the discomfort of our fellow-creatures, and the danger of our own souls".

To the mind of Jane Austen, the time allotted to us on earth is critical, since for every act and omission within it we shall be answerable. Hence the cry,

Teach us, almighty father, to consider this solemn truth, as we should do, that we may feel the importance of every day, and every hour as it passes, and earnestly strive to make a better use of what thy goodness may yet bestow on us, than we have done of the time past.

It surely brings completeness to this intimation in the heroine, and confirmation of its place in the novel, that we are told of Tom Bertram at the end, and similarly in minor utterance, that after his harrowing experience "He became what he ought to be, useful to his father, steady and quiet, and not living merely for himself".

With utmost discretion, Jane Austen has kept to the conditions of her craft, allowing herself no more than a hint of anything beyond the secular – her words at this point being an almost exact repetition of those which conveyed Fanny Price's "keener solicitude" as to "how little useful, how little self-denying" Tom's life had been. But the touch has been added in terms of events and sentiments in a novel which, if examined in themselves – and brought into relation with strong emphases in her *Prayers* which alone can fully explain them – cast a new light upon the inspiration of her work as a whole.

Though it is, and can only be, small, and though it is brought in and handled with particular care, the theme so considered is in fact proof that these otherwise entirely secular novels arise from a devotedly and uncompromisingly Christian appraisement of the human scene. Dear and real to Jane Austen as were her earthly associations, and full of interest the world she knew, immeasurably more joyous and desirable than them all was the final reality of the human situation, the *unum necessarium* of our being. Thomas Carlyle's affirmation, "It is well said, in every sense, that a man's religion is the chief fact with regard to him",[44] is surely borne out in Jane Austen. For it is this commitment to a higher service, obedience and love that gives her literary achievement its quality, and, to an indefinable extent, its greatness.

ix

How Silly is Mrs. Bennet?

To his wife, we are informed, Mr. Bennet "was very little otherwise indebted, than as her ignorance and folly had contributed to his amusement". For the more personable of his daughters, she is the source of constant embarrassment; and for their cultivated neighbours, the object of their united derision. By generations of grateful readers she has been revered as a captivating purveyor of mindless blunders. Jane Austen herself refers to her as "a woman of mean understanding, little information and uncertain temper", who, when she is discontented, "fancied herself nervous", and who can find solace only in the trivialities of "visiting and news". As if this were not enough, her creator dubs her the possessor of an "illiberal mind" which, being so, cannot be subject to change; for the accomplishment at the end of so much of her heart's desire in the marrying-off of three of her daughters leaves her still "occasionally nervous and invariably silly".

Is not this judgement final? Must not any attempt to justify her be a case of defending the indefensible? And why take the trouble? Surely it would be better to conclude – with apologies to the shade of Polonius – that "to define true silliness, What is't but to be nothing else but silly?"

Certainly the matter can be left there. Yet Mrs. Bennet is a significant character in the novel. She cannot in every respect be laughable: there must be some positive elements in her, if only to enact the folly. She had been pretty in her youth, and must have had some engaging qualities to attract a man like Bennet; in maturity she is mother of five daughters, the director of a considerable household. For all that may be her absurdities, she is closely involved in village activities, with numerous acquaintances and fellow-gossips, to judge from the likes of Lady Lucas and Mrs. Long. And at all times she displays, with a vigour of disposition, a wealth of opinions, not all of which can be devoid of rationality. Why then should she not be a subject for consideration? The process we may be assured can do no harm; and it is not likely to consign us to solemnity.

The relationship between husband and wife is most clearly defined in the opening interchanges on the young Mr. Bingley's having acquired Netherfield Park. But immediately it becomes apparent that it is to Mr. Bennet's manner of proceeding, rather than to Mrs. Bennet, that the closest scrutiny must be applied. For we have from him nothing other than a series of intellectual sallies and manoeuvres whose sole aim is to put his wife in the wrong and make her look silly. In an ordinary reading, what gains the attention is not the urbane, calculated ridiculing of Mrs. Bennet, but its diverting effect upon the distraught recipient. To make a fair judgment, therefore, it is essential that we be alive to exactly what Bennet is up to.

His first device is a pretence of complete indifference: a negative as to having heard the news about Nethefield followed by a silence, which provokes from the lady, "Don't you want to hear who has taken it?" Bennet's reply is as coldly distant as an affirmative can be: "*You* want to tell me, and *I* have no objection to hearing". The particulars now excitedly given, he poses two terse questions as to Bingley's age and marital status in a total of nine words.

Mrs. Bennet's relapsing into the sentiment of the coming of a single man of large fortune being a "fine thing for our girls!" now heralds a professed incomprehension of her meaning. His "How so? how can it affect them?" is sufficiently nonsensical to earn Mrs. Bennet's, "how can you be so tiresome? You must know that I am thinking of his marrying one of them". Incomprehension is ingeniously extended into naiveté in her husband's, "Is that his design in settling here?"

The preposterous question gains a prompt reward in Mrs. Bennet's, "Design! nonsense, how can you talk so!" followed by her correct mention of the required social call by the master of the house. To this he returns a seeming and repeated refusal: and he can intensify the dismay it causes with the playful suggestion of the females visiting

Bingley instead – at the same time laying a bait for the touch of vanity in his wife which will exist in any woman, in the caution that she should exclude herself from going: "for as you are as handsome as any of them, Mr. Bingley might like you the best of the party". Her polite, "My dear, you flatter me" leads only into an admission of former beauty, and the natural remark that a mother of grown-up children should give over thinking of such a thing. Whether it is born of frustration or malice at being thus baulked, or both, Bennet's rejoinder of, "In such cases, a woman has not often much beauty to think of", uttered as a platitude, is in fact a jeer, if not an intended insult.

But Mrs. Bennet's mind is preoccupied with the necessity for the family of Bennet's calling on their new neighbour. "Indeed, you must go, for it will be impossible for us to visit him if you do not". The fact is dismissed as if it were fancy. She, Bennet tells her, is to go to Bingley alone – armed now with a note giving her husband's consent to his marrying whichever of the girls he chooses: "though I must throw in a good word for my little Lizzy". The tailpiece he knows will be annoying, his constant openly favouring Elizabeth having been a slight upon her sisters; and his inserting it will be the means of driving their mother to as near anger as she can get in his presence – the more so because her anticipated accusation of his always giving Lizzy the preference is to be followed by a positively inflammatory mock denial, the assertion that "They none of them have much to recommend them; they are all silly and ignorant like other girls".

The desired effect is obtained. Mrs. Bennet is provoked to indignation at the affront to her offspring, and exclamation as to the state of her nerves. But the master-stroke is yet to come. Its prelude is a hint of sympathy for her nerves, and kindly hope that she will soon "get over" them: but then ensues the prediction of a recovery by which she will live "to see many young men of four thousand a year come into the neighbourhood". This open taunting drives her to hyperbole, in the irate retort, "It will be no use to us if twenty such should come since you will not visit them". Bennet thereupon makes gracious numerical accommodation for her fears with the infuriating assurance, "Depend upon it, my dear, that when there are twenty, I will visit them all".

Not to dwell upon the family conference on the evening of the day Bennet has made the visit he "had always intended" would be to miss a masterly performance in dissimulation. It is engineered by his withholding throughout the fact of his having paid it, and employing the contrary impression to tease, mock and vex not his wife alone, but all his daughters – and to make the eventual admission itself an instrument of his purpose.

It is introduced, and the hateful topic determined, by the innocent remark to his second daughter, now engaged in trimming a hat, "I hope Mr. Bingley will like it, Lizzy". As expected, Mrs. Bennet reproves him with the resentful and accurate, "We are not in a position to know *what* Mr. Bingley likes, since we are not to visit"; and she dismisses Elizabeth's mention of Mrs. Long's having promised to introduce him at the assemblies, on the grounds of that lady's having two grown-up nieces of her own, and – in the warmth of the moment – being "a selfish, hypocritical woman". With this hasty judgment he has goaded her into, Bennet offers an amiable concurrence, designed to extinguish hope: "I am glad to find you do not depend upon her serving you". A sudden burst of coughing from Kitty is the occasion for a further example of insidious goodwill. Her mother rounding upon her in the fraught situation for upsetting her nerves, Bennet contributes the speciously compassionate, "Kitty has no discretion in her coughs; she times them ill" – to that girl's indignation, and Mrs. Bennet's further discomfiture: for she is now accredited with the senseless notion of regulated coughing.

So far, there has been a hint of reason in her husband's irrelevances; but, with the moment for telling of his morning's visit to Bingley now upon him, Bennet reduces truth to incomprehensibility. With the further mild inquiry of Elizabeth as to the date of her next ball, he precipitates the factual interjection from his wife that Mrs. Long will not be back till the day before, and it will thus be impossible for her to introduce him, for she will not know him herself. "Then, my dear," she is told, "you may have the advantage of your friend, and introduce Mr.

Bingley to her". Not for nothing does the astonished Mrs. Bennet call this proposition "Impossible", when she herself is not acquainted with Bingley; nor further ask her husband, "how can you be so teasing?" And she finds herself oddly agreed with: "A fortnight's acquaintance is certainly very little". But, Bennet goes on, there is an obligation upon them to venture the introduction: and "if you decline the office," he informs the astonished family, "I will take it on myself".

Her girls staring at their father, their mother can pronounce only a blank, "Nonsense, nonsense". These words, seized upon, inspire Bennet to further heights. In the tones of a moralistic preacher he demands, "Do you consider the forms of introduction, and the stress that is laid on them, as nonsense?" As if dismayed, and in need of support, he asks the unhappy Mary for her opinion, on the grounds of her learning; and, upon her silence, declares, "Let us return to Mr. Bingley".

Understandably now beyond the limits of fortitude and constraint, Mrs. Bennet cries, "I am sick of Mr. Bingley". The outburst is what her husband was waiting for, and dissimulation can now come to its climax. Strange accents, endearing in their very absurdity, close upon the ears of the afflicted woman. "I am sorry to hear that; but why did you not tell me before? If I had known as much this morning, I certainly would not have called on him. It is very unlucky; but as I have actually paid the visit, we cannot escape the acquaintance now".

Amidst the ensuing tumult of the ladies' astonishment and delight, Bennet ought to have reached the fullest satisfaction in his dénouement. But, in keeping with the motivation which has brought it about, he cannot make his exit without a *sotto voce* dig at the nervous irritation of the woman upon whom he has so deliberately inflicted it. "Now, Kitty, you may cough as much as you chuse".

*   *   *

When, after returning from her fateful encounter with Mr. Darcy at Pemberley, Elizabeth tells her sister of the change in her feelings for its master, from aversion to respect, she laments her former manner of derisive incivility towards him. "It is such a spur to one's genius," she says to Jane, "such an opening for wit to have a dislike of that kind". She speaks as her father's daughter. Whatever else the proximity of a person he disdains might challenge him to, it stimulates Bennet's mental powers in the cause of ridicule. Due allowance must be made for his bitterness after the hurt suffered through disillusionment in his spouse; and there must also be admiration for the consummate skill he uses in taunting her. But his unrelenting endeavour to do so, thereby reducing her to a fretful and petulant state, is for all its veneer of civility the opposite of gentlemanly, and by some standards little short of villainous. For in this instance it must be remembered that he and Mrs. Bennet are of one mind upon the importance of making early acquaintance with Mr. Bingley, that Bennet was "among the first" to pay his respects to their new neighbour: that, indeed, a normal husband's, "Yes, of course" to the urging of a visit would have given its quietus to the bizarre, heady, pointless if hilarious extravaganza we have here. The whole thing has been perversely designed by Bennet for his own entertainment. That the power, and the deadliness, of such an intention was uppermost in Jane Austen's mind is clear from the words she puts upon the lips of a nettled Mr. Darcy responding to Elizabeth's jibe at Netherfield, that he is "not to be laughed at!" – "The wisest and best of men, nay, the wisest and best of their actions, may be rendered ridiculous by a person whose first object in life is a joke". If Mr. Darcy can feel himself thus endangered by this young lady's taunting, what chance has Mrs. Bennet of not being made a laughing-stock by such an accomplished and assiduous jester as her husband?

But it is important that we observe her at this juncture – for all ill-feeling, any resentment she might have felt at her husband's conduct, not to mention her posited nerves, have been swept aside by a wave of happiness and gratitude upon news of the visit now paid. She can see nothing but kindness in him. "How good it was in you, Mr. Bennet!" She had been sure his love for his daughters, and her own persuasions, would move him at last. And his flagrant deception, and the dismay it has plunged them into, have become "such a good joke, too!" All is gladness: Bennet is "an excellent father" to his daughters: there is no shred of ill-feeling in his wife's consciousness. Not only this; for she does not know how the girls "will ever make him amends for his kindness; or me, either, for that matter", she concludes, not permitting any hampering modesty to obscure the reality of her own efforts on their behalf.

If there is folly in this state of mind, it would have been much greater folly to nurse resentment; and of this, Mrs. Bennet appears incapable. The truth is that she will not or cannot think ill of any member of the family – herself included, it must be admitted. Her loyalty to them seems an overwhelming passion to which all other considerations must give way. Such devotion, or love, does not require cleverness; but there can certainly be no wisdom in being without it. It can grieve her to hear Mr. Bennet call the girls "silly and ignorant"; but the same cause ensures that she will never see him as other than the head of the family, and honoured husband. It lies at the heart of the sense of right by which she is moved in all her dealings – or perhaps propelled would be the better word, for it can run into excess. There is no harm in her rejoicing at Jane's looks not being affected by unhappiness over Bingley; but the same cannot be said for "Their affectionate mother" sharing the grief of Kitty and Lydia upon the regiment's leaving Meryton, or for there being "No sentiment of shame" to dampen her rapture at Lydia's questionable wedlock. There are however other examples of the fond and doting mother in Jane Austen's novels; but Mrs. Bennet is distinguished by the joy that floods through her at her daughters' prospects being enhanced: her "delight" at Jane's rain-soaked ride to Netherfield, the transport that will deny her sleep all night at the achievement of the wish and certainty that Jane would get Bingley at last; and the speed of her transition from abhorrence of Mr. Darcy to ardent admiration of the prospective son-in-law as being "such a charming man! so handsome! so tall!" In the last instance it might be thought that the mother deserves a modicum of credit for reversal of sentiment within the space of a few minutes, when it has taken the daughter half the novel to effect the same.

Can silliness be predicated for this overbearing concern in Mrs. Bennet for her family and their needs? Her creator seems on the point of it, in casually telling us at a chapter's end that "The business of her life was to get her daughters married". But for a woman of that age, with five almost dowerless grown-up daughters on her hands, and the family estate destined to go to a stranger and leave them poor and excluded from society, anything much less than obsession with finding husbands for the girls would have been reprehensible. Not only is Mrs. Bennet's behaviour in this respect both reasonable and natural, but her husband, for all his protestations, is as quick as she to spot a matrimonial opportunity and exert himself to exploit it.

*   *   *

What brings about the marriages of Jane and Elizabeth Bennet, and makes the novel itself a possibility, is Mrs. Bennet's stratagem to oblige Jane to undertake her visit to Bingley's sisters at Netherfield on horseback, with the likelihood of rain meaning that she will have to stay all night, since "the gentlemen will have Mr. Bingley's chaise to go to Meryton, and the Hursts have no horses to theirs". The plan is perfect in scope and detail. It is critical to note Mr. Bennet's reaction to it. Her mother counters Jane's wish for the coach with the eager supposition to Bennet that the horses are wanted at the farm. The response she gets from him is strangely evasive: "They are wanted in the farm much oftener than I can get them". His thoughts are upon his wife's scheme. So are Elizabeth's. She intervenes to obtain an answer from him – and, we are told, "did at last extort from her father an acknowledgement that the horses were engaged". Mrs. Bennet is thus enabled to attend Jane to the door "with many cheerful prognostics of a bad day".

That Bennet has closed with his wife's suggestion is proved the next day; for upon Elizabeth's declaring herself determined to walk the three miles through muddy fields to Netherfield on news that Jane is indisposed, her father asks, "Is this a hint to me, Lizzy, to send for the horses?" The last thing he would have done is admit concurrence in Mrs. Bennet's stratagem; and the only thing left for him is to utter his sardonic, "Well, my dear, if your daughter should have a dangerous fit of illness, if she should die, it would be a comfort to know that it was all in pursuit of Mr. Bingley, and under your orders". From this single happening it is clear that, whatever may be her idiosyncracies, Mrs. Bennet is no fool: it is evidence of decided cleverness.

And this is by no means the only occasion. She displays at times – particularly when she is agitated or provoked by a threat to family interests – an ability to sum up a situation with clarity and conciseness. Affronted by Elizabeth's look of unconcern at having rejected Collins, and accusing her of "caring no more for us than if we were at York, provided she can have her own way", she goes on: "But I tell you what, Miss Lizzy, if you take it into your head to go on refusing every offer of marriage in this way, you will never get a husband at all – and I am sure I do not know who is to maintain you when your father is dead. – I shall not be able to keep you – and so I warn you. – I have done with you from this very day". While the latter remark is the effect of irritation, the rest shows Mrs. Bennet's accurate and urgent estimation of her penniless daughter's small chance of a reputable suitor, and of the penury threatened by the entail.

Similarly, when the news of Lydia's elopement has burst upon her, Mrs. Bennet is vividly aware of its potential outcome for them all. True, in her distress she does blame everyone but herself for the event, and protest that she had been overruled as always; but her analysis of what could follow is practical and perceptive enough to alarm her hearers.

"Poor dear child. And now here's Mr. Bennet gone away, and I know he will fight Wickham, whenever he meets him, and then he will be killed, and what is to become of us all? The Collinses will turn us out, before he is cold in his grave; and if you are not kind enough, brother, I do not know what we shall do".

Such outpourings as these are no less apt for their giving immediate relief to her feelings; but they would certainly have been more effective if delivered in a moderate and distinguished way.

Though to say so is contrary to modern tastes, Mrs. Bennet had been right, by the standards of that age, in her determination that Elizabeth should marry Mr. Collins. We tend to think of it simply as occasioning one of the most laughable incidents in the novel. Her calling upon Mr. Bennet to insist upon Elizabeth accepting him, upon pain of her mother never seeing her again, enables Bennet to put before his daughter what he gravely terms an unhappy alternative. "From this day you must be a stranger to one of your parents. – Your mother will never see you again if you do *not* marry Mr. Collins, and I will never see you again if you *do*". The reader being aware – as Mrs. Bennet is not – of Mr. Collins's pompous stupidity, and what it provokes in Elizabeth, will applaud what seems the good sense of Mr. Bennet's position, and be diverted by the perceived silliness of that of his wife. What is almost sure to escape them, however, is the contemporary view of marriage as a family contract, its deprecation of romance, its harsh equating of social acceptability and wealth, of a woman's desirability with the amount of her dowry, the disaster – it was no less – of social deprivation through want of means. These considerations determine the motives and actions of many in Jane Austen's novels. They are reflected in Willoughby's jilting of the loving Marianne, and Wickham's of the less deeply committed Elizabeth; in Lady Russell's resolve that Anne Elliot's marriage to the fortuneless Capt. Wentworth "must not be, if by any fair interference of friendship, any representations from one who had almost a mother's love, and mother's right, it would be prevented". And at their sternest they are represented in Sir Thomas Bertram, whose reaction to his ward Fanny Price's forestalling of the wealthy Henry Crawford's proposal, with her, "I – I cannot like him, sir, well enough to marry him", is that her attitude is so "very strange" as to be beyond his comprehension: the deplorable act of an immature and "heated fancy" – wilful, selfish, indifferent to the needs and wishes of the family, and disrespectful of those, himself especially, having "the right to guide" in such a matter. For Mrs. Bennet, in her state of knowledge, to call upon her husband to insist that the marriage of Collins and Elizabeth should take place, and thereby secure to them all the Longbourn estate and their respectability, is not a foolish demand. And if it is to be counted an insensitive one, the same can be said for the worthy Sir Thomas, not only with regard to Fanny, but in consenting to his daughter Julia's marriage to the rich but stupid James Rushworth for the sake of family alliance and advantage, knowing that she has neither love nor respect for him.

*　　*　　*

We might better understand these indications of shrewdness and commonsense in Mrs. Bennet if it were not for the social blunders she is constantly making. She does, in a lesser sense, appear to be socially aware: in knowing precisely who danced with whom at Meryton, or of the Hursts having no horses to their carriage, or the shortness of Bingley's lease of Netherfield, or even which are the best London warehouses for wedding clothes. Her judgments of persons, too, can be perceptive: of Darcy, walking about at Meryton without dancing, and "thinking himself so very great"; or in contradicting Jane's plea in Darcy's defence that he is "remarkably agreeable" amongst those he is intimate with, by insisting, rightly, that "If he were so agreeable he would have talked to Mrs. Long". And her winking at Elizabeth and Kitty "for a considerable time" to prompt them to vacate the room and leave Jane and Bingley together would have been appropriate, if Kitty had not inanely called out, "What is the matter, mama? What do you keep winking at me for? What am I to do?"

These are scarcely gaffes; and at other demanding moments Mrs. Bennet can be seen as conducting herself quite correctly. For example, upon the Bennet and Lucas ladies meeting after the Meryton ball, she properly compliments Charlotte, despite preoccupation with Jane, on having been Mr. Bingley's first choice. She knows to give respectful complaisance to the mannerless Lady Catherine de Bourgh upon her unheralded appearance at Longbourn – and to answer her haughty, "You have a very small park here" with deference yet dignity, in her, "It is nothing in comparison with Rosings, my lady, I dare say; but I assure you it is much larger than Sir William Lucas's". And it is with propriety and delicacy that she has responded to Mr. Collins's airy hint of a wish to make Jane the mistress of his parsonage-house at Hunsford, uttering,

> amid very complaisant smiles and general encouragement, a caution against the very Jane he had fixed on. – "As to her *younger* daughters she could not take it upon her to say – she could not positively answer – but she did not *know* of any prepossession; – her eldest daughter, she must just mention – she felt it incumbent on her to hint, was likely to be very soon engaged".

Much the same qualities are present in her apologising to Elizabeth for having to walk with the "disagreeable" Mr. Darcy to Oakham Mount, in company with Jane and Bingley, and impressing upon her, "it is all for Jane's sake, you know; and there is no occasion for talking to him, except just now and then". The advice, sensitive in itself, is ridiculous only in the light of what is in the heads of the two concerned.

For the greater part, however, Mrs. Bennet is guilty of indiscretion, and even blindness, socially speaking. It is as if she is constrained to pursue her objects and wishes without regard to how others are disposed. She can, though, be defended in her blurting out to Collins, when on his arrival he declares himself assured that her fine family of daughters will be "in due time well disposed in marriage", that she wishes with all her heart it may prove so, "for else they will be destitute enough. Things are settled so oddly." Uncouth this may be, but it is a fitting rejoinder to his obtuse compliment; and it may be we should approve her for having instantly realised her potential to engage with a mind as insensitive as her own can be.

Otherwise tactlessness abounds. What else is Mrs. Bennet's crying up the bed-ridden Jane's charms at Netherfield, in terms of her having "the greatest patience in the world", and "the sweetest temper I ever met with. I often tell my other girls that they are nothing to her". Or for that matter, upon Bingley's kind hope that she has not found Miss Bennet worse than she expected, her indignantly pronouncing to all present, "Indeed, I have, Sir. She is a great deal too ill to be moved". It is the same when, during supper at the Netherfield ball, Mrs. Bennet, placed within Mr. Darcy's hearing, talks to Lady Lucas "freely, openly, and of nothing else but her expectation that Jane would soon be married to Mr. Bingley"; and, upon being urged by the blushing Elizabeth to moderate these very audible rejoicings for fear of offending Bingley's friend Mr. Darcy, retorts even more audibly, "What is Mr. Darcy to me, pray, that I should be afraid of him? I am sure we own him no such particular civility as to be obliged to say nothing *he* may not like to hear". And things are not made easier for her second daughter by the mother's manoeuvre of delaying their departure until everyone else was gone, so giving them "time to see how heartily they were wished away by some of the family".

It requires no high degree of imagination to sense Elizabeth's "misery" later upon hearing her mother complain to Bingley of the "awkward business" her brother Gardiner had made of drawing up so minimal announcement of Lydia's marriage in the newspapers – or her ingratiating invitation, "When you have killed all your own birds, Mr. Bingley, I beg you will come here and shoot as many as you please, on Mr. Bennet's manor. I am sure he will be vastly happy to oblige you, and will save all the best of the covies for you". These are serious failings, typifying someone who at times is difficult if not impossible to deal with.

Elizabeth's sufferings, indeed, are a measure of the depth her mother's insensitivity can reach. But there are social blunders on Mrs. Bennet's part which can be more charitably regarded: put down to natural weaknesses in an ordinary human being. One, surely, is her protesting to Sir William Lucas, on his coming to announce Charlotte's engagement to Mr. Collins, "with more persistence than politeness", that he was entirely mistaken. A shock of surprise can produce such immoderation in anyone; and Elizabeth had outdone her mother when, previously, Charlotte confided the event to her: "Engaged to Mr. Collins! my dear Charlotte, impossible!"

Prominent amongst Mrs. Bennet's pleasing vagaries is her proneness to unconscious inconsistency. Angrily addressing Elizabeth on her entering the breakfast-room with Jane after the Collins affair, she can say, "I told you in the library, you know, that I should never speak to you again, and you will find me as good as my word". In the same fashion, agog at the rumour that Bingley is returning to Netherfield after his long absence, and torn between wounded pride and revived hope where Jane is concerned, she addresses a fine example of the art to Mrs. Phillips.

"Well, so much the better. Not that I care about it, though. He is nothing to us, you know, and I am sure *I* never want to see him again. But, however, he is very welcome to come to Netherfield, if he likes it. And who knows what *may* happen? But that is nothing to us. You know, sister, we agreed long ago never to mention it. And so, is it quite certain he is coming?"

Upon Mr. Darcy being seen riding to Longbourn with Bingley, he is declared in the same breath welcome as the latter's friend and the object of her detestation. Mrs. Long, aunt to two grown-up nieces, is before the Meryton ball "a selfish, hypocritical woman"; but when, after Bingley's dining at Longbourn, she has prophesied concerning Jane, "Ah! Mrs. Bennet, we shall have her at Netherfield at last", she becomes "as good a creature as ever lived – and her nieces are very pretty-behaved girls, and not at all handsome: I like them exceedingly".

In entertaining contradictory views of the same persons, Mrs. Bennet is not alone. Isabella Knightley and Mary Musgrove are particularly good at it, without being notably silly. The former, having stated of Mr. Weston that "there could not be a more feeling heart nor a better man in existence", is immediately maintaining that she "really never could think well of anybody" who, like him, has parted with his own child for adoption. The latter, complaining in the first part of a letter to Anne Elliott that Admiral and Mrs. Croft offer neither civility nor attention as neighbours, writes in the second part to give news of their forthcoming stay in Bath, and declaring, "I shall be truly glad to have them back again. Our neighbourhood cannot spare such a pleasant family". But neither would have been capable of such inconsistency as to urge that a marriage should be speedily arranged and the wedding clothes purchased afterwards, or that a young daughter who has lived with a man unmarried, "is not the kind of girl to do such a thing, if she had been well looked after".

Mrs. Bennet is also addicted to vagueness in speech, a failing which her husband finds an excellent means of exploiting in the subject of the entail. Her distress at its providing that she will have to give place to Charlotte Lucas as mistress of Longbourn House moves her to exclaim, "I cannot bear to think they should have all this estate. If it was not for the entail I should not mind it". Fastening upon the expression, Bennet inquires, "What should you not mind?" and, being rewarded with a vacant, "I should not mind anything at all", sanctimoniously responds, "Let us be thankful that you are preserved from a state of such insensibility".

Mercifully, Mrs. Bennet's offering upon the probability that Bingley will not return from London to claim Jane – "Well, my comfort is, I am sure Jane will die of a broken heart, and then he will be sorry for what he has done" – does not bring a Bennet-like demand from Elizabeth that she should specify what that comfort comprises.

*   *   *

Weak her words at times may be; but Mrs. Bennet is a headstrong woman, to put it plainly, and her impulses are compelling. It is not that persons of this kind cannot act rationally, but that reason in them often fails to remain uppermost. Reasoning as such is not lacking in Mrs. Bennet: it is there in abundance, in her constantly explaining her actions and arguing her cause of the moment. But the querulous tone of many of her outgivings denotes the emotion simmering as it were beneath them; and very often we are fortunate enough to encounter in her the intriguing process of reason put to use as emotion's servant.

Upon Sir William Lucas's taking leave of Mrs. Bennet after imparting Charlotte's engagement, "her feelings found rapid vent", the author tells us, in six lucid mental positions.

> In the first place, she persisted in disbelieving the whole matter; secondly, she was very sure that Mr. Collins had been taken in; thirdly, she trusted they would never be happy together; and fourthly, that the match might be broken off. Two inferences, however, were plainly deduced from the whole; one, that Elizabeth was the real cause of all the mischief; and the other, that she herself had been barbarously used by them all; and on these two points she principally dwelt during the rest of the day.

Invariably, this lady has good cause for drastic shifts of attitude. Reasonably enough, she foresees with trepidation that Mr. Bennet in London will fight Wickham and be killed – "and what is to become of us all?": but his intending later to come home without having traced Lydia is very reasonably denounced in terms of, "Who is to fight Wickham and make him marry her, if he comes away?" When, upon the marriage being arranged, Jane gravely impresses on her mother the certainty that Gardiner has pledged a great deal of his own money to secure it, her illiberal response is couched in the most rational terms. "Well, it is all very right, who should do it but her own uncle? If he had not a family of his own, I and my children must have had all his money you know, and it is the first time we have ever had anything from him, except a few presents".

And, upon a lesser issue, reason does not fail the momentarily dispirited Mrs. Bennet when, after the departure of the scapegrace wedded pair, Elizabeth is prompted in her father's style to point out that her eagerness to marry Lydia off is responsible for her present gloom.

She is answered by a superb display of limited logic on the maternal achievement. "It is no such thing. Lydia does not leave me because she is married; but only because her husband's regiment happens to be so far off. If that had been nearer, she would not have gone so soon".

But, in moments of happiness, as well of dejection, reason is vanquished by emotion's sheer force within her. The phenomenon, in what Jane Austen calls its "exuberance", can be contemplated and enjoyed in her reception of the news of Lydia's marriage settlement, which projects her into "an irritation as violent from delight, as she had ever been fidgety from alarm and vexation", and excludes both fear for the girl's happiness with such a man and remembrance of her misconduct. As for Elizabeth's telling her of her engagement to Mr. Darcy, "Its effect", we are informed, "was most extraordinary": first, an unnatural and prolonged silence, next, a slow progress to comprehension, then a fidgeting, a getting up and sitting down, a wondering, a murmuring, a blessing herself – and, at last, a paean of elation so extreme that Elizabeth quits the room as soon as she can, "rejoicing that such an effusion was heard only by herself".

Mrs. Bennet's emotional tendencies are without doubt responsible for some of her lack of comprehension. The outstanding example is her inability to understand what an entail is. Jane and Elizabeth have often tried to explain it to her, "but it was a subject on which Mrs. Bennet was beyond the reach of reason". One might wonder at this being so, in a woman as astutely able as she to devise the means of Jane's making Bingley's better acquaintance – and so keenly perceptive of the minutiae of the neighbourhood's affairs and neighbours' business as we know her to be. But this, without taking into account the degree to which she is incensed by the entail's injustice to her loved ones, and their wretchedness that must ensue: the fact, in this respect, that her whole being reacts against understanding, blinding her to the manner of the entail's application. There is an emotional barrier, a mental block – and, we might note, a certain similarity to that sense in Elizabeth of the injustice in the custom of 'coming out' which drives her to denounce it so boldly, if not rudely, in the decorous precincts of Rosings as to make the startled Lady Catherine to remark, "Upon my word, you give your opinion very decidedly for so young a person". And it might also be well to bear in mind that Elizabeth's failure at the Netherfield ball to check her mother's flow of words upon her anticipation of Bingley's marrying Jane, her intransigence, and so audibly expressed indifference to Darcy's feelings, could have arisen, not from lack of intelligence, but from residual anger against the man who had scorned and humiliated her daughter at Meryton.

Might it not be, after all, that Mrs. Bennet's seeming silliness is almost wholly due to her being the victim of her own emotions? On the surface we find in her a frequent lack of comprehension, occasional ignoring of obvious fact, and an almost invariable insensitivity to what is going on in the minds of others. But, at the same time, we are aware of a vehemence in her which bestows prominence and pretention upon the self – making the firstlings of her heart, happily not the firstlings of her hand, as with Macbeth, but of her tongue. The two are inseparably linked; and the question arises whether it is Mrs. Bennet's want of understanding which generates the emotionalism, or the power of emotion which clouds and limits the understanding – and bears the blame for what silliness there is. Sadly, we must resign ourselves to never knowing. For we are dealing with nothing else than a chicken and egg situation, that must ever rank with the ultimate mysteries.

*   *   *

Once this is appreciated, there is enlightenment as to that related and impressive feature of Mrs. Bennet's personality, her nerves. We are introduced to them at an early stage of events, upon her husband's slighting reference to their daughters as being silly and ignorant. "Mr. Bennet, how can you abuse your children in such a way? You take delight in vexing me. You have no compassion upon my poor nerves". She is not mollified by his assurance of high respect for them as his old friends of twenty years' acquaintance. Following Elizabeth's rejection of Mr. Collins we are given a further indication of the woes they inflict.

At the end of a long speech from Mrs. Bennet to her girls, we hear: "People who suffer as I do from nervous complaints can have no inclination for talking. Nobody can tell what I suffer! – But it is always so. Those who never complain are never pitied".

But it is when Mr. Gardiner declares his intention of going to London and assisting Mr. Bennet in the potentially dangerous task of retrieving his daughter that we are favoured with the most revealing account of her nervous condition.

> "Tell him what a dreadful state I am in, – that I am frightened out of my wits; and have such tremblings, such flutterings, all over me, such spasms in my side, and pains in my head, and such beatings at heart, that I can get no rest by night or day".

Here we have, all too obviously, physical symptoms of a mental state. Or is it better called one of frustration? Mrs. Bennet's everyday life must be full of bewilderment at people's behaving as far as she can make out unreasonably and irresponsibly. A potent will in her finds itself powerless to check unaccountable doings both in those near and dear to her, and in her wider circle: and her only resort, within the puzzling and anxious milieu in which she finds herself, must be to live, feel, think and act for the moment – instinctively to fight for what appear to be her interests, and the true interests of all, against every manifestation which seems to oppose them. She is a vigorous personality naturally repressed by the conditions life imposes on her – just as her spirited daughter Elizabeth experiences frustration through the social norms which curb her instincts. The one certainty, to which Mrs. Bennet must ever cling, is the duty of promoting the well-being of the family for which she has such deep and heart-felt concern. And her nerves, which contrive so greatly to amuse us, are the somewhat less than honourable scars of the battle she is constantly engaged in.

But how far is this battling necessary? It is without doubt most marked in her relations with her husband; but would it not be entirely done away in this regard if she could grasp that the positions he takes are all a dissembling: if she had wit enough to realise, in the process of being ridiculed, that what Bennet is so blandly putting forth is utter nonsense?

An answer – if not *the* answer – Jane Austen herself provides at the very outset, in her comment,

> Mr. Bennet was so odd a mixture of quick parts, sarcastic humour, reserve, and caprice, that the experience of three and twenty years had been insufficient to make his wife understand his character.

The man's complexity and inscrutability, that is to say, has set Mrs. Bennet an impossible task; and instead, therefore, of being laughed at for the absurdities he can drive her into, she might preferably be congratulated on an undiminished respect for him.

Further, is the assumption commonly made that she has not the intelligence to see through Bennet's pretence sustainable, in face of the evidence she so frequently gives, in such expostulations as, "Nonsense, nonsense", and, "How can you be so tiresome?" and, "You take delight in vexing me", that she is to the contrary perfectly conscious of the unreasonableness of his conduct, and of its artificiality? Its moving her on occasion to outright contradiction and condemnation is not surprising: but what is noteworthy, and admirable, is that it never drives her to acrimony.

Mrs. Bennet's harshest rejoinders do not amount to more than a passing reproof; and perhaps the most telling of them is in the word "tiresome". She reacts to her mocking husband as one would to a wayward and difficult child: with indulgence, almost a gentleness; and the touches of irritation and ill-humour she exhibits are no more than momentary.

Can it be that, amidst all provocation, she cannot bring herself to think so ill of her husband, or so demean herself, as remotely to suspect him of offensive intent? In fact, is Bennet's manner less an affront to folly in his wife than to her good-nature? As has been mentioned, it is intended that we should be amused by his teasing her throughout the novel, and be diversely charmed by the cleverness of the one and confusion of the other: but so doing we are at risk of being carried away by Bennet's impressive feats, sardonic and ironic, to the extent of failing to appreciate the plain and kindly commonsense in Mrs. Bennet that is their butt.

Eliza Dolittle, now transformed through the professional attentions of Henry Higgins, remarks to Colonel Pickering that what makes the difference between a lady and a flower-girl is not how she behaves, but how she is treated. If we are tempted to apply this maxim to defend Mrs. Bennet's frequent lapses, we should be wiser to conclude that they cannot be so excused: that her presumed upbringing, and innate and highly individual characteristics, have in this case been determinative. But the distinction Eliza makes could well apply to readers' own treatment of Mrs. Bennet: to an insensitivity in themselves more marked than any that may exist in her.

Mrs. Bennet may not be quite a lady. But she is with all her faults and foibles a lady-like person: and being so, she is conscious of, and in general constrained by, those contemporary standards of social conduct which set the limits to feminine assertiveness. It is hard for us today to see them in their stringency and universality. But their influence is plain in the mild comment of Mr. Knightley to the newly-wed Mrs. Weston at Randalls that, while as Miss Taylor nominally mistress to young Emma, she had in fact been dictated to by her pupil. Smiling, he tells her,

> "You are better placed *here*; very fit for a wife, but not for a governess. But you were preparing yourself to be an excellent wife all the time you were at Hartfield. You might not give Emma such a complete education as your powers would seem to promise; but you were receiving a very good education from *her*, on the very matrimonial point of submitting your own will, and doing as you were bid; and if Weston had asked me to recommend him a wife, I should certainly have namend Miss Taylor".

To attribute to Mrs. Bennet a blameable passivity in her relation to her spouse is to disregard that dutiful submission to a husband's will, the respect for male dominance, which it was incumbent upon a woman of those times in no way to challenge. Whatever were Mrs. Bennet's attempts in self-justification would have been tempered and conditioned by the ruling convention that a husband's word is the wife's law.

*   *   *

Any who have in the past tended to view Mrs. Bennet as simply silly (among which number the present writer has been one) ought to find it salutary to turn their attention to other ladies whom the novels introduce to us. There is, for instance, Lady Catherine de Bourgh, whose name only needs mention; and Lady Bertram, who, spending her days decorously on a sofa doing needlework, guided in concerns large and small by those around her, is inertia personified; Mrs. Allen, wife of the chief property-owner about Fullerton, a woman "of a trifling turn of mind", who can evoke in others "no other emotion than surprise at there being any man in the world who would like them well enough to marry them"; or Lady Middleton, distinguished by "a calm of manner, with which sense had nothing to do", and masks "a cold insipidity" for which there was no other possible description than "repulsive". Mrs. Jenning's other daughter, married to the intelligent Mr. Palmer, has amongst similar accomplishments the capacity to find the greatest amusement in her husband's irritation and annoyance at her stupidity; whilst her mother takes jovial vulgarity to the point of threatening decorum, and is saved from ostracism only by her wealth.

One reason for our not classing these women as fools is their having escaped the destiny of being wedded to a Bennet. Another is that, despite any consequence they may possess, they are all virtual nonentities in having nothing particularly apposite to say – although without practising the verbal economy of their astringent compeer Mrs. Ferrars, who is "not a woman of many words, for, unlike people

205

in general, she proportioned them to the number of her ideas". There exists in none of them that grain of cleverness discernible – at intervals – in Mrs. Bennet; nor, looks apart, does any display as much womanly prepossession.

By comparison, therefore, Mrs. Bennet comes off rather well. She is, far from being a nobody, or an offensive person, a vibrant, considerate creature. In her devotion to her family and unfailing esteem for her provocative husband; in the general beneficence of her outlook, her contentedness with life, and her wakefulness to joy, she is admirable. Her purposes in themselves are irreproachable, and her thinking, at its best, can be acute; and if she often is uncomprehending and insensitive, and the cause of difficulty or displeasure to others, it is through natural incapacities rather than unjust or unworthy intention. – We have ourselves in reality been guilty of faults not unlike her own: the mistaken judgement, momentary ill-feeling, undue prominence of self, flimsy reasoning in support of doubtful motive, blindness to others' needs and attitudes, clinging to resentments, and so forth.

In her many failings and aberrations, Mrs. Bennet is, to be sure, very like other people – is she not? This observation, if correct, suggests a further possibility: that, in delineating this fallible but endearing character, Jane Austen is mischievously creating a lively caricature of us all. Mrs. Bennet's fault lies not in silliness – though improvement in this aspect would not be amiss – but rather in the fact that she is incorrigibly, grievously, and triumphantly human: a representation of deficiencies abundantly present in the persons of the novels, in mankind at large, and, naturally enough, in our good selves.

Notes

1 Milton, *Lycidas,* 1.87
2 *Much Ado About Nothing,* IV. ii. 85-92
3 I.ii.31
4 IV.vi.110-11
5 III.iii.416-7
6 *Johnson on Shakespeare,* ed. W. Raleigh, London: O.U.P., 1957, p. 196
7 I.vii.39-41
8 T. B. Macaulay, 'The Diaries and Letters of Mme D'Arblay', *Edinburgh Review* (January 1843) lxxvi, 561-2; cited by B. C. Southam, *Jane Austen: The Critical Heritage,* London: Routledge & Kegan Paul, 1968, p. 122
9 Letter 142, to James Edward Austen, 9 July 1816, *Letters* ed. D. Le Faye, O.U. P., 1996, p.316
10 II.iii.248-9
11 *Jane Austen,* The Novelists Series, 2nd edn, London: Arthur Barker, 1966, p. 50
12 I.iii.211-12
13 *Measure for Measure,* I. iv. 34
14 op. cit., pp. 67, 73
15 *The Merchant of Venice,* II. ix. 32-3
16 I.iv.35
17 op. cit., pp. 74-5
18 ibid., p. 88
19 *Jane Austen: A Biography,* 1938, revised edn, Indigo, 1996, p. 161
20 ibid., p. 162
21 *Knightes Tale,* l. 1761
22 op. cit., p. 88
23 II.ii.52
24 op. cit., p. 82
25 *The Two Gentlemen of Verona,* V. iv. 110-12
26 *An Ideal Husband,* First Act, Mrs. Cheveley to Sir Robert Chiltern.

27 Letter 155, 23 March 1817, *Letters*, ed. D. Le Faye, p. 335
28 *Jane Austen: A Biography*, p.293
29 op. cit., p.296
30 op. cit., p.137
31 I.ii.158
32 D. Le Faye, op. cit. p.333
33 *An Essay on Criticism*, ll. 232-3.
34 *L'Allegro*, ll. 121-3.
35 *Love's Labour's Lost*, III. iv. 327.
36 *The Rape of the Lock*, I, ll. 13-4.
37 *The Novels of Jane Austen*, London: O.U.P. (3rd edn, 1932-), VI, pp. 453-7 The new Cambridge edition of the novels places the *Prayers* in an appendix of its final volume, *Later Manuscripts*.
38 *Christian Devotion*, London: O.U.P., 1962, p.23
39 'North British Review' (April, 1870), lii, pp.129-52; B.C. Southam (ed.), *Jane Austen: The Critical Heritage*, London: Routledge & Kegan Paul, 1968, p. 249
40 'Quarterly Review' (January, 1821), xxiv, pp.352-76; Southam, *op.cit.*, p.155
41 Unsigned notice of *Northanger Abbey* and *Persuasion*, 'Blackwood's Edinburgh Magazine' (May, 1818), n.s.ii, p.455; Southam, *op. cit.*, p.268
42 Philip Doddridge, *The Rise and Progesss of Religion in the Soul*, 1744; Kessinger Publishing Co., 2003, p.2
43 *op.cit.*, pp.30,33
44 *On Heroes and Hero-Worship*, 1841; London: O.U.P. (The World's Classics), 1974, i, p.2